How Can I Help My Child?

Early Childhood Resource Directory for Parents and Professionals

Caring About Children Ages 2 through 5 in the Washington Metro Area

DISTRICT OF COLUMBIA

MARYLAND
MONTGOMERY COUNTY • PRINCE GEORGE'S COUNTY

VIRGINIA
ALEXANDRIA • ARLINGTON COUNTY • FAIRFAX COUNTY

Compiled by

THE EARLY CHILDHOOD CONSULTATION CENTER

Irene Shere, Editor

How Can I Help My Child?
Early Childhood Resource Directory
for Parents and Professionals
Caring About Children Ages 2 through 5
In the Washington Metro Area

Compiled by The Early Childhood Consultation Center
Edited by Irene Shere
Published by The Early Childhood Consultation Center
11506 Michale Court
Silver Spring, MD 20904-2704
(301) 593-5992

Cover Design by Ross & Jeannette Feldner, Letterforms, Bethesda, Maryland
Layout Design and Production by Letterforms, Bethesda, Maryland

Fall 1997 Edition
ISSN 1094-7434
ISBN 0-9658244-0-3

Disclaimer

The Early Childhood Resource Directory is compiled to provide information and resources for parents and professionals caring about and for young children. Every effort has been made to provide up-to-date, accurate, and reliable information, but errors may exist. The Directory is sold with the understanding that the editor shall have no liability for any error, problem, or loss caused or alleged to have been caused directly or indirectly by any information or resource contained in this book. Individuals with any complaint or claim regarding a service listed in this Resource Directory should contact the person or organization in question.

For additional copies, use order form at the back of the Directory.

Printed in the United States of America

DEDICATION

To Steve, Holly, and Brett, always my best resources for love and encouragement

And to Bea, my own personal resource guide

ACKNOWLEDGMENTS

Thank you to all of the people and organizations listed in this guide. As the number of listings grew from ten pages to twenty pages to fifty pages to three hundred pages, it was truly heartwarming to know that there are so many people in the community dedicated to helping young children and their families.

Special thank you to Chuck Simpkinson of Common Boundary for being a valuable book consultant and enthusiastic supporter.

Special thank you to graphic artists Jeannette and Ross Feldner for their expertise in creating an attractive, easy-to-use book from a computer printout.

Thank you to Alison Farber for being such a thorough, enterprising, and sweet research assistant.

Thank you to Carol Smalls for her patient proofreading and helpful suggestions, from large details to small.

Thank you to Jane Beveridge of Luther Rice Coop Nursery School for her help with online computer listings.

Introduction

"My son is extremely distractible and very active. I'm worried that he has ADD. Where can I go to have him checked out?"

"My daughter's sick and I have to go to work. Is there a daycare center that will accept sick children?"

"Do you know of a dentist that specializes in children?"

"Our son will be three soon. What's the name of a good preschool close to my home?"

"My kids' fighting drives me crazy! Who can help us?"

"I'm a home care provider. One of the children I care for has delayed language. Where can her parents take her for an evaluation? It needs to be free because they can't afford testing."

"Where can I learn CPR for young children?"

"HELP!! I'm a single parent and I need to talk to other single parents like me!"

"I'm a preschool teacher and I need help managing my wild class. Where can I take a course about class discipline?"

"I'm a grandparent. Raising kids is different today. How can I brush up on my parenting skills?"

Over the years, as a parent, a preschool director and teacher, and an educational consultant, I have heard many people ask questions like these about their children. Parents seek help from other parents, parents ask professionals, and professionals turn to other professionals for answers. Often it seems that finding someone to help with a problem is as difficult as dealing with the problem itself. And, in the Washington metropolitan area, the search is complicated by resource listings only serving the District of Columbia or Maryland or Virginia.

How Can I Help My Child? Early Childhood Resource Directory contains important general, health care, mental health, child care, school, parent, and early childhood professional resources to ease the problem of finding help. District of Columbia, suburban Maryland, and northern Virginia listings are all included, as well as many national listings. This Directory is, as one parent previewing it said, "a serious guide" for answering the more serious questions asked by parents and professionals.

This Resource Directory is the resource directory that, as a parent, teacher, and consultant, I have always wanted at my fingertips. Hopefully, this guide will be helpful for you, too, while you are searching in the Washington metropolitan area for answers about your young child.

Table of Contents

USING THE EARLY CHILDHOOD RESOURCE DIRECTORY 7
ABOUT THE EARLY CHILDHOOD CONSULTATION CENTER 11
ABOUT THE EDITOR 11
GLOSSARY 303
INDEX 305
RESOURCE DIRECTORY UPDATE FORM 311
RESOURCE DIRECTORY ORDER FORM 313

GENERAL RESOURCES   13

TABLE OF CONTENTS 14
Advocacy Groups 15
Books, Etc. 17
    Book Finders
    Book Stores
    Catalogs and Distributors
    Library Resources
    Magazines for Adults
    Magazines for Children
    Newsletters about Books
    Newsletters and Newspapers
    Personalized Books
    Resource Guides
Computer Resources 34
    Consultants
    Courses for Children and Adults
    Online Services: General, Books and Literature, For Children, Security
    Software
Conferences and Speaker Series 40
Government Information and Resources 42
Helplines 44
    Multi-lingual Helplines
HOTLINES 47
    Multi-lingual Hotlines
Play Equipment and Playgrounds 49
    Consultants
    Equipment
Toys, Etc. 52
    Catalogs and Distributors
    Craft Supplies
    Educational Supply Stores
    Toy Recommendations
    Toy Rentals
    Toy Replacement Parts
    Toy Safety
    Toy Stores
    Used Toys
Videos 70
    Videos for Adults
    Videos for Children
    Video Reviews

HEALTH CARE RESOURCES 73

TABLE OF CONTENTS 74
Courses in CPR, First Aid, and Health 75
Dentists, Pediatric 77
    Referrals and Information
    District of Columbia
    Maryland
    Virginia
Drug Stores, Open 24 Hours 80
Health Information and Resources 82
Hospitals and Clinics 86
    Hospitalization Resources
    District of Columbia
    Maryland
    Virginia
Nutritionists and Nutritional Resources, Pediatric 90
    National
    Metro Area
Optometrists and Visual Training, Pediatric 92
    Referrals and Information
    District of Columbia
    Maryland
    Virginia
Pediatricians 94
    Referrals and Information
    ADD/ADHD Specialists
    Allergists
    Dermatologists
    Ear, Nose, and Throat Specialists
    Gastroenterologists
    Nephrologists
    Neurologists
    Ophthalmologists
    Orthopedists
    Special Needs
Physical and Occupational Therapists, Pediatric 102
    Referrals and Information
    District of Columbia
    Maryland
    Virginia
Speech and Hearing Specialists, Pediatric 106
    Referrals and Information
    District of Columbia
    Maryland
    Virginia

MENTAL HEALTH RESOURCES 111

TABLE OF CONTENTS 112

Counseling Centers 113
    District of Columbia
    Maryland
    Virginia
    Multi-cultural Counseling Centers

Mental Health Information and Resources 121
    National
    District of Columbia
    Maryland
    Virginia

Mental Health Practitioners, Child and Family 124
    Referrals and Information
    Psychiatrists
        Metro Area
        District of Columbia
        Maryland
        Virginia
    Psychologists
        Metro Area
        District of Columbia
        Maryland
        Virginia
    Social Workers
        District of Columbia
        Maryland
        Virginia
    Specialists
        Art Therapists
        Movement/Dance Therapists
        Music Therapists
        Special Needs

Testing and Assessment, Pediatric 141
    District of Columbia
    Maryland
    Virginia

CHILD CARE AND SCHOOL RESOURCES 145

TABLE OF CONTENTS 146
Babysitting Referrals 147
Child Care Referrals and Information 148
 Metro Area
 District of Columbia
 Maryland
 Virginia
Child Care Special Resources 151
 Background Checks and Surveillance
 Drop-In Child Care Centers
 Scholarships and Sliding Fee Child Care
 Sick Children Child Care
Consultants about Child Care and Schools 155
 Educational Consultants
 Multi-cultural Educational Consultants
 Special Needs Educational Consultants
Educational Information and Resources 159
Nannies 160
 Agencies
 Health Insurance for Nannies
 Hiring
 Newsletters and Publications
 Support and Training for Nannies
 Tax Guidance for Household Employers
Private Preschools and Kindergartens 163
 General School Referrals and Information
 Cooperative Preschool Information
 Montessori School Information
 Reggio Emilia Preschool Information
 Special Needs Schools Information
 Waldorf School Information
Public Preschools and Kindergartens 169
 National Information
 District of Columbia Public School Information
 Maryland Public School Information
 Virginia Public School Information
 Special Needs Programs

PARENT RESOURCES 173

TABLE OF CONTENTS 174
Child Safety 175
    Child Photo-ID Registration
    Child Safety Education
    Home and Product Safety
Child Transportation 177
Computer Online Services for Parents 178
Consultants for Parents 179
    Family Consultants
    Special Needs Family Consultants
Organizations for Parents 182
    Cooperative Preschool Parent Organizations
    Parent Teacher Associations (P.T.A.s)
Parent Education Classes 183
    Referrals and Information
    National
    Metro Area
    District of Columbia
    Maryland
    Virginia
    Multi-cultural, Multi-lingual Parent Education
    Special Needs Parent Education
Parent Information and Support 195
    Adoption
    African-American Families
    Allergy and Asthma
    Asian-American Families
    Attention Deficit Disorder (ADD)
    Attention Deficit Hyperactivity Disorder (ADHD)
    Autism
    Bedwetting
    Cancer
    Cerebral Palsy
    Challenging Children
    Child Abuse Prevention
    Death and Bereavement
    Diabetes
    Disabled and/or Chronically Ill Children
    Divorce and Separation
    Down's Syndrome
    Emotionally Disturbed Children
    Epilepsy
    Fathers
    Foster Care
    Gay and Lesbian Parents
    Grandparents
    Hearing-Impaired Children
    Home Schooling
    Latino-American Families
    Learning Disabilities
    Low Income Resources
    Mothers
    Multicultural Resources
    Parents of Multiple Births
    Playgroups
    Sibling Relationships
    Single Parents
    Special Needs
    Stepfamilies
    Stuttering
    Support Groups
    Tourette's Syndrome
    Visually-Impaired Children
    Working Parents
Parent Resource Centers 249
    National
    Maryland
    Virginia

EARLY CHILDHOOD PROFESSIONAL RESOURCES   **253**

TABLE OF CONTENTS 254
Child Care and Schools: Business Management Resources 255
    Grant Resources
    Insurance
    Management and Operation
    Start-up Resources
    Tax Services
Child Care and Schools: Educational Resources 259
    Assessments for Children
    Computer On-site Services
    Curriculum
    Organizations
    Scholarships
Child Care and Schools: Licensing and Accreditation 264
    General Child Care and School Licensing
    Montessori School Accreditation
    NAEYC Accreditation
Computer Resources for EC Professionals 267
    Online Services
    Information and Resources
Conferences and Speaker Series 270
Consultants for EC Professionals 272
    General School Consultants
    Cooperative Preschool Consultants
    Multi-cultural Consultants
    Reggio Emilia Preschool Consultants
    Special Needs Consultants
Courses: College Programs 277
    Graduate Programs
    Undergraduate Programs
Courses: General Training 282
    General EC Professional Courses
    Maryland Certification Courses
    Montessori School Training
    Reggio Emilia Preschool Training
Courses: Mentoring Programs and Training for Trainers 288
Courses: Scholarships For EC Professionals .289
Helplines for EC Professionals 290
Job Clearinghouses for EC Professionals 291
Organizations for EC Professionals 292
    General Organizations
    Cooperative Preschool Organizations
    Directors' Organizations
    Family Child Care Organizations
Publications for EC Professionals 296
    Books for EC Professionals
    Journals and Magazines for EC Professionals
    Library Resources for EC Professionals
    Newsletters for EC Professionals
Videos for EC Professionals 301

Using
The Early Childhood Resource Directory

The Resource Directory is divided into six sections:

GENERAL RESOURCES includes general listings of interest to both parents and professionals.

HEALTH CARE RESOURCES includes listings concerning the physical, neurological, visual, speech, and hearing growth and development of young children.

MENTAL HEALTH RESOURCES includes listings concerning the emotional, social, behavorial, and cognitive growth and development of young children and their families. Testing and assessment resources are included in this section.

CHILD CARE AND SCHOOL RESOURCES includes listings about child care and schools. Information about nannies, home care providers, daycare centers, and private and public preschools and kindergartens are included in this section. Resources for child care professionals and child care centers and schools are in EC PROFESSIONAL RESOURCES.

PARENT RESOURCES includes listings for parent information and support.

EARLY CHILDHOOD PROFESSIONAL RESOURCES includes listings for early childhood education professionals and for child care centers and schools. Listings about child care and schools are in CHILD CARE AND SCHOOL RESOURCES.

The Resource Directory covers the following geographic areas:

District of Columbia

Maryland: Montgomery County
Prince George's County

Virginia: Alexandria
Arlington County
Fairfax County

Metro Area resources listed are resources available throughout the entire Washington metropolitan area: DC, MD, and VA.

Resources in other cities and counties in Maryland and Virginia are listed when relevant.

National Resources are listed when relevant.

The Resource Directory includes:

TABLE OF CONTENTS: A Table of Contents is provided at the beginning of the Directory. A more detailed Table of Contents is included at the beginning of each main section.

GLOSSARY: A glossary explaining special abbreviations and terms is at the back of the Directory.

RESOURCE DIRECTORY UPDATE FORM: A form is provided at the back of the Directory for those individuals or organizations wishing to have information included or updated in the next edition of the Resource Directory.

ORDER FORM: Order forms for additional copies of the Directory are included in the back.

INDEX: An index has been provided at the back of the Directory.

Listing Notes:

Be sure to look in "Metro Area" when available. Metro Area resources are available throughout the entire Washington metropolitan area. These resources are not repeated in the separate District of Columbia, Maryland, and Virginia listings.

See also at the beginning of resource listings provides cross-references.

Multi-lingual, multi-cultural, and special needs resources are included as available. Special sections and annotations in the listings indicate these resources.

Inclusion in the Resource Directory is free of charge to the individuals and organizations listed in an effort to provide an information directory rather than a commercial directory.

All professional licensing and accreditation is through federal and/or state government regulatory agencies and/or professional organizations. Licensing, accreditation, and degrees should always be verified by the consumer.

Looking for a Topic:

(1) <u>First look in the Table of Contents</u> at the beginning of the Resource Directory. Look in General Resources first. When a topic is relevant to both parents and professionals, it is listed in the General Resources section.

(2) <u>Check the other main sections in the Table of Contents.</u> Each section has a helpful introduction.

(3) <u>Try the Index</u> at the back of the Resource Directory.

(4) <u>Locate a similar category</u> and look at the "See also" cross-references for help.

(5) <u>Try the "Information and Resources" section</u> of the relevant section.

(6) <u>Go to "Helplines" in GENERAL RESOURCES</u> and see if anyone at the helpline has an answer.

Looking for a Specific Resource:

First look in the Index at the back of the Resource Directory.

Example of a Search:

"How can I find someone to check my child for ADD or developmental delays?"

<u>Search Options:</u>

(1) <u>Using the Table of Contents</u>, look in MENTAL HEALTH RESOURCES. Check out "Counseling Centers," or individual "Mental Health Practitioners," noting the listings that refer to "ADD" or "testing," or . . .

(2) <u>Using the Index</u>, look under "ADD," "Developmental Delays," "Special Needs" or "Testing and Assessment," or . . .

(3) <u>Look in PARENT RESOURCES:</u> Parent Info for "ADD," or . . .

(4) <u>Go to "Helplines" in GENERAL RESOURCES</u> and call a helpline phone number.

"How Can I Help My Child?" Early Childhood Resource Directory

9

About
The Early Childhood
Consultation Center

This Resource Directory was compiled by The Early Childhood Consultation Center (ECCC) in Silver Spring, Maryland. The ECCC, "Helping Parents with Preschoolers," provides services and support to parents and early childhood professionals caring about children ages 2 through 7. The Center provides both educational workshops and consultations to families, preschools, and child care providers concerning child development issues.

Educational workshops focus on young children's emotional and social development through exploration of issues such as creative discipline, anger management, separation concerns, sibling relationships, and age-appropriate behavior. Workshops are conducted at ECCC facilities in Silver Spring as well as on-site at schools, daycare centers, and places of business.

The ECCC provides services and support for families dealing with the challenges of raising children in today's world. Family consultations are provided through home visits where family communication and parent-child issues are explored. Consultations may deal with issues such as anger management, separation problems, toilet training, sleep problems, school adjustment, divorce, moving, fears, and dealing with death.

Consultations to schools, day care centers, and home care providers may address issues such as staff development, classroom curriculum, and child behavior concerns.

Any inquiries concerning The Early Childhood Consultation Center are welcome at 301-593-5992.

About the Editor

In 1994, Irene Shere founded The Early Childhood Consultation Center. Believing that the first several years in a child's life are crucial to who they are in the world and how they are in the world, Irene conducts workshops and provides consultations to families, schools, daycare centers, and businesses.

Irene has been an educator for over 20 years. She is a member of the American Counseling Association, a former preschool teacher and director, president of the Potomac Association of Cooperative Teachers (P.A.C.T.), and a trainer approved by the Maryland Child Care Administration in seven areas of preschool development. In addition, Irene has consulted on articles about young children for *The Washington Post, Maryland Family Magazine,* and *Working Mother.* She is the co-author of three children's books featured on the television show *Reading Rainbow: Cat's Out of the Bag, In the Doghouse,* and *Grin and Bear It.*

Irene is married and has two children. She is a native of the Washington metro area.

12

"How Can I Help My Child?" Early Childhood Resource Directory

General Resources

Resources for Both Parents and Professionals

GENERAL RESOURCES includes:

- **Advocacy Groups**
- **Books, Etc.**: includes other Resource Guides
- **Computer Resources**
- **Conferences and Speaker Series**
- **Government Information and Resources**
- **Helplines**: staffed during regular business hours
- **HOTLINES**: staffed 24 hours a day, 7 days a week
- **Play Equipment and Playgrounds**
- **Toys, Etc.**: includes craft supplies and educational supplies
- **Videos**: educational videos for adults and quality videos for children

The Table of Contents on the next page provides a detailed listing of this section.

Note:

Be sure to look in "Metro Area" when available. Metro Area resources are available throughout the entire Washington metropolitan area. These resources are not repeated in the separate District of Columbia, Maryland, and Virginia listings.

"How Can I Help My Child?" Early Childhood Resource Directory

13

General Resources
Table of Contents

Advocacy Groups 15
Books, Etc. 17
   Book Finders 17
   Book Stores 17
   Catalogs and Distributors 21
   Library Resources 23
   Magazines for Adults 24
   Magazines for Children 25
   Newsletters about Books 26
   Newsletters and Newspapers 27
   Personalized Books 29
   Resource Guides 30
Computer Resources 34
   Consultants 34
   Courses for Children and Adults 34
   Online Services: General 35
   Online Services: Books and Literature 37
   Online Services: For Children 37
   Online Services: Security 37
   Software 38
Conferences and Speaker Series 40
Government Information and Resources 42
Helplines 44
   Multi-lingual Helplines 46
HOTLINES 47
   Multi-lingual Hotlines 48
Play Equipment and Playgrounds 49
   Consultants 49
   Equipment 50
Toys, Etc. 52
   Catalogs and Distributors 52
   Craft Supplies 57
   Educational Supply Stores 60
   Toy Recommendations 62
   Toy Rentals 62
   Toy Replacement Parts 62
   Toy Safety 63
   Toy Stores 64
   Used Toys 69
Videos 70
   Videos for Adults 70
   Videos for Children 71
   Video Reviews 72

14

"How Can I Help My Child?" Early Childhood Resource Directory

Advocacy Groups

See also **PARENT RESOURCES: Organizations, Advocacy Groups**
EC PROFESSIONAL RESOURCES: Organizations

NATIONAL

Children's Defense Fund 1-800-233-1200
25 E Street, NW   202-628-8787
Washington, DC 20001   FAX: 202-662-3540
    legislative programs and policies for children

Children's Foundation 202-347-3300
725 15th Street, NW, Suite 505   cfwashdc@aol.com
Washington, DC 20005
    advocacy group for children and parents; issues such as health care,
    child support, publications

KidsCampaigns 1-888-661-KIDS
    information on Coalition for America's Children   http://www.kidscampaigns.org
    and children's issues and advocacy organizations

Multicultural Education Training and Advocacy, Inc. (META) 617-628-2226
240A Elm Street, #22   FAX: 617-628-0322
Sommerville, MA 02145
    advocacy for immigrant youth from low-income households; training for
    parents and teachers

National Association for the Education of Young Children 202-232-8777
1509 16th Street, NW   1-800-424-2460
Washington, DC 20036   FAX: 202-328-1846
    services and advocacy for young children ages birth to 8; books, brochures,
    conferences for parents and professionals

National Association of Child Advocates 202-289-0777
                                                                                      FAX: 202-289-0776
                                                                                      HN1315@handsnet.org

National Black Child Development Institute 1-800-556-2234
1023 15th Street, NW, Suite 600   202-387-1281
Washington, DC 20005   FAX: 202-234-1738
    information for parents and providers; publications; advocacy; quarterly
    publication "Child Advocate"; focus on health, child welfare, education and
    child care, early childhood education

National Center for Missing and Exploited Children .1-800-843-5678
2101 Wilson Blvd., Suite 550   FAX: 703-235-3900
Arlington, VA 22201   202-635-9821
                                                        http://www.missingkids.org/publication.html

Parent Action 410-727-3687
2 North Charles Street, Suite 960
Baltimore, MD 21201
    provides advocacy, programs, and access to local networks

GENERAL RESOURCES

Stand for Children 202-234-0095
    Department P, 1834 Connecticut Avenue, NW   FAX: 202-234-0217
    Washington, DC 20009   tellstand@stand.org
        child advocacy group   www.stand.org
Stand for Children Action Center 1-800-663-4032
        resource guides developed from the Stand for Children March;   http://www.stand.org
        guides such as the <u>Everyday Action Guide</u>

United Families of America 202-546-1600
    220 I Street, NE, Suite 150
    Washington, DC 20002
        public policy and legislation; training for lobbying

DISTRICT OF COLUMBIA

DC Association for the Education of Young Children (DCAEYC)
    Mattie Edwards, President 202-332-3680
        services and advocacy for people concerned with the well-being of
        young children, ages birth to 8

MARYLAND

Maryland Committee for Children 410-752-7588
    608 Water Street
    Baltimore, MD 21202
        speaker series; parent and professional training public policy reports; child
        care referral; school selection; newsletters

Maryland Association for the Education of Young Children (MAEYC)
    Rivalee Gitomer 410-455-4236
    Vickie Kaneko, 3928 Rolling Road, 7-C, Baltimore, MD 21208 410-767-6890
    Arundel-Bowie AEYC, ...301-206-2082
        Ester Parker, 2307 Westport Lane, Crofton, MD 21114
    Central MD AEYC 410-296-2955
        Cathy Owings, 1015 Winsford Road, Towson, MD 21204
    Maryland Community AEYC (MCAEYC) 301-229-4146
        Ann Byrne, 5905 Namakagan Road, Bethesda, MD 20816
    Southern MD AEYC 301-855-4714
        Brenda Tyrrell, 8816 Donald's Way, Owings, MD 20736
    Western MD AEYC 301-689-2808
        Denise Payne, University Children's Center, 104 Pullen Hall, Frostburg, MD 21532
            services and advocacy for people concerned with the well-being of
            young children, ages birth to 8

VIRGINIA

Virginia Association for the Education of Young Children (VAEYC)
    Mary Landis, membership 757-272-9266
    Sharon Stottlemyer, information 540-786-2065
    VAEYC President 804-560-2700
        services and advocacy for people concerned with the well-being of
        young children, ages birth to 8

Books, Etc.

See also **EC PROFESSIONAL RESOURCES: Publications**

BOOK FINDERS

BooksNow 1-800-962-6651
      one-stop book shop has every title in   ext. 7000
      print; books, CDs, videos; full research department   http://www.booksnow.com
      specializing in finding hard-to-get titles

Children's BookAdoption Agency 301-565-2834
      Barbara B. Yoffee, M.S.Ed., Director
      P.O. Box 643
      Kensington, MD 20895
            buying, selling, searches, want lists; out-of-print and nostalgia books; phone
            anytime; visits by appointment

BOOK STORES

See also **GENERAL RESOURCES: Toys, Etc., Toy Stores**
              EC PROFESSIONAL RESOURCES: Publications, Books

District of Columbia

Barnes and Noble 202-965-9880
      3040 M Street, NW
      Washington, DC 20007

Cheshire Cat Children's Books 202-244-3956
      5512 Connecticut Ave, NW
      Washington, DC 20015
            books, storytime, author visits; call for newsletter

Crown Books, Super Crown
      3335 Connecticut Avenue, NW 202-966-7232
      11 Dupont Circle, NW 202-319-1374
      2020 K Street, NW 202-659-2030
      1275 K Street, NW 202-289-7170
      1200 New Hampshire Avenue, NW 202-822-8331

Fairy Godmother 202-547-5474
      319 7th Street, SE
      Washington, DC

Health Source Bookstore 1-800-713-7122
      1404 K Street, NW   202-789-7303
      Washington, DC 20005   FAX: 202-789-7899
            health books for children and parents

Metropolitan Family Bookstore 202-332-7590
1225 R Street, NW
Washington, DC 20009

Politics and Prose 202-364-1919
5015 Connecticut Avenue, NW   FAX: 202-966-7532
Washington, DC 20008   http://www.politics-prose.com
    children's book room, parenting books   books@politics-prose.com

Travel Books and Language Center 202-237-1322
4437 Wisconsin Avenue
Washington, DC 20016
    books on travelling with children

Tree Top Toys & Books, Inc 202-244-3500
3301 New Mexico Avenue, NW
Washington, DC 20016

Maryland

Audubon Naturalist Bookshop 301-652-3606
8940 Jones Mill Road at Woodend
Chevy Chase, MD 20815
    nature books for children

Barnes and Noble 301-986-1761
4801 Bethesda Avenue
Bethesda, MD 20814

Book Nook 301-474-4060
9933 Rhode Island Avenue
College Park, MD 20740
used books

Bookoo Books for Kids, etc! 301-652-2794
4945 Elm Street
Bethesda, MD 20814
    books; storytime; birthday parties

Borders Books and Music
11301 Rockville Pike, Kensington 301-816-1067
534 N. Frederick Avenue, Gaithersburg 301-921-0990
    children's books, parenting books; storytime; special orders

Chuck and Dave's 301-891-2665
7001 Carroll Avenue
Takoma Park, MD 20912
    children's books

Cricket Book Shop, The 301-774-4242
17800 New Hampshire Avenue
Ashton, MD 20861
    children's books

Crown Books, Super Crown
  4601 East-West Highway, Bethesda 301-656-5775
  5265 River Road, Bethesda 301-986-0091
  6828 Race Track Road, Bowie 301-352-0446
  295 Kentlands Blvd., Gaithersburg 301-258-9330
  7495 Greenbelt Road, Greenbelt 301-441-8220
  5110 Nicholson Lane, Kensington 301-770-6729
  18153 Village Mart Drive, Olney 301-774-3917
  7727 Tuckerman Lane, Potomac 301-299-4104
  13826 Outlet Drive, Silver Spring 301-890-6177
  11181 Veirs Mill Road, Wheaton 301-942-7995

Toys...Etc. 301-299-8300
  11325 Seven Locks Road, Cabin John Mall
  Potomac, MD 20854
    books, storytime

Zany Brainy
  2522 Solomon's Island Road, Annapolis 410-266-1447
  9097 Snowden River Pkwy, Columbia 410-312-0783
  1631 Rockville Pike, Rockville 301-984-0112
    books; storytime

Virginia

Aladdin's Lamp Children's Bookstore 703-241-8281
  126 West Broad Street, Route 7
  Falls Church, VA 22046
    "Children's Books and Other Treasures"; books, storytime

A Likely Story Children's Bookstore 703-836-2498
  1555 King Street   ALS@Chandler.com
  Alexandria, VA 22314
    books, educational games, audio and video tapes

Book Nook 703-591-6545
  10312 Main Street
  Fairfax, VA

Borders Books and Music
  5871 Crossroads Center Way, Baileys Crossroads 703-998-0404
  22054 Lee Highway, Fairfax 703-359-8420
    children's books, parenting books; storytime; special orders

Color Book Gallery 703-768-9698
  2903A Arlington Drive
  Alexandria, VA 22306
    books; large multi-cultural selection, storytime

Crown Books, Super Crown

501 King Street, Alexandria	703-548-3432
6244 Little River Turnpike, Alexandria	703-750-3553
6230 N. Kings Highway, Alexandria	703-765-1858
4017 S. 28th Street, Arlington	703-931-6949
9246 Ole Keene Mill Road, Burke	703-451-0350
6011 Centreville Crest Lane, Centreville	703-968-6617
13005 Lee Jackson Memorial Highway, Fairfax	703-378-2052
9508 Main Street, Fairfax	703-425-9188
7511 Leesburg Pike, Falls Church	703-506-0339
6286 Arlington Blvd., Falls Church	703-534-4830
7271 Arlington Blvd., Falls Church	703-573-3500
1451 Chain Bridge Road, McLean	703-893-7640
2924 Chain Bridge Road, Oakton	703-281-0820
11620 Plaza America Drive, Reston	703-834-6160
6758 Springfield Mall, Springfield	703-313-8370
46301 Potomac Run Plaza, Sterling	703-450-8705
8365 Leesburg Pike, Vienna	703-442-0133

Imagination Station Children's Books 703-522-2047
4524 Lee Highway
Arlington, VA 22207

Why Not 703-548-4420
200 King Street
Alexandria, VA 22314

Zany Brainy

3513 Jefferson Street, Bailey's Crossroads	703-998-1203
2890 Prince William Pkwy, Dale City	703-680-9870
9484 Main Street, Fairfax	703-323-3658
12180 West Ox Road, Fairfax	703-691-1896
11870 Spectrum Center, Reston	703-319-1875
6575 Frontier Drive, Springfield	703-719-9585
46262-115 Cranston Street, Sterling	703-404-8850

    books; storytime; special activities

CATALOGS AND DISTRIBUTORS

National

Children's Book Council 212-966-1990
Book Week Catalog
568 Broadway, Suite 404
New York, NY 10012
> information about Book Week (week before Thanksgiving) and other
> materials about children's books and authors

Chinaberry Books 1-800-776-2242
2780 Via Orange Way, Suite B   FAX: 1-619-670-5200
Spring Valley, CA 91978
> quality children's books and tapes by mail; free catalog

Edu-Kinesthetics Publications 805-650-3303
P.O. Box 3396   FAX: 805-650-0524
Ventura, CA 93006
> books on learning through movement; "brain gym" activities

Faber/Mazlish Workshops, LLC 1-800-944-8584
Dept. 103A   FAX: 914-967-8130
P.O. Box 37   customer counselor: 914-967-8130
Rye, NY 10580
> workbooks, audio tapes, video tapes from the award-winning book *How to
> Talk So Kids Will Listen and Listen So Kids Will Talk*

Magination Press 1-800-825-3089
19 Union Square West, 8th Floor
New York, NY 10003
> books written by professionals to help parents help their children

National Association for the Education of Young Children 202-232-8777
1509 16th Street, NW   1-800-424-2460
Washington, DC 20036   FAX: 202-328-1846
> books, brochures, and videos for parents & professionals; free
> *Early Childhood Resources Catalog*

National Maternal and Child Health Clearinghouse .703-821-8955
8205 Greensboro Drive, Suite 600
McLean, VA 22102
> distributors of catalogs for professional and self-help organizations

Parenting Press, Inc 1-800-992-6657
P.O. Box 75267
Seattle, WA 98125
> children's books about emotional and social issues; parenting books

Scholastic, Inc. 1-800-724-6527
P.O. Box 7502   FAX: 573-636-2749
Jefferson City, MO 65102
> early childhood catalog

Soundprints 1-800-577-2413
353 Main Avenue
Norwalk, CT 06851
> interactive toys, books, tapes, and puppets for kids

Metro Area

Dorling Kindersley Family Learning
Hildegard B. Groves, Independent distributor 301-340-6621
    14913 Talking Rock Court, Gaithersburg, MD 20878
Marcia Helms, Independent distributor 703-690-0159
    9400 Crosspointe Drive, Fairfax, VA 22039
Julie Kind, Independent Distributor 301-977-2993
    educational books, videos, and CD-ROMS

Gryphon House, Inc. 1-800-638-0928
    P.O. Box 207   FAX: 301-595-0051
    Beltsville, MD 20704   http://www.ghbooks.com
    quality books for children ages 2-8

Usborne Books At Home
Mary Bond 703-569-5331
Other Distributors 301-774-1723
                                                    703-266-2682
    children's books and kits sold through book fairs or catalog   703-768-4624

LIBRARY RESOURCES

District of Columbia

Martin Luther King, Jr, Memorial Library 202-727-1111
901 G Street, NW
Washington, DC
main library

Maryland

Children's Resource Center 301-217-3800
Rockville Regional Library
99 Maryland Avenue
Rockville, MD 20850
extensive educational book and video collection for parents and
professionals; borrowers do not need to be Montgomery County residents

InfoConnect 301-217-3875
fee-based research service by appointment only

Night Owl Reference Service 1-800-325-NITE
toll-free Maryland State Library Resource Center

Special Needs Library 301-897-2212
6400 Democracy Blvd.   TDD: 301-897-2217
Bethesda, MD 20817
special format reading material; information on special needs, disabilities

Virginia

Alexandria Libraries 703-838-4555
Arlington County Libraries 703-358-5990
Fairfax County Libraries 703-222-3155
www.co.fairfax.va.us/library
On-line Library catalog; modem phone # 703-802-7447
Library Administration
13135 Lee Jackson Highway, Suite 301
Fairfax, VA 22033

Falls Church City Libraries 703-241-5030

Special Education Parent Resource Center 703-358-7238
Clarendon Education Center   703-358-7239
2801 Clarendon Blvd, Suite 304
Arlington, VA 22201
resource library for support and education for parents and staff working
with children with disabilities

GENERAL RESOURCES

MAGAZINES FOR ADULTS

See also EC PROFESSIONAL RESOURCES: Publications

National

Child, The Essential Guide for Today's Parents 212-499-2000
    Gruner and Jahr USA Publishing
    375 Lexington Avenue
    New York, NY 10017
        monthly magazine

Family Life 303-604-1464
    P.O. Box 52220   FAX: 303-604-7455
    Boulder, CO 80322
        monthly magazine

Freebies
    1135 Eugenia Place, Box 5025
    Carpinteria, CA 93014
        free mail-order items for children; sample copy for $2.50; specify edition for
        kids and families

Kidsnet Media Guide and News 202-291-1400
    Kidsnet
    6856 Eastern Avenue, NW, Suite 208
    Washington, DC 20012
        monthly media guide reviewing children's television, radio, audio, video,
        and multimedia

Modern Dad, For a New Generation of Fathers .312-465-8088
    Next Generation Publishing, Inc.   FAX: 312-465-8299
    7628 N.Rogers Avenue
    Chicago, IL 60626
        bi-monthly magazine

Mothering, The Magazine of Natural Family Living 505-984-8116
    Mothering Magazine, Inc.   FAX: 505-986-8335
    P.O. Box 1690   mother@ni.net
    Santa Fe, NM 87504
        monthly magazine

Parenting 303-678-8475
    Parenting Magazine
    P.O. Box 56861
    Boulder, CO 80322
        ten issues per year

Parents 212-499-2000
    Gruner and Jahr USA Publishing
    375 Lexington Avenue
    New York, NY 10017
        monthly magazine

P*R*A*C*T*I*C*A*L Parenting, From Pregnancy to Preschool
    Kings' Reach Towers
    Stamford Street
    London, England SE1 9LS
        monthly magazine available at Borders Books and Music

Working Mother 212-551-9500
    MacDonald Communications Corporation
    135 West 50th Street
    New York, NY 10020
        ten issues per year

Metro Area

Maryland Family Magazine 410-366-7512
        materials for parents of children of all ages in Baltimore area   FAX: 410-366-7601

MAGAZINES FOR CHILDREN

Chickadee 1-800-387-4379
    The Magazine for Young Children from Owl   FAX: 416-971-5294
    25 Boxwood Lane
    Buffalo, NY 14227

Ladybug, The Magazine for Young Children 1-800-827-0227
    The Cricket Magazine Group
    315 Fifth Street
    P.O. Box 300
    Peru, IL 61354
        magazine for children ages 2 to 6; features stories, songs, crafts, with a
        parent's guide

Let's Find Out 1-800-631-1586
    Scholastic Magazine Corporation
    Scholastic, Incorporated
    P.O. Box 3710
    Jefferson City, MO 65102
        reading and activities magazine for young children

Sesame Street 303-604-1465
    P.O. Box 52000
    Boulder, CO 80322
        magazine based on the TV show characters, for ages 2-6

Your Big Back Yard 703-790-4000
    National Wildlife Federation
    8925 Leesburg Pike
    Vienna, VA 22184
        nature magazine for children ages 3-5

NEWSLETTERS ABOUT BOOKS

See also **EC PROFESSIONAL RESOURCES: Publications**

Book Links, Booklist 1-800-545-2433
    American Library Association
    50 East Huron Street
    Chicago, IL 60611
        newsletters about books, videos, and audio-tapes

Children's Literature Newsletter 301-469-2070
    7513 Shadywood Road
    Bethesda, MD 20817
        monthly review of children's literature

Parent's Choice 617-965-5913
    Parent's Choice Foundation
    P.O. Box 185
    Newton, MA 02168
        quarterly journal of Parent's Choice books and videos

School Library Journal 1-800-456-9409
        monthly review of new books for children of all ages; available at public
        library or by subscription

NEWSLETTERS AND NEWSPAPERS

National

Choice Music for Kids
Clifton Press
P.O. Box 583083
Minneapolis, MN 55485
    bimonthly newsletter about music for young children; send request for a
    free issue to above address

Joyful Child Journal
P.O. Box 566
Buffalo, NY 14213
    quarterly publication offering educational and inspirational articles for
    parents and professionals, along with values-based stories for children

Love and Logic Journal 1-800-338-4065
2207 Jackson Street
Golden, CO 80401
    quarterly journal on psychological and educational issues concerning
    children; $15 per year

Parent and Preschooler Newsletter 1-800-726-1708
Preschool Publications, Inc.   516-626-1971
P.O. Box 1167   FAX: 1-516-765-4927
Cutchogue, NY 11935
    a monthly exploration of early childhood topics for parents and educators;
    an international resource for parents and professionals; articles reproducible
    for school/center use; available in English and English/Spanish

Parenting Psychology News 714-369-7573
Barbara U. Hammer, Ph.D., and Charles H. Hammer, Ph.D.
2438 Calle Aquamarina
San Clemente, CA 92673
    newsletter providing latest information to help guide families toward
    psychological wellness

Raising Your Child's Self-Esteem
P.O. Box 1003
North Wales, PA 19454
    newsletter of original articles and articles from other publications
    encouraging parents to develop the potential that is in each child

Safety P.I.N., The 301-681-1584
P.O. Box 86031
Gaithersburg, MD 20886
    child safety newsletter providing up-to-date safety info for children birth to 8;
    six issues per year

Metro Area

El Montgomery 301-309-0129
    biweekly newspaper in Spanish

Family Times 202-363-3333
    The Washington Times newspaper, Tuesday edition
    weekly section addressing the issues and challenges of families

Foreign-born Parent Network 703-812-8716
2700 N. Wakefield Street
Arlington, VA 22207
    interactive newsletter focusing on how a second language and culture affect
    a foreign-born family; also offers workshops for families

Kidstreet News 410-730-9308
P.O. Box 205   301-596-6180
Columbia, MD 21045
    monthly newspaper for families; no July issue

Maryland Child Care Resource Network Training Calendar
Susan Thorpe, Editor 410-752-7588
Maryland Childcare Resource Network
608 Water Street
Baltimore, MD 21202
    quarterly publication of the MD Committee for Children and MD Child Care
    Administration; lists workshops throughout Maryland that are presented by
    organizations with MD Child Care Administration approval

Maryland Council of Parent Participation Nursery Schools (MCPPNS) Newsletter
Cooperatively Speaking
Kirsten Rhoades 301-933-9840
    newsletter for cooperative preschool parents and schools; published three
    times per school year; winter issue contains information about March
    Conference

Parentline: Parents Supporting Parents 301-424-0656
    newletter published quarterly by the Mental Health Association of
    Montgomery County

Virginia Cooperative Preschool Council Newsletter
Cooperative Voice
Kathryn Conklin, President 703-361-0146
Leslie Sirriani, Vice President 703-533-3181
    newsletter for cooperative parents and preschools; published twice a year

Washington Families
3 Bethesda Metro Center, Suite 750, Bethesda, MD 20814 301-656-0901
462 Herndon Parkway, Suite 206, Herndon, VA 20170 703-318-1385
                                                                                     FAX: 703-318-5509
                                                                                     WashFAMILS@aol.com
    monthly newspaper for active families in MD, DC, and Northern VA

Washington Parent 301-320-2321
The Parent Connection   washpar@washingtonparent.com
5606 Knollwood Road   http://washingtonparent.com
Bethesda, MD 20816
    monthly newspaper for families

PERSONALIZED BOOKS

Books About Me 1-888-855-6874
P.O. Box 5461   719-390-3212
Colorado Springs, CO 80931
personalized books; call or write for free brochure

Create-a-Book
customized book in which your child is the lead character; birthday books,
dinosaur adventures, farm adventures, Hanukkah books, Christmas books;
ordered through Learningsmith Toy Stores

Just for You 703-451-4225
P.O. Box 2758   FAX: 703-569-5705
Springfield, VA 22152
personalized books and tapes; Create-A-Book available

My-Name Gifts 301-670-5202
your child is the star of the story; washable, hardcover

Personalized Children's Books 301-773-4583
G & G Enterprise, Dept. PRG0196
P.O. Box 1298
Landover, MD 20785
your child is the star of the story

Uncle John's Create-a-Book 540-439-8621
personalized children's storybooks; free catalog listing over 30 titles

RESOURCE GUIDES

National

American Academy of Pediatrics Parent Resource Guide
AAP Publications 1-800-433-9016
P.O. Box 927
Elk Grove Village, IL 60009

Best Toys, Books, Videos & Software for Kids 1997, The
Joanne Oppenheim, author
Oppenheim Toy Portfolio/Energizer Toy Line 1-800-544-8697
Prima Publishing 1-800-632-8676

Parents' Resource Almanac, The 1-800-872-5627
Beth DeFrancis, author
Bob Adams, Inc., publisher
260 Center Street
Holbrook, MA 02343
resource almanac extensively covering parent issues; endorsed by *Parents'
Choice* magazine; over 750 pages

Reaching Out 703-821-8955
National Maternal and Child Health Clearinghouse   ext. 254 or 265
8205 Greensboro Drive, Suite 600   FAX: 703-821-2098
McLean, VA 22102
free 180 page directory of over 400 national organizations related to
maternal and child health

Resources for Early Childhood: A Handbook,
edited by Hannah Nuba et al.; Garland, 1994
resource book includes essays and annotated bibliographies by experts on all aspects
of child development and early childhood education; available at local libraries

Self-Help Resource Book, The 201-625-7101
American Self-Help Clearinghouse   http://www.cmhc.com/selfhelp
Northwest Covenant Medical Center
Denville, NJ 07834
contacts for any national self-help group; $9; help starting a support group

Spirit of Excellence, National Black Child Development Institute Resource Catalog
National Black Child Development Institute 1-800-556-2234
1023 15th Street, NW, Suite 600   202-387-1281
Washington, DC 20005   FAX: 202-234-1738
free catalog of books and videos on advocacy, health, and education

Stand for Children Action Center 1-800-663-4032
http://www.stand.org
resource guides from the Stand for Children March

Who to Call, The Parent's Source Book
Daniel Starer, author
William Morrow and Company, Inc., Publishers
1350 Avenue of the Americas
New York, NY 10019
resource guide to 800 numbers, hotlines, and organizations for raising
children; over 600 pages; available at local bookstores

Metro Area

Directory of Self-Help Support Groups 703-838-7535
National Mental Health Association Information Center
1021 Prince Street
Alexandria, VA 22314
> over 1200 listings of support groups in the Washington metro area;
> $30 plus $5 shipping and handling

"How Can I Help My Child?" Early Childhood Resource Directory For
Parents and Professionals Caring About Children Ages 2 through 5
in the Washington Metro Area
Irene Shere, editor
The Early Childhood Consultation Center 301-593-5992
11506 Michale Court
Silver Spring, MD 20904
> directory of general, health care, mental health, child care and school,
> parent, and EC professional resources

Independent School Guide for Washington DC & Surrounding Area
Independent Schools Guides 301-986-5370
7315 Brookville Road   301-652-8635
Chevy Chase, MD 20815   301-986-0698
> over 340 private schools from preschool up; includes summer programs, day
> care LD/ED; area book stores or send $14.95 + $2.00 postage & handling

Metropolitan Washington Preschool and Day Care Guidebook
Merry Cavanaugh 202-338-7257
3833 Calvert Street, NW
Washington, DC 20007
> descriptive guide of over 1,000 listings in MD, DC, and VA; available by
> phone or at Crown Books and The Cheshire Cat bookstore

Parent Resource Guide for the Metropolitan Washington Area, The 703-698-8066
Vienna, VA 22182   FAX: 703-698-8067
> parent resource guide; $6.95 + shipping

Raising Your Child in Washington, A Guide for the Growing Years
Piccolo Press/Dept. WP 703-519-0376
901 King Street, Suite 102
Alexandria, VA
> parenting resource guide written by Washington area child development
> experts; call for a free brochure; $15.95 + $2.25 shipping

Washington's CHILD Project (WCP) 202-966-7543
3031 Oregon Knolls Drive
Washington, DC 20015
> directory of area parenting education programs and services for
> economically disadvantaged, single parent families

WISER, Directory of Educational Services in the Washington Area 301-816-0432
11140 Rockville Pike, #105
Rockville, MD 20852
> referral network for educational resources

Metro Area Activities

Frommer's Washington, D.C., with Kids 212-698-7200
    Beth Rubin, author
    Macmillan Travel, A Simon & Schuster Macmillan Company
    1633 Broadway
    New York, NY 10019
        activity guidebook for children ages 2-14; $15.95; area book stores

Going Places With Children in Washington, DC 301-881-4100
    Green Acres School Publication
    11701 Danville Drive
    Rockville, MD 20852
        activity guidebook for Alexandria, Baltimore, Annapolis, Frederick, and points
        in-between; book stores $11.95; mail orders $13.50

Kidding Around Washington, D.C. 505-982-4078
    Debbie Levy, author
    John Muir Publications
    P.O. Box 613
    Santa Fe, NM 87504
        travel and activity book for children; area book stores

Kid's Guide to Washington, D.C., A 407-345-2000
    Diane C. Clark, author
    Gulliver Books
    Harcourt Brace & Company
    6277 Sea Harbor Drive
    Orlando, FL 32887
        children's guide to DC; area book stores

Places to Go with Children in Washington, D.C. 415-777-7240
    Judy Colbert, author
    Chronicle Books
    275 Fifth Street
    San Francisco, CA 94103
        activity guidebook for children; $10.95 in area bookstores

Maryland

Montgomery County, Maryland, Quick Guide to Community Resources
Montgomery County Information and Referral 301-217-6500
101 Monroe Street, 2nd Floor   http://www.co.mo.md.us/inforef.html
Rockville, MD 20850
      44 page guide to services; $.25 each

Parent Resource Guide: How to Get Through the First 21 Years
Montgomery County Community Partnership 301-929-8550
The Healthy Montgomery Coalition   301-217-1708
      parent resource guide for Montgomery County

Virginia

Parenting Education Resource Guide for Arlington County
Clarendon Education Center 703-358-7215
2801 Clarendon Blvd., Suite 306
Arlington, VA 22201
      free directory of services in Arlington County

Parenting Program Guide 703-846-8670
Parenting Education Center, PPG
Lacey Instructional Center
3705 Crest Drive
Annandale, VA 22203
      free reference guide to parenting programs, classes and activities in Fairfax
      County; printed two times a year

Resources for Parents in Fairfax County 703-846-8670
Parenting Education Center, PPG
Lacey Instructional Center
3705 Crest Drive
Annandale, VA 22003
      free brochure offered in 10 different languages

Computer Resources

See also EC PROFESSIONAL RESOURCES: Computer Resources

CONSULTANTS

PC Solutions 301-593-2753
    10706 Blossom Lane   pcsolve@nicom.com
    Silver Spring, MD 20903
        complete systems; upgrades and maintenance; tutoring; installations

COURSES FOR CHILDREN AND ADULTS

Computer Clubhouse 301-258-0166
    843-B Quince Orchard Blvd   FAX: 301-990-2545
    Gaithersburg, MD 20878
        computer classes for children ages 3 and up

Computer Kids 301-983-9600
    10324 Windsor View Drive   301-983-4965
    Potomac, MD 20854
        on-site computer courses for children ages 4 through 12

Computer Tutors 301-384-ABCD

Computertots 301-365-8687
    serving Montgomery and Frederick Counties
Computertots 1-800-531-5053
    on-site computer instruction for schools and centers

Comsoft 301-652-MATH
    Bethesda, MD
        computer learning center for children of all ages

Even Start Family Learning Center 301-808-8106
    H. Winship Wheatley Special Center
    8801 Ritchie Drive
    Capital Heights, MD 20743
        family computer courses for adults with low literacy skills with a child
        between ages of birth to 7 years

FutureKids Computer Learning Centers
    Herndon, VA 703-707-0619
    McLean, VA 703-821-0847
        computer classes for children ages 3 and up

Kidz Online 703-442-9580
    Sharon Cruver, President   703-821-8309
        teaches computer skills to kids; allows parents to screen software before
        purchasing

ONLINE SERVICES

See also **EC PROFESSIONAL RESOURCES: Computer Resources**

Online Services: General

America Online . . . . .at keyword "Families"

American Self-Help Clearinghouse . . . . .http://www.cmhc.com/selfhelp
        contacts for any national self-help group

Children Now . . . . .http://www.childrennow.org/
        lists of resources and information on www relating to children locally,
        nationally, and internationally

Community LINC Computer Bulletin Board 301-424-5123
        Montgomery County, MD, information and referral source

Dr. Toy . . . . .http://www.drtoy.com
        recommendations on the best toys to buy

ERIC-Clearinghouse on Elementary and Early Childhood Education
                            http://ericps.crc.uiuc.edu/ericeece.html
                                 ericeece@uiuc.edu
University of Illinois at Urbana-Champaign 1-800-583-4135
51 Gerty Drive   217-333-1386
Champaign, IL 61820   FAX: 217-333-3767

ERIC-Educational Resources Information Center 1-800-LET-ERIC
        special needs resource   http://www.cec.sped.org./ericec.htm

ERIC-Listservs . . . . .ericeecel.cso.uiuc.edu
        sponsored listservs include the following:

                ECENET-L-listserv for discussion of issues related to development, education
                and care of children from birth through age 8

                ECPOLICY-listserv provides forum for those interested in discussing policy
                issues related to young children; co-sponsored with NAEYC

                REGGIO-L-listserv provides opportunity to discuss educational philosophy
                of Reggio Emilia preschools; co-sponsored with Merrill-Palmer Institute at
                Wayne State University

                SAC-listserv provides discussion for those interested in school-age care;
                co-sponsored with School-Age Child Care Project, Wellesley College Center
                for Research on Women

Family Education Network . . . . .www.familyeducation.com
        free online service that gives parents information, advice and discounts on
        education products

Family Planet .... .family.starwave.com
   "The Thinking Parent's Playground" 1-800-775-7891
      call for free Family Planet Starter Kit and one month free access to Family
      Planet and www through Netcom; parenting advice, family activities and
      travel; reviews on toys, movies, products, support from other parents

HeadStart .... http://www.acf.dhhs.gov/ACFPrograms/HeadStart/index.html

National Child Care Information Center .... http://ericps.ed.uiuc.edu/nccic/nccichome.html
      sponsored by the Child Care Bureau of the Dept. of Health and
      Human Services

National Center for Missing and Exploited Children
                              http://www.missingkids.org/publication.html

National Foundation for Gifted and Creative Children, The
                              http://www.nfgcc.oa.net/index.html

National Parent Information Network (NPIN)-ERIC 1-800-583-4135
                                                  ericeece@uiuc.edu
                                          http://ericps.crc.uiuc.edu/npin
      educational resource for parents and professionals; offers articles,
      question-answering service, discussions, access to other parents and
      organizations serving parents; ERIC digests

Parenting Advice .... .http://www.wholefamily.com
      psychologists and educators provide advice on parenting

Parenting Q & A .... .www.parenting-qa.com
      searchable database of answers from experts in child development and
      behavior

Parents AskERIC—ERIC 1-800-583-4135
                                                  askeric@ericir.syr.educ
      service for parents with questions about development, education and care
      of children from birth through high school years; part of ERIC

Washington Families
   Maryland 301-656-0901
   Virginia 703-318-1385
                                                  WashFAMILS@aol.com
      monthly newspaper for active families in MD, DC, and Northern VA

Washington Parent 301-320-2321
      monthly newspaper for families   washpar@washingtonparent.com
                                          http://washingtonparent.com

U.S. Dept. of Health & Human Services .... .http://www.acf.dhhs.gov/
      federal agency serving children and families

Online Services: Books and Literature

Children's Literature Web Guide, The . . . . .http://www.ucalgary.ca/~dkbrown/

Gryphon House . . . . .http://www.ghbooks.com/
       quality books for young children and ECE professionals

Vandergrift's Children's Literature Page . . .http://www.scils.rutgers.edu/special/kay/childlit.html
       discussion and reference materials

Online Services: For Children

Kids . . . . .http://www.lightspeed.net/kids.htm
       children's site on the www

KidsWeb . . . . .http://www.npac.syr.edu/textbook/kidsweb
                                           http://www.cccnet.com
       funded by New York State; access to instructional information for children
       in grades K-12

Yahoo Kids Links . . . . .http://www.yahoo.com/Society_and_Culture/Children/Links_for_Kids/

Online Services: Security

Cyber Patrol, Microsystems Software 1-800-828-2608
                                           http://www.cyberpatrol.com
       blocks access to Internet sites that have sexual or violent content

CYBERsitter, Solid Oak Software 1-800-388-2761
       http://www.solidoak.com
       blocks access to Internet sites that have sexual or violent content

Microsoft Plus! for Kids . . . . .http://www.microsoft.com/kids
       security features packaged with children's programs; password-protected
       parental controls

Net Nanny 1-800-340-7177
                                          http://www.netnanny.com
       logs sites visited or shuts down unapproved sites; prevents use of
       unauthorized diskettes and CD-ROMS

Net-Rated 1-800-404-9913
                                          http://www.netrated.com
       blocks Web sites, CD-ROMS and diskettes that are not pre-approved

PICS-Compatible Blocking Software http://www.w3.org/pub/WWW/PICS/
       www consortium's site for an interactive demonstration on how blocking
       software works

Recreational Software Advisory Council . . . . .http://www.rsac.org
       independent ratings system

SafeSurf . . . . .http://www.safesurf.com
        parent groups on independent ratings systems

SurfWatch 1-800-458-6600
                                        http://www.surfwatch.com
        screens Web sites; subscription automatically updates list of blocked sites

Time's Up!, The Fresh Software 1-800-846-3787
        blocks access to Internet sites that have sexual or violent content; also sets
        time limits for use

SOFTWARE

Booklist
        American Library Association 1-800-545-2433
        50 East Huron Street
        Chicago, IL 60611
            reviews of software, books, videos, audio tapes; twice monthly, with single
            issues in July and August

Brittman International Inc. . . . . .http://www.totalmarketing.com/brittman
        catalog on the Internet; 7000 special interest video and CD-ROM titles

Children's Software Revue 1-800-993-9499
        uses families to test computer software   www.childrenssoftware.com

Computer Clubhouse 301-258-0166
        843-B Quince Orchard Blvd   FAX: 301-990-2545
        Gaithersburg, MD 20878
        children's software

Disney's Animated Storybook 1-800-900-9234
        Disney Interactive

Eager to Learn, Sierra On-Line 1-800-757-7707
        60 creative learning activities

Edutainment Catalog, The 1-800-338-3844
        P.O. Box 21330   FAX: 1-800-226-1942
        Boulder, CO 80308
        PC and Mac software for the whole family

Houghton Mifflin Interactive 617-351-3333
        222 Berkeley Street   http://www.hmco.com
        Boston, MA 02116

JumpStart Pre-K, Knowledge Adventure 1-800-542-4240
        animated learning adventures

Kidsnet Media Guide and News 202-291-1400
    Kidsnet
    6856 Eastern Avenue, NW, Suite 208
    Washington, DC 20012
        monthly media guide reviewing children's electronic media

Kidz Online 703-442-9580
    teaches computer skills to kids; allows parents to screen software before
    buying it

Living Books 1-800-397-4240
    Dr. Seuss comes to life on CD-ROM

McGraw Hill Home Interactive 1-800-786-HOME
    entertaining and unique CD-ROMS   www.mmhi.com

Multi-media Craft Kits 1-800-774-6860
                                             http://www.printpaks.com
    craft kits to order with CD-ROMs and craft materials

My Very First Software 1-800-9-T-Maker
    software for children ages 2 to 5 in English, Spanish, French, and German

Notable Films/Videos, Recordings and Microcomputer Software
    Association for Library Service to Children
    50 East Huron Street
    Chicago, IL 60611
        compiled annually; free; send self-addressed, stamped envelope with request

Only the Best: Annual Guide to Highest-Rated Education Software/
Multimedia for Preschool-Grade 12 1-800-407-7377
    High/Scope Buyer's Guide to Children's Software
    High/Scope Press
    600 North River Street
    Ypsilanti, MI 48198
        annual edition of best software for parents, teachers, schools

Pico 1-800-588-8674
    Sega turns your TV into your child's first computer

School Zone's Alphabet Express 1-800-253-0564
    alphabet and beginning phonics

Stanley's Sticker Stories, Edmark 1-800-691-2985
    preschoolers create stories

Conferences and Speaker Series

See also PARENT RESOURCES: Parent Education Classes
EC PROFESSIONAL RESOURCES: Conferences and Speaker Series

DISTRICT OF COLUMBIA

Coalition for Marriage, Family and Couples Education Conference
Diane Sollee, Director, CMFCE, L.L.C. 202-966-5376
5310 Belt Road, NW   FAX: 202-362-0973
Washington, DC 20015   CMFCE@his.com
                                                                       info@smartmarriages.com
    annual spring conference on strengthening families   http://www.his.com/~CMFCE

Lowell School Lecture Series 202-726-9153
16th and Decatur Streets, NW   FAX: 202-723-8469
Washington, DC 20011
    lecture series on child development and parenting issues

ZERO TO THREE 202-638-1144
National Center for Infants, Toddlers, and Families   FAX: 202-638-0851
734 15th Street, NW, Suite 1000   0-3@zerotothree.org
Washington, DC 20005
    annual conference for parents and professionals working with children
    ages zero to three

MARYLAND

Ivymount School Speaker Series 301-469-0223
11614 Seven Locks Road
Rockville, MD 20854
    speaker series on special needs children; babysitting available

Maryland Committee for Children 410-752-7588
608 Water Street
Baltimore, MD 21202
    speaker series of early childhood experts

**Maryland Community Association for the
Education of Young Children (MAEYC)** 301-863-2322
                                                                       301-373-8360
    annual November conference in Towson, MD, for educators and parents

Maryland Council of Parent Participation Nursery Schools:MCPPNS
Kirsten Rhoades 301-933-9840
    annual conference for parents and professionals on a Saturday in March

Maryland Week of the Working Parent 410-752-7588
    yearly celebration of contributions of parents to Maryland's work force

Potomac Association of Cooperative Teachers Conferences
Jeanne Porter 703-549-8037
Irene Shere 301-593-5992
      conferences for professionals working in cooperative preschools; parents
      welcome; Fall Conference in November in Alexandria, VA;
      Spring Conference in February in Bethesda, MD.

Week of the Young Child Fair 301-279-1260
      Children's Resource Center, Montgomery County
      annual fair celebrating young children in April at Wheaton Plaza;
      weeklong celebration of informational, educational, and fun activities for
      young children; sponsored by many private and public agencies

VIRGINIA

Virginia Cooperative Preschool Council (VCPC)
Kathryn Conklin 703-361-0146
      conferences for parents and professionals in cooperative preschools

Government Information and Resources

See also GENERAL RESOURCES: Computer Online Services
HEALTH CARE RESOURCES: General Information and Resources
MENTAL HEALTH RESOURCES: Mental Health Information
CHILD CARE AND SCHOOL RESOURCES: Educational Information
EC PROFESSIONAL RESOURCES: Child Care, Licensing

NATIONAL

Americans with Disabilities Act Information Center 1-800-949-4232
2111 Wilson Blvd., Suite 400   703-525-3268
Arlington, VA 22201

Child Care Law Center 415-495-5498
22 Second Street, 5th Floor
San Francisco, CA 94105

Consumer Product Safety Commission Hotline 1-800-638-2772
Washington, DC 20207   http://www.cpsc.gov
    provides current and past recall information for products; reporting agency
    for a product hazard or product-related injury

Office of Research Reporting 301-496-5133
National Institute of Child Health and Human Development
National Institutes of Health
9000 Rockville Pike, Blg 31, Rm 2A-32
Bethesda, MD 20892
    free government publications on topics such as Down's Syndrome,
    nutrition, and developmental disabilities

DISTRICT OF COLUMBIA

CHILDFIND Testing and Assessment 202-727-8300

Department of Health and Human Services, DC 202-727-8500

MARYLAND

CHILDFIND Testing and Assessment
Montgomery County 301-279-FIND
Prince George's County 301-952-6341

Department of Health and Human Services, MD 301-217-3500

Department of Human Resources, MD
Child Care Administration 410-767-7810
311 West Saratoga Street, First Floor
Baltimore, MD 21202

Governor's Office for Children, Youth, and Families 410-225-4160
301 W. Preston Street, 15th Floor   FAX: 410-333-5248
Baltimore, MD 21201

Governor's Office for Individuals with Disabilities .410-333-3098
1 Market Center
300 W. Lexington Street, Box 10
Baltimore, MD 21201

Infants and Toddlers Program, MD 410-333-2263
One Market Center, Suite 204
300 West Lexington Street, Box 10
Baltimore, MD 21201
see also CHILDFIND

VIRGINIA

CHILDFIND Testing and Assessment
Alexandria 703-824-6708
Arlington 703-358-6042
Falls Church 703-241-7695
Fairfax County, Devonshire Center 703-876-5244
Fairfax County, Lorton 703-446-2100

Department of Health and Human Services, VA 703-838-0710

Helplines

(<u>not</u> 24 hours, <u>not</u> 7 days a week)

See also EC PROFESSIONAL RESOURCES: Helplines

GENERAL

Child Support Enforcement 1-800-723-5437
1-800-795-5437
1-800-892-4813

Disability Information 202-205-8241

National Coalition on Domestic Violence 202-638-6388

Parents 1-900-680-KIDS
child care information sponsored by *Parents* magazine; many topics;
95 cents per minute

Parents Anonymous, Parents Stressline 1-909-621-6184
1-800-243-7337

parent support, crisis intervention and referral service; "breaking the cycle
of abuse for generations"

Psychiatric Institute of Washington Helpline 202-965-8521
staffed 24 hours

Self-Help Clearinghouse of Greater Washington 703-941-LINK

Toy Safety Information Hotline 1-800-638-2772

DISTRICT OF COLUMBIA

Child Abuse Reporting 202-727-0995

Child Care Information and Referral 202-737-7226

Human Services Information and Referral Line 202-724-5466

Public School Information 202-724-4044
Special Education 202-724-4800

Psychiatric Institute of Washington Helpline 202-965-8521
staffed 24 hours

Self Help Clearinghouse of Greater Washington 703-941-LINK

MARYLAND

Child Abuse Reporting
Montgomery County 301-217-4417
Prince George's County 301-699-8605

Child Care Information and Referral
Montgomery County, Child Care Connection 301-279-1773
Prince George's County 301-772-8400

Child Care Connection/Montgomery Co.Public Schools 301-942-5374
child-rearing questions and referrals to professionals as necessary

Children's Resource Center 301-279-1260

Community LINC of Montgomery County 301-217-0500
TTY: 301-424-1087
computer bulletin board 301-424-5123
information and referral service for Montgomery County

Health Information Center (HIC) 301-929-5520
Wheaton Regional Library   TTY: 301-929-5524
11701 Georgia Avenue
Wheaton, MD 20902
free telephone research for medical issues (through MEDLINE);
free book referral research for medical issues

Hispanic Hotline 301-230-3073
school-related questions

Parenting Helpline 301-929-2025
8:30 am - 5 pm; parenting, child development concerns

Parent Resource Centers
Montgomery County 301-840-4508
Prince George's County 301-805-2710

Parent Warmline 301-929-WARM
TDD users, call MD Relay: 1-800-735-2258
free telephone consultation; responds to parent and caregivers questions
about child development, discipline, and other concerns for children
of all ages

Parent Warmline 301-881-3700
sponsored by Jewish Social Services

Public School Information
Montgomery County 301-279-3391
Montgomery County, Special Education 301-657-4969
Prince George's County 301-952-6000
Prince George's County, Special Education 301-731-4571

"How Can I Help My Child?" Early Childhood Resource Directory

45

VIRGINIA

ADHD/LD Counseling Services Helpline 703-849-9476
  sponsored by Virginia Pediatric Group

Alexandria Citizen Assistance/Public Information 703-838-4800
Alexandria Health-Line 703-845-1243
Alexandria Information and Referral 703-548-3810

Child Abuse Reporting
  Alexandria 703-838-0800
  Arlington County 703-358-5100
  Fairfax County 703-324-7400

Child Care Resource and Referral, Virginia 703-358-5101
  Alexandria 703-838-0750
  Arlington County 703-358-5101
  Fairfax County 703-449-9555

Korean Community Service Center 703-354-6345

Public School Information
  Alexandria 703-824-6600
  Alexandria, Special Education 703-824-6631
  Arlington County 703-358-6000
  Arlington County, Extended Day . . . .-358-6069
  Fairfax County 703-246-2502
  Fairfax County, Special Needs 703-691-7826

MULTI-LINGUAL HELPLINES

Andromeda, Spanish Hotline 202-722-1245

Center for Multicultural Human Services 703-533-3302
  serving children and families in 15 languages

Hispanic Hotline 301-230-3073
  school-related questions

Hispanos Unidos de Virginia 703-533-9300

Korean Community Service Center
  7720 Alaska Avenue, NW, Washington, DC 202-882-8270
  7610 New Castle Drive, Annandale, VA 703-354-6345

Montgomery County Public Schools
  Counseling Center 301-230-0675
  Parent Center 301-230-0674
  ESOL/Bilingual Parent Services 301-231-5930
    counseling services in Spanish, Chinese, Vietnamese, Cambodian, Russian,
    French, Yiddish, Hindi, and Korean

Naim Foundation 202-462-5715
  serving Arabic families

Hotlines
(24 hours a day, 7 days a week)

GENERAL

EMERGENCY POLICE, FIRE, AMBULANCE 911

Center for Missing and Exploited Children 703-235-3900

Parents Anonymous, Parents Stressline 1-909-621-6184
1-800-243-7337
> parent support, crisis intervention and referral service; "breaking the cycle of abuse for generations"

Poison Control Center 202-625-3333

Toy Safety Information Hotline 1-800-638-2772
http://www.cpsc.gov
> provides current and past recall information for products

DISTRICT OF COLUMBIA

DC Crisis and Referral Hotline 202-223-2255
DC Crisis Line 202-561-7000
DC Hotline 202-574-5442

Parents Anonymous, Parents Stressline 1-909-621-6184
1-800-243-7337
> parent support, crisis intervention and referral service; "breaking the cycle of abuse for generations"

Poison Control Center 202-625-3333

MARYLAND

Abused Persons Hotline
> General Hotline 301-654-1881
> Charles County and Southern Maryland 301-843-1110

Montgomery County Crisis Center 301-656-9161
Montgomery County Hotline 301-738-2255
> crisis intervention
301-738-CALL

Parents Anonymous, Parents Stressline, MD 1-800-243-7337
410-243-7337
> Montgomery County, upcounty 301-963-4138
> Montgomery County, downcounty 301-565-8272
> Self-help and Supportive Listening Groups Hotline 301-738-2255
>> (24-hour anonymous listening service)
>> parent support, crisis intervention and referral service; "breaking the cycle of abuse for generations"

"How Can I Help My Child?" Early Childhood Resource Directory

47

Poison Control Center 1-800-492-2414
301-528-7701

Prince George's County Crisis Center 301-731-0004
Prince George's County Hotline 301-577-4867

Virginia

ACTS Hot Line 703-368-4141
    crisis intervention serving Prince William County, Manassas, and
    Manassas Park

Alexandria Hot Line 703-548-3810
Alexandria Mental Health Center 703-836-5751
Alexandria Poison Center 703-379-3070

Arlington County After Hours Mental Health Emergency 703-358-4256
Arlington County Child Protective Services 703-358-5100
Arlington County Hot Line 703-358-5150
    after 5pm, weekends & holidays 703-358-4848
        crisis intervention; domestic violence

Commonwealth Psychological Associates 703-734-0787
    24 hour emergency service

Dominion Hospital 703-538-2872
    2960 Sleepy Hollow Road
    Falls Church, VA 22044
        First Step program for family crisis interventions

Fairfax County Child Abuse and Neglect Hotline 703-324-7400
Fairfax County Mental Health 24-Hour Emergency Service 703-573-5679

Northern Virginia Hot Line 703-527-4077
    crisis intervention

Parents Anonymous, Parents Stressline 1-909-621-6184
1-800-243-7337
    parent support, crisis intervention and referral service; "breaking the cycle
    of abuse for generations"

Poison Control Center 1-800-552-6337

MULTI-LINGUAL HOTLINES

Andromeda, Spanish Hotline 202-722-1245
Hispanic Hotline 301-230-3073
    school-related questions

Play Equipment and Playgrounds

CONSULTANTS

Creative Leisure Products, Inc 301-428-9008
David Hammett & Kent Miller
15130 Barnesville Road
P.O. Box 104
Boyds, MD 20841

Creative Playgrounds, Ltd 1-800-338-0522
play structures made of wood; free design and purchasing assistance;
free catalog

Custom Playground Child Care & Design Consultants 1-800-413-0998
Esther Grossman   410-358-8343
P.O. Box 1283   FAX: 410-358-8760
Brooklandville, MD 21022
independent playground distributor

PlayDesigns 1-800-327-7571
P.O. Box 529   FAX: 717-966-3030
315 Cherry Street
New Berlin, PA 17855
free guide: "Playground 101: Everything You Need to Know About Selecting
Playground Equipment"

Playgrounds, Inc. 1-800-638-9663
2735 Door Avenue   FAX: 703-698-8610
Fairfax, VA 22031
commercial and residential play equipment; free catalog; demonstration
park; certified playground safety inspections; Woodset and Lions Pride play
equipment

Schappet, Jean, CPSI 703-698-4334
playground safety and design consultant   1-800-638-9663

EQUIPMENT

National

American Playgrounds 1-800-552-5270
        wooden playsets; free color catalog; free delivery and installation

Creative Playgrounds, Ltd. 1-800-338-0522
        play structures made of wood
        free design and purchasing assistance; free catalog

Early Works, BigToys 1-800-553-2446
    7717 New Market Street
    Olympia, WA 98501
        play structures, playhouses, swings, and climbers

Genesis by Burke 1-800-356-2070
    BCI Burke Company
    660 Van Dyne Road, P.O. Box 549
    Fond du Lac, WI 54936
        play systems and play equipment for children ages 2-5

Little Tikes Exploration Centers for Sand/Water Play 1-800-325-8828
        modular play systems

PlayDesigns 1-800-327-7571
    P.O. Box 529   FAX: 717-966-3030
    315 Cherry Street
    New Berlin, PA 17855
        free catalog of park and school equipment; free guide: "Playground 101:
        Everything You Need to Know About Selecting Playground Equipment"

Playground Environments 1-800-622-0922
        free catalog

Step 2 1-800-446-1135
        heavy-duty plastic play equipment for young children; free catalog

Metro Area

Backyard Billy's 1-800-300-3856
2144 Red Apple Plaza   410-643-8800
Kent Island, MD 21619
  Amish-made wooden swing and play sets, furniture & toys

Creative Leisure Products, Inc. 301-428-9008
David Hammett and Kent Miller
15130 Barnesville Road
P.O. Box 104
Boyds, MD 20841

Custom Playground Child Care & DesignConsultants 1-800-413-0998
  Esther Grossman, independent playground distributor

Educational Media, Inc. 202-583-9594
3191 Westover Drive, SE
Washington, DC 20020
  residential and commercial grade playground equipment

Playgrounds, Inc. 1-800-638-9663
2735 Door Avenue   FAX: 703-698-8610
Fairfax, VA 22031
  commercial and residential play equipment; free catalog; demonstration
  park; distributors of Woodset and Lions Pride play equipment

Play N'Learn, Inc. 1-800-22-SWING
5800 Old Centreville Road, Fairfax, VA 703-502-1864
9398-A Baltimore National Pike, Ellicott City 410-750-8575
  play equipment

Schirmer's
5041 Nicholson Lane, Rockville, MD 301-881-2200
2916 Annandale Road, Falls Church, VA 703-534-1400
9208 Enterprise Court, Manassas, VA 703-631-0144
  back yard wooden play systems; pre-assembled, pre-drilled

Turtle Park Toys 202-362-8697
4115 Wisconsin Avenue, NW
Washington, DC 20016
  wooden playsets

Woodset 1-800-638-9663
4460 Printers Court
Waldorf, MD 20695
  commercial and residential play equipment; free catalog; demonstration
  park; certified playground safety inspections97

Toys, Etc.

CATALOGS AND DISTRIBUTORS

National

ABC School Supply, Inc. 1-800-669-4222
3312 North Berkeley Lake Road   FAX: 1-800-933-2987
P.O. Box 100019
Duluth, GA 30136
    toys and educational supplies

Angeles Group, The 314-257-0533
9 Capper Drive
Dailey Industrial Park
Pacific, MO 63069
    classroom supplies and equipment

Animal Town 1-800-445-8642
P.O. Box 485   FAX: 1-800-837-9737
Healdsburg, CA 95448
    toys and educational supplies

Back-to-Basics Toys 1-800-356-5360
31333 Agoura Road   FAX: 818-865-9771
Westlake Village, CA 91361
    classic toys that stimulate the imagination

Beckley-Cardy 1-800-622-2101
P.O. Box 2358
Lufkin, TX 74902
    toys and educational toys

Book of Early Learning, The 1-800-628-8608
New England School Supply   FAX: 1-800-272-0101
609 Silver Street
P.O. Box 3004
Agawam, MA 01001
    complete line of educational toys, equipment, arts & crafts, games;
    24-hour, free ordering

Carpets for Kids 503-232-1203
115 SE 9th Avenue   FAX: 503-232-1394
Portland, OR 97214
    creative innovative carpets for teaching spaces

Childcraft 1-800-631-5652
250 College Park, P.O. Box 1811   FAX: 717-397-1943
Peoria, IL
Janet Zahm, local distributor 1-800-631-5652

ChildsWork/ChildsPlay 1-800-962-1141
  Center for Applied Psychology
  P.O. Box 61586
  King of Prussia, PA 19406
      catalog addressing the mental health needs of children and their families
      through play

Community Playthings 1-800-777-4244
  P. O. Box 901, Route 213   FAX: 914-658-8065
  Rifton, NY 12471
      free catalog of wooden furniture and play equipment

Constructive Playthings 1-800-448-4115
  1227 East 119th Street   FAX: 816-761-9295
  Grandview, MO 64030
      toys and educational supplies

Creative Educational Surplus 1-800-886-6428
  1000 Apollo Road   FAX: 1-800-681-2245
  Eagon, MN 55121
      recycled products at bargain prices for educators

Discount School Supply 1-800-627-2829
  P.O. Box 7636   http://www.earlychildhood.com/dss.html
  Spreckles, CA 93962
      discount toys and educational supplies

Environments, Inc. 1-800-EI-CHILD
  P.O. Box 1348   FAX: 1-800-EI-FAXUS
  Beaufort Industrial Park
  Beaufort, SC 29901
      free 384 page catalog of toys and educational supplies

Fisher-Price Consumer Affairs 1-800-432-5437
  636 Girard Avenue
  East Aurora, NY 14052
      free replacement parts catalog; $5 for Toy Fair catalog

Great Kids Company, The 1-800-533-2166
  P.O. Box 609   FAX: 1-800-977-TOYS
  Lewisville, NC 27023
      winner of Parents' Choice Catalog award; educational toys

Hand in Hand 1-800-872-9745
  Catalogue Center   FAX: 207-539-4415
  891 Main Street
  Oxford, ME 04270
      educational toys

Hearth Song 1-800-325-2502
  6519 N. Galena Road, P.O. Box 1773
  Peoria, IL 61656
  children's toy catalog for families

Holbrook-Patterson, Inc. 1-800-KID-8121
    633 Race
    P.O. Box 447
    Coldwater, MI 49036
        free catalog of educational, play, and storage equipment

J. L. Hammett Co. 1-800-333-4600
                                       FAX: 1-800-873-5700
        quality classroom furniture and materials for birth through grade 12

Jonti-Craft 1-800-543-4149
    P.O. Box 30, Highway 68   FAX: 1-800-860-5617
    Wabasso, MN 56293
    wooden and classroom furniture at discount prices

Kaplan School Supply Company 1-800-334-2014
    600 Jamestown Road
    Winston-Salem, NC 27103
        toys and educational supplies

Kids Club 1-800-363-0500
    7425 Whipple Avenue, NW   FAX: 330-494-0265
    North Canton, OH 44720
        discount toys and supplies

Kidsrights 1-800-892-KIDS
    10100 Park Cedar Drive   FAX: 704-541-0113
    Charlotte, NC 23210
        catalog for books, videos, brochures, concerning difficult emotional issues

Lakeshore Learning Materials 1-800-421-5354
    2695 E. Dominguez Street   FAX: 1-310-537-5403
    Carson, CA 90749   customer service: 1-800-428-4414
        educational toys, furniture, supplies, & equipment

Learn & Play/Troll Learn & Play 1-800-247-6106
    45 Curiosity Lane, P.O. Box 1822
    Peoria, IL 61656
        toys and educational supplies

Music for Little People 1-800-727-2233
    Department BKR, P.O. Box 1720   FAX: 1-800-722-9505
    Lawndale, CA 90260   customer service: 1-800-707-8522
        musical instruments, audio tapes, books, videos, puppets

NASCO's Learning Fun Catalog 1-800-558-9595
    P.O. Box 901   FAX: 414-563-8296
    Fort Atkinson, WI 53538   info@nascofn.com
                             http://www.nascofn.com

Oriental Trading Co. 1-800-228-2269
    Mail Order   FAX: 1-800-327-8904
    P.O. Box 3407   customer service: 1-800-228-0475
    Omaha, NE 68103
        small toys, stickers, etc.

PlayFair Toys 1-800-824-7255
P.O. Box 18210
Boulder, Colorado 80308
    nonviolent, non-sexist educational toys for children

Play Therapy Associates 1-800-542-9723
1750 25th Avenue #200   FAX: 1-800-628-6250
Greeley, CO 80631   Re-Print: 1-800-248-9171
    "early learning discounter"; free catalog of   http://www.re print.com
    discount art supplies, play equipment

Puppet Petting Zoo, The 860-872-6899
213 Crystal Lake Road
Tolland, CT 06084
    animal and fantasy puppets; hand puppets, rod puppets, and cone puppets

Re-print Corporation 1-800-248-9171
P.O. Box 830677   FAX: 1-800-628-6250
Birmingham, AL 35283   http://www.re-print.com/
    early childhood supplies, art supplies, etc.

Sensational Beginnings 1-800-444-2147
P.O. Box 2009
987 Stewart Road
Monroe, MI 48162
    toys and educational supplies

Theraplay Products 1-800-308-6787
P.O. Box 2030   FAX: 209-368-6787
Lodi, CA 95241
    educational and therapeutic toys and games

This Country's Toys 1-800-359-1233
P.O. Box 41479   FAX: 1-800-359-6144
Providence, RI 02940   TCTOYS@AOL.COM
    American-made toys, kits, games; discount with membership

Toys to Grow On 1-800-542-8338
P.O. Box 17   customer service: 1-800-874-4242
Long Beach, CA 90801
    toys and educational supplies

Troll Learn & Play 1-800-247-6106
45 Curiosity Lane, P.O. Box 1822
Peoria, IL 61656
    toys and educational supplies

Virco Preschool Furniture 1-800-448-4726
P.O. Box 5000   ext. 209
Conway, AR 72033
    free full-color catalog

Young Explorers 1-800-239-7577
825 S. Frontage Road   1-800-777-8817
Ft. Collins, CO 80522   FAX: 1-970-484-8067
    creative educational products

Metro Area

Back to Basics Toys 703-707-9150
305 Sunset Park Drive
Herndon, VA 20170
classic toys for children

Beckley-Cardy 703-779-1710
Eric Lay
775 Gateway SE #109
Leesburg, VA 22075
educational supplies, arts and crafts

Chaselle School Supplies 410-381-9611
8300 Guilford Road
Columbia, MD 21046
complete line of educational supplies, games, arts & crafts, and equipment

Crown Educational and Teaching Aids 301-948-4207
211 Perry Parkway, Suite B
Gaithersburg, MD 20877
educational supplies, arts and crafts

Hammett, J.L.
2914 Chain Bridge Road, Oakton, VA 703-938-0047
6420 Brandon Avenue, Springfield Mall, VA 703-569-2303
educational supplies, books; classroom supplies

Story Teller, The 410-647-4464
Teresa Avery
Felt Educational Products
1246 Timber Turn
Arnold, MD 21012
feltboards and felt storyboards; mail order available

Terri's Puppets 540-349-3271
Terri Taggart
7931 Leeds Manor Road
Marshall, VA 20115
animal puppets; puppets from classic books; mail order

CRAFT SUPPLIES

See also **GENERAL RESOURCES: Toys, Etc., Catalogs**
GENERAL RESOURCES: Toys, Etc., Educational Supply Stores
GENERAL RESOURCES: Toys, Etc., Toy Stores

National

Multi-media Craft Kits 1-800-774-6860
http://www.printpaks.com
craft kits that come with everything from CD Rom to craft materials

District of Columbia

Lura's Crafts 202-723-6003
5804 Georgia Avenue, NW
Washington, DC

Point of It All 202-966-9898
3301 New Mexico Avenue, NW
Washington, DC 20016

Utrecht Art and Drafting Supplies 202-898-0555
1250 I Street, NW
Washington, DC 20005
arts and crafts supplies

Visual Systems 202-331-7090
1019 19th Street, NW
Washington, DC 20036
arts and crafts supplies

"How Can I Help My Child?" Early Childhood Resource Directory

57

Maryland

Craft Country 301-774-0810
18149 Town Center Drive
Olney, MD 20832
arts and crafts supplies

Family Crafts 301-577-3345
9354 Lanham-Severn Road
Seabrook, MD 20706
arts and crafts supplies

Frank's Nursery and Crafts
5610 Linda Lane, Camp Springs 301-894-7832
6300 Greenbelt Road, Greenbelt 301-982-9240
9457 Annapolis Road, Lanham 301-306-9898
201 Laurel Bowie Road, Laurel 301-725-3200
arts and crafts supplies

Michael's 410-766-0720
16 Mountain Road
Glen Burnie, MD 21060
arts and crafts supplies

MJ Designs
660 Quince Orchard Road, Gaithersburg 301-330-0031
13850 Georgia Avenue, Aspen Hill 301-871-0300
arts and crafts supplies

Pearl Art and Craft Supplies 301-816-2900
12266 Rockville Pike
Rockville, MD 20852
arts and crafts supplies

reSTORE
Maryland Committee for Children 410-752-7588
608 Water Street
Baltimore, MD 21202
low-cost recycled materials for creative art projects; schedule varies;
call before coming; usually open on first and last Friday and Saturday
each month from 10-4

Total Crafts
597 B Ordinance Road, Glen Burnie 410-766-2224
3445 Fort Meade Road, Laurel 301-470-6033
arts and crafts supplies

Visual Systems
1009 Cathedral Street, Baltimore 410-625-9000
7825 Old Georgetown Road, Bethesda 301-718-8500
8610 Cherry Lane, Laurel . . . . .301-470-4300 ext. 1750
1596 Rockville Pike, Rockville 301-770-0500
arts and crafts supplies

Virginia

Craft Shop, The 703-524-2832
2102 W. Pollard Avenue
Arlington, VA
arts and crafts supplies

Frank's Nursery and Crafts
7702 Richmond Highway, Alexandria 703-799-0228
10930 Lee Highway, Fairfax 703-591-6851
arts and crafts supplies

Michael's
11630 Plaza America Drive, Reston 703-736-0530
6303 Richmond Highway, Alexandria 703-768-0306
arts and crafts supplies

MJ Designs
3524 S. Jefferson St., Baileys Crossroads .703-578-0664
3089 Nutley Street, Fairfax 703-207-0277
46301 Potomac Run Center, Sterling 703-406-0840
arts and crafts supplies

Pearl Art and Craft Supplies 703-960-3900
5695 Telegraph Road
Alexandria, VA 22303
arts and crafts supplies

Total Crafts
6910C Bradlick Shopping Center, Annandale 703-256-7110
6096 Rose Hill Drive, Alexandria 703-922-4208
9960 Main Street, Fairfax 703-359-9800
490-B Elden Street, Herndon 703-481-9204
arts and crafts supplies

Visual Systems
5900A Leesburg Pike, Baileys Crossroads .703-820-4650
3045 Nutley Street #17, Pan Am Shopping Center, Fairfax 703-280-4500
art supplies

"How Can I Help My Child?" Early Childhood Resource Directory

59

EDUCATIONAL SUPPLY STORES

See also **GENERAL RESOURCES: Toys, Etc., Catalogs**
GENERAL RESOURCES: Toys, Etc., Toy Stores

District of Columbia

Crown Educational and Teaching Aids 202-529-3470
304 Riggs Road, NE
Washington, DC 20011
educational supplies

Maryland

ABC's and 1-2-3's 301-881-5133
12219 Nebel Street
Rockville, MD 20852
educational games and equipment

Chaselle School Supplies 410-381-9611
8300 Guilford Road
Columbia, MD 21046
complete line of educational supplies, games, arts and crafts, and
equipment; catalog ordering available

Crown Educational and Teaching Aids 301-948-5710
15914 Shady Grove Road
Gaithersburg, MD
educational toys and games; catalog orders available

Educate & Celebrate 410-535-2771
136 W. Dares Beach Road
Prince Frederick, MD 20678

Learning Ideas 301-420-9211
5570 Silver Hill Road, Penn Station Shopping Center
District Heights, MD 20747

Kaybee Montessori 301-963-2101
7895 K Cessna Avenue   FAX: 301-963-2197
Gaithersburg, MD 20879
Montessori teaching materials

Potomac ABC 301-439-0700
8400 Carroll Avenue
Takoma Park, MD 20912
educational supplies

School Box 301-770-5577
5054 Nicholson Lane
Rockville, MD 20852
classroom supplies

School Stuff 301-645-4488
3087 Old Washington Road
Waldorf, MD
educational supplies

Virginia

Beckley-Cardy 703-779-1710
Eric Lay
775 Gateway SE #109
Leesburg, VA 22075
catalog ordering available

Crown Educational and Teaching Aids 703-631-8066
14215 N. Centreville Square
Centreville, VA 20121
educational toys and games; catalog ordering available

Hammett, J.L.
2914 Chain Bridge Road, Oakton, VA 703-938-0047
6420 Brandon Avenue, Springfield Mall, VA 703-569-2303
educational supplies, books; catalog orders available

Jackie's Teacher Store 703-670-2406
4321 Dale Blvd.
Dale City, VA
educational supplies

K.T.'s 703-560-KIDS
8558-F Lee Highway
Merrifield, VA 22031
resource center for children, teachers, and schools

School Box 703-914-0656
7112 Columbia Pike
Annandale, VA 22003
classroom supplies

Teacher's Edition 703-369-2521
9756 Center Street, Cavalry Village
Manassas, VA
educational supplies

Teacher's Mart 703-250-6777
5765-M Burke Center Parkway   FAX: 703-250-3114
Burke, VA
parent, student, and teacher supplies

TOY RECOMMENDATIONS

American Academy of Pediatrics, Dept. C
Toy Safety
P.O. Box 927
Elk Grove Village, IL 60009
> send a self-addressed, stamped envelope for a free brochure on toy
> recommendations for children birth through 14

"Dr. Toy" . . . . .http://www.drtoy.com
Institute for Childhood Resources
268 Bush Street
San Francisco, CA 94104
> send self-addressed, stamped, business-size envelope for toy
> recommendations

Oppenheim Toy Portfolio/Energizer Toy Line 1-800-544-8697
40 East 9th Street, Suite 14M
New York, NY 10003
> toy tips, free brochure on toys; publication on best toys, books, videos
> and software; quarterly pamphlet

Parents' Choice Awards 617-965-5913
Parents' Choice Foundation
P. O. Box 185
Waban, Mass. 02168
> $4 for list of Parents' Choice Award toys

TOY RENTALS

Lend A Toy 301-231-6670
> toy rental and delivery service for ages birth to 5; rent a variety of toys
> delivered monthly to your home

TOY REPLACEMENT PARTS

Fisher-Price Consumer Affairs .1-800-432-5437
636 Girard Avenue
East Aurora, NY 14052
> free replacement parts catalog; $5 for Toy Fair catalog

Lauri Crepe Rubber Puzzle Replacements 1-800-451-0520
P.O. Box F-ECT
Phillips-Avon, ME 04966
> free catalog of replacement parts for Lauri puzzles

TOY SAFETY

American Academy of Pediatrics, Dept. C
Toy Safety
P.O. Box 927
Elk Grove Village, IL 60009
free brochure on toys that includes toy safety; send a self-addressed, stamped envelope

Consumer Product Safety Commission 1-800-638-2772
Washington, DC 20207   http://www.cpsc.gov
current and past recall information for products; reporting agency for product hazard or product-related injury

"Play Smart Holiday Guide to Toy Safety" 1-800-697-6446
National Safe Kids Campaign and Toy Manufacturers of America free guide

"Trouble in Toyland" 202-546-9707
U.S. Public Interest Research Group
218 D Street, SE
Washington, DC 20003
e-mail, send with subject line "toy" . . . . .watchdog@pirt.org
$10 report

"How Can I Help My Child?" Early Childhood Resource Directory

63

TOY STORES

See also **GENERAL RESOURCES: Toys, Etc., Catalogs**
GENERAL RESOURCES: Toys, Etc., Craft Supplies
GENERAL RESOURCES: Toys, Etc., Educational Supply Stores

District of Columbia

Another Universe 202-333-8651
3060 M Street, NW
Washington, DC 20036

Barston's Child's Play 202-244-3602
5536 Connecticut Avenue, NW
Washington, DC 20015
educational toys

FAO Schwartz 202-965-7000
3222 M Street, NW
Washington, DC 20007

Learningsmith 202-337-0800
3222 M Street, NW, Georgetown Park
Washington, DC 20007
"A General Store for the Curious Mind"; toys, books, games

Sullivan's Toy Store 202-362-1343
3412 Wisconsin Avenue, NW
Washington, DC 20016
toys and games

Tree Top Toys & Books 202-244-3500
3301 New Mexico Avenue, NW, Foxhall Square
Washington, DC 20016
educational toys

Turtle Park Toys 202-362-TOYS
4115 Wisconsin Avenue, NW, First Floor
Washington, DC 20016
"quality toys at affordable prices"

64

"How Can I Help My Child?" Early Childhood Resource Directory

Maryland

Anglo Dutch Pools and Toys 301-951-0636
    5460 Westbard Avenue
    Bethesda, MD 20816
        Playmobil, LEGO, Brio, Fisher-Price, Playskool, etc.

Chaselle School Supplies 410-381-9611
    9645 Gerwig Lane
    Columbia, MD 20816
        complete selection of educational toys

Chuck and Dave's 301-891-2665
    7001 Carroll Avenue
    Takoma Park, MD 20912
        games, puppets, puzzles

Crown Educational and Teaching Aids 301-948-5710
    15914 Shady Grove Road
    Gaithersburg, MD 20877
        educational toys and games

Discovery Toys
    Susan Crawford, Silver Spring 301-946-9148
    Gaithersburg 301-251-6126
    Kensington 301-942-7770
    Rockville 301-762-2662
    Upper Marlboro 301-855-4215
        toys and games

Kay-Bee Toys
    Montgomery Mall, Bethesda 301-469-6199
    11301 Rockville Pike, Kensington 301-881-3120
    6200 Annapolis Road, Landover Hills 301-386-5848
    Briggs Chaney Plaza, Silver Spring 301-890-2213
    3101 Donnell Drive, Forestville 301-568-6631
    Prince George's Plaza, Hyatsville 301-853-3392
    701 Russell Avenue, Gaithersburg 301-840-0465
    3765 Branch Avenue, Hillcrest Heights .301-899-0723
    11160 Veirs Mill Road, Wheaton 301-942-0725

Learningsmith
    Columbia Mall, Columbia 410-740-4100
    Lakeforest Mall, Gaithersburg 301-208-2600
        "A General Store for the Curious Mind"; toys, books, games

Mother May I? 1-800-770-6294
    St. Charles Town Center Mall, Rte. 301 South 301-870-4465
    Waldorf, MD 20603

Toys...etc 301-299-3800
    11325 Seven Locks Road, Cabin John Mall
    Potomac, MD 20854
        educational toys and equipment

Toys-R-Us

4721 Auth Place, Suitland	301-423-6614
1308 W Patrick Street, Frederick	301-694-7278
11810 Rockville Pike, Rockville	301 770-3376
2277 University Blvd, Silver Spring	301-422-4080
8201 Annapolis Road, Lanham	301-459-6070
600 N Frederick Road, Gaithersburg	301-869-5510
160 Mall Circle, Waldorf	301-705-9800
10901 Georgia Avenue, Wheaton	301-946-2954
933 Washington Blvd, Laurel	301-497-6325

Toys Unique 301-983-3160
9812 Falls Road
Potomac, MD 20854

Whirligigs & Whimsies 301-897-4940
10213 Old Georgetown Road, Wildwood Center
Bethesda, MD 20814

Zany Brainy

2522 Solomon's Island Road, Annapolis	410-266-1447
9097 Snowden River Pkwy, Columbia	410-312-0783
1631 Rockville Pike, Rockville	301-984-0112
educational toys, games, and books	

Virginia

Another Universe
Fair Oaks Mall, Fair Oaks, Fairfax 703-273-3355
Springfield Mall, Springfield 703-313-0404

Back to Basics Toys 703-707-9150
305 Sunset Park Drive
Herndon, VA 20170
classic toys for children

Children's Toy Connection Co. 540-785-0211
Melvey Brown
2500 Lucas Street
Fredericksburg, VA 22407
toys and educational supplies

Children's Toy Lab 703-356-6448
1380-A Chain Bridge Road
McLean, VA 22101
educational toys

Counterpane Gallery of Toys 703-525-4551
2900 Clarendon Blvd.
Arlington, VA
educational toys

Creative Playthings Factory Outlet 703-968-2901
14080-H Sullyfield Circle
Chantilly, VA 22101
educational toys outlet

Crown Educational and Teaching Aids 703-631-8066
14215 N. Centreville Square
Centreville, VA 20121
educational toys and games

Discovery Toys
Elizabeth Faria, Alexandria 703-960-5227
Fairfax 703-591-0908
Vienna 703-560-8080
educational toys, books, games, and software

Earth Toys 703-684-1407
322 S. Washington Street
Alexandria, VA
educational toys, art and craft supplies

FAO Schwartz 703-917-9600
1651 International Drive
McLean, VA 22102

"How Can I Help My Child?" Early Childhood Resource Directory

67

TOYS, ETC., TOY STORES

FuncoLand

Landmark Plaza, Alexandria	703-642-0991
Fair City Mall, Fairfax East	703-978-0295
Willston Centre 1, Falls Church	703-533-1523
Best Buy Metro Center, Springfield	703-971-5597

Imaginarium 703-847-0011
Tyson's Corner Center
McLean, VA 22102

Kay-Bee Toys

21800 Towncenter Plaza, Sterling	703-406-3227
4238 N Wilson Blvd, Arlington	703-527-2617
7235 Arlington Blvd, Falls Church	703-280-9355
5801 Duke Street, Alexandria	703-914-2109
1100 S. Hayes Street, Arlington	703-418-6762
Fair Oaks Mall, Fair Oaks, Fairfax	703-591-6007
Springfield Mall, Springfield	703-971-5656
Tyson's Corner Center, McLean	703-848-0910

Kinderhaus Toys 703-527-5929
4510 Lee Highway
Arlington, VA
educational toys

Learningsmith

Tysons Corner Center, McLean	703-556-0200
Springfield Mall, Springfield	703-922-3400

"A General Store for the Curious Mind"; toys, books, games

Once Upon A Time 703-255-3285
120 Church Street, NE
Vienna, VA 22180
educational toys

One Two Kangaroo 703-845-9099
4022 S. 28th Street, Shirlington Village
Arlington, VA 22206
learning store

Toy Corner, The 703-255-3232
2918 Chain Bridge Road
Oakton, VA 22124

Toys-R-Us

5521 Leesburg Pike, Baileys Crossroads	703-820-2428
13035 Fairlakes Shopping Center, Fairfax	703-803-1050
8449 Leesburg Pike, Tysons Corner	703-893-2223
6715 Commerce Street, Springfield	703-922-7876
10318 Portsmouth Road, Manassas	703-330-8304
14603 Telegraph Road, Woodbridge	703-490-1466

Why Not 703-548-4420
    200 King Street
    Alexandria, VA 22314
       toys and games

Zany Brainy
    3513 Jefferson Street, Bailey's Crossroads 703-998-1203
    2890 Prince William Pkwy, Dale City 703-680-9870
    9484 Main Street, Fairfax 703-323-3658
    12180 West Ox Road, Fairfax 703-691-1896
    11870 Spectrum Center, Reston 703-319-1875
    6575 Frontier Drive, Springfield 703-719-9585
    46262-115 Cranston Street, Sterling 703-404-8850
       educational toys, games, and books

USED TOYS

Toy Traders
    14390 Layhill Road, Silver Spring 301-598-5588
    536 N. Frederick Avenue, Gaithersburg 301-258-1023
       used toys bought and sold

Videos

See also **EC PROFESSIONAL RESOURCES: Videos**

VIDEOS FOR ADULTS

National

Active Parenting Publishers 1-800-825-0060
810 Franklin Court, Suite B
Marietta, GA 30067
book and video kits on parenting skills

California Department of Education 1-800-995-4099
parenting videos available in Spanish

Committee for Children 1-800-634-4449
2203 Airport Way South, Suite 500   FAX: 206-343-1445
Seattle, WA 98134
educational videos for parents on early childhood issues; free catalog; free
information packet on teaching social skills

Faber/Mazlish Workshops, LLC 1-800-944-8584
Dept. 103A   FAX: 914-967-8130
P.O. Box 37   customer counselor: 914-967-8130
Rye, NY 10580
workbooks, audio tapes, video tapes series from the award-winning book
How to Talk So Kids Will Listen and Listen So Kids Will Talk

Floor Time: Tuning in to Each Child 1-800-325-6149
Scholastic, Inc.
child psychiatrist Stanley Greenspan's video on the importance of adults
engaging children in meaningful play

Library Video Company 1-800-843-3620
523 Righters Ferry Road   610-667-0200
Bala Cynwyd, PA 19004   FAX: 610-667-3425
educational videos for parents and professionals

Small Fry Productions 1-800-521-5311
4016 Flowers Road, Suite 440   http://www.ttsbn.com/~smallfry
Atlanta, GA 30360   smfryprod@aol.com

Successful Parenting 1-800-544-2219
Richards and Taylor Video Productions
P.O. Box 11851
Winston-Salem, NC 27116
videos, workbooks, and audiocassettes focusing on self-esteem,
communication, and discipline for parents

Metro Area

Children's Resource Center 301-217-3800
Rockville Regional Library
99 Maryland Avenue
Rockville, MD
educational videos for parents and professionals; borrowers do not have to
be Montgomery County residents

Fairfax County Libraries 703-222-3155
www.co.fairfax.va.us/library
On-line Library catalog; modem phone # 703-802-7447
Library Administration
13135 Lee Jackson Highway, Suite 301
Fairfax, VA 22033
collection of educational videos

VIDEOS FOR CHILDREN

Children's Circle Videos 1-800-KIDS-VID
Children's Circle
Weston, CT 06883
based on classic children's books

KIDS Home Video 1-800-451-4340

Lightyear Entertainment 1-800-229-7867

Mother's Lode Entertainment, Inc. 1-800-665-9210

Small Fry Productions 1-800-521-5311

Sony Wonder 1-800-338-7834

Taking Care of Corey 919-233-9767
American Kennel Club, Attention: Corey Video
5580 Centerview Drive, Suite 200
Raleigh, NC 27606
write for free animated program about dogs and responsibility

Toons Productions 1-800-350-5197
1700 K Street, NW, Suite 650
Washington, DC 20006

"How Can I Help My Child?" Early Childhood Resource Directory

71

VIDEO REVIEWS

Booklist 1-800-545-2433
American Library Association
50 East Huron Street
Chicago, IL 60611
reviews of books, videos, audio tapes; twice monthly, with single issues in
July and August

Children's Video Report, The 718-935-0600
390 Court Street, #76
Brooklyn, NY 11231
independent review of children's videos; 8 issues per year

Child Magazine's MediaKids Hotline 1-900-407-4KID
hotline features what it considers best movies, videos, TV programs for
children; new features weekly; 95 cents per call

Kidsnet Media Guide and News 202-291-1400
Kidsnet
6856 Eastern Avenue, NW, Suite 208
Washington, DC 20012
monthly media guide reviewing children's videos and electronic media

Notable Films/Videos, Recordings and Microcomputer Software
Association for Library Service to Children 312-332-0941
50 East Huron Street
Chicago, IL 60611
compiled annually; free; send self-addressed, stamped envelope with request

Parent's Choice 617-965-5913
Parent's Choice Foundation
P.O. Box 185
Newton, MA 02168
quarterly journal of Parent's Choice Award videos and books

PG-14, Parental Guidance for Teens, Preteens, and Children 1-800-681-PG14
PG-14, Inc.
2713 Calgary Avenue
Kensington, MD 20895
monthly newsletter reviewing movie contents for parents of teens, preteens
and children; $18 per year

Health Care Resources

Resources Concerning the Physical, Neurological, Visual, Speech, and Hearing Growth and Development of Young Children

HEALTH CARE RESOURCES and **RESOURCES**

HEALTH CARE RESOURCES includes:

- **Courses in CPR, First Aid, and Health**
- **Dentists, Pediatric**
- **Drug Stores, Open 24 Hours**
- **Health Information and Resources**
- **Hospitals and Clinics:** includes Hospitalization Resources
- **Nutritionists and Nutritional Resources, Pediatric**
- **Optometrists and Visual Training, Pediatric**
- **Pediatricians:** includes specific pediatricians for certain specialties
- **Physical and Occupational Therapists, Pediatric**
- **Speech and Hearing Specialists, Pediatric**

The Table of Contents on the next page provides a detailed listing of this section.

Notes:

1. **Be sure to look in "Metro Area" when available.** Metro Area resources are available throughout the entire Washington metropolitan area. These resources are not repeated in the separate District of Columbia, Maryland, and Virginia listings.

2. Low-income health care resources are listed in PARENT RESOURCES: Parent Information under "Low Income Resources."

3. Testing and assessment are performed by the health care specialists listed. Testing and assessment resources for emotional, social, cognitive, and behavioral concerns are listed in MENTAL HEALTH RESOURCES: Testing and Assessment.

Health Care Resources
Table of Contents

Courses in CPR, First Aid, and Health .... .75
Dentists, Pediatric .... .77
    Referrals and Information .... .77
    District of Columbia .... .78
    Maryland .... .78
    Virginia .... .79
Drug Stores, Open 24 Hours .... .80
Health Information and Resources .... .82
Hospitals and Clinics .... .86
    Hospitalization Resources .... .86
    District of Columbia .... .87
    Maryland .... .88
    Virginia .... .89
Nutritionists and Nutritional Resources, Pediatric .... .90
    National .... .90
    Metro Area .... .91
Optometrists and Visual Training, Pediatric .... .92
    Referrals and Information .... .92
    District of Columbia .... .92
    Maryland .... .92
    Virginia .... .93
Pediatricians .... .94
    Referrals and Information .... .94
    ADD/ADHD Specialists .... .96
    Allergists .... .97
    Dermatologists .... .99
    Ear, Nose, and Throat Specialists .... .99
    Gastroenterologists .... .99
    Nephrologists .... .99
    Neurologists 100
    Ophthalmologists 100
    Orthopedists 100
    Special Needs 101
Physical and Occupational Therapists, Pediatric 102
    Referrals and Information 102
    District of Columbia 102
    Maryland 103
    Virginia 104
Speech and Hearing Specialists, Pediatric 106
    Referrals and Information 106
    District of Columbia 107
    Maryland 107
    Virginia 109

Courses in CPR, First Aid, and Health

DISTRICT OF COLUMBIA

American Red Cross 202-728-6400

In Safe Hands 202-884-3851
Children's National Medical Center
111 Michigan Avenue, NW
Washington, DC 20010

Personal-Touch 202-537-7200
infant and child CPR taught by pediatric registered nurse

Sibley Memorial Hospital 202-537-4058
5255 Loughboro Road, NW
Washington, DC 20016
infant and child safety and CPR classes

MARYLAND

Bethesda Emergency Assistance Training (BEAT) 301-840-1057
9013 Shady Grove Court   301-208-1911
Gaithersburg, MD
infant and child CPR and safety courses on-site or at training center for
teachers, day care providers, parents

Child Care Connection 301-294-4954
Children's Resource Center
332 West Edmonston Road
Rockville, MD 20852
first aid and childhood emergencies courses at various sites

Health Quest, Inc. 410-869-0454
9 Newburg Avenue   FAX: 410-869-0452
Catonsville, MD 21228
courses also offered in Baltimore County, Ellicott City, Columbia, Frederick
County, and Harford County

Montgomery Child Care Association 301-946-1213
2730 University Blvd, West, Suite 616
Wheaton, MD 20902
infant and child CPR and first aid

Shady Grove Adventist Hospital 1-800-542-5096
9901 Medical Center Drive
Rockville, MD 20850
pediatric safety and CPR classes

Washington Adventist Hospital 1-800-542-5096
7600 Carroll Avenue
Takoma Park, MD 20912
pediatric safety and CPR classes

VIRGINIA

Alexandria Hospital Women's and Children's Education Services
Alexandria Hospital 703-750-0754
4320 Seminary Road
Alexandria, VA 22205

Alexandria Public Health Nurses 703-838-4884
home visits for health and wellness teaching and health care supervision

American Red Cross
4333 Arlington Blvd, Arlington 703-527-3010
123 N. Alfred Street, Alexandria 703-549-8300
CPR and first aid classes; Spanish classes also offered

Inova Health Source 703-208-5600
2832 Juniper Street
Fairfax, VA 22031
family health classes on various topics

HEALTH CARE
RESOURCES

Dentists, Pediatric

REFERRALS AND INFORMATION

National

Academy of Dentistry for Persons with Disabilities. 312-440-2660
611 E. Chicago Avenue
Chicago, IL 60611

American Dental Association Referral Service 703-642-5297

Dental Guidance Council for Cerebral Palsy 212-947-5770
UCP Association-Professional Services Program Department
66 E. 34th Street
New York, NY 10016

Dental Referral Service 1-800-DENTIST
private referral service to pediatric dentists in DC, MD, VA

National Foundation of Dentistry for the Handicapped .303-573-0264
1600 Stout Street, Suite 1420
Denver, CO 80202

District of Columbia

District of Columbia Dental Society 202-547-7613
502 C Street, NE
Washington, DC 20002

Maryland

Southern Maryland Dental Society 301-345-4196
4920 Niagara Road
College Park, MD 20740

Virginia

Northern Virginia Dental Society 703-642-5297
4201 John Marr Drive
Annandale, VA 22003

DENTISTS, PEDIATRIC

District of Columbia

Cuervo, Liliana, D.D.S. 301-840-0635
3801 Northampton Street, NW
Washington, DC 20015
Spanish-speaking

Ehudin, Helga, D.D.S. 202-362-2932
4105 Wisconsin Avenue, NW, No. 111
Washington, DC 20016

Greenwald, Dana S., D.D.S. 202-966-0045
5028 Wisconsin Avenue, NW, Suite 101
Washington, DC 20016

Lee, Fred M., D.D.S. 202-483-4237
1824 Calvert Street, NW
Washington, DC 20009

Maryland

Bethesda Dental Specialties 301-654-3011
Starr, Ronald M., D.D.S..   FAX: 301-986-1452
Etessami, Michael, D.D.S.
4405 East West Highway
Bethesda, MD 20814

Biederman, Paul D., D.D.S. 410-465-6000
Columbia, MD   301-740-0606

Blanton, Melanie J., D.M.D. 410-465-6000
Columbia, MD   301-740-0606

Camps, Robert D., D.D.S. 301-989-8994
2415 Musgrove Road, Suite 301
Silver Spring, MD 20904

Crafton, B. Casey, D.D.S. 410-740-4021
Ellicott City, MD

Dental Health Clinic, Montgomery County 301-217-1875
dental services for low-income families

Guy, Steven F., D.D.S. 301-593-5500
10301 Georgia Avenue
Wheaton, MD 20902
family dentistry

Hatfield, Dennis, D.D.S. 301-622-1116
12316 New Hampshire Avenue
Silver Spring, MD 20904
family dentistry

Kiesel, Nancy E., D.D.S. 301-656-4810
    5454 Wisconsin Avenue, #1045
    Chevy Chase, MD 20815
        family dentistry

Mintz and Pincus Dental Group
    6192 Oxon Hill Road, Oxon Hill 301-839-1330
    2955 Crain Highway, Waldorf 301-843-9330

Morgenstein and Levy, Drs., P.A. 301-881-6170
    White Flint Mall, 3rd level
    North Bethesda, MD 20895
        pediatric dentistry and special needs

Pediatric Dental Associates 301-989-8994
    2415 Musgrove Road, Suite 301
    Silver Spring, MD 20904

Weir-Gladstone, Yvette, D.D.S. 301-984-1968
    5940 Hubbard Drive, Montrose Rd. and Rockville Pike
    Rockville, MD
        family dentistry

Virginia

Averne, Robert M., D.D.S. 703-437-5700
    11503 Sunrise Valley Drive
    Reston, VA 20191

Bethel, Shirley F., D.D.S. 703-830-5566
    14245-M Centreville Square
    Centreville, VA 20121

Leaf, Scott H., D.D.S.
    7841 Rolling Road, Springfield 703-455-1339
    9316 Old Keene Mill Road, Burke 703-455-9683

McIlveen, Lezley P., D.D.S. 703-689-3900
    150 Elden Street, #130
    Herndon, VA 20170

Nelson, Edward J., D.D.S. 703-525-8200
    2501 N. Glebe Road, Suite 100
    Arlington, VA 22207

Sears, Robert S., D.D.S. 703-707-2070
    150 Elden Street, Suite 200
    Herndon, VA 20170

Ternisky, Michael J., D.D.S.
Ternisky, Cris Ann, D.D.S.
    1760 Reston Parkway, #204, Reston 703-481-9200
    6711 Whittier Avenue, McLean 703-356-1875

Drug Stores, Open 24 Hours

DISTRICT OF COLUMBIA

Dupont Circle CVS 202-785-1466
7 Dupont Circle, NW
Washington, DC

Thomas Circle CVS 202-628-0720
14th Street and Thomas Circle, NW
Washington, DC

MARYLAND

Bethesda CVS 301-656-2522
6917 Arlington Road
Bethesda, MD

Bethesda Giant 301-530-3271
Georgetown Square
Bethesda, MD

Bowie CVS 301-249-6515
1334 Crain Highway
Bowie, MD
open until midnight

District Heights CVS 301-736-3994
5870 Silver Hill Road, Silver Hill Plaza
District Heights, MD

Gaithersburg CVS 301-948-3250
Gaithersburg Square
Gaithersburg, MD

Greenbelt CVS 301-441-8810
5910 Greenbelt Road
Greenbelt, MD

Greenbelt Giant 301-982-2359
Beltway Plaza
Greenbelt, MD

Langley Park Giant 301-434-3121
7939 New Hampshire Avnue
Langley Park, MD

VIRGINIA

Arlington CVS 703-522-0260
Lyons Village Park Shopping Center
Arlington, VA

Bailey's Crossroads Giant 703-931-1333
3480 South Jefferson Street
Falls Church, VA

Fairfax CVS 703-631-1493
Greenbrier, Route 50
Fairfax, VA

Falls Church CVS 703-560-7280
Yorktown Center
Falls Church, VA

Manassas CVS 703-368-9146
8041 Sudley Road
Manassas, VA

Springfield CVS 703-451-1400
Springfield Plaza
Springfield, VA

HEALTH CARE RESOURCES

Health Information and Resources

See also GENERAL RESOURCES: Government Information and Resources
HEALTH CARE RESOURCES: Helplines
PARENT RESOURCES: Parent Info, specific topics

NATIONAL

Association for the Care of Children's Health 301-654-6549
7910 Woodmont Avenue   FAX: 301-986-4553
Bethesda, MD 20814
    publications; advocacy; group membership

Children's Environmental Health Network 510-450-3729
                                                                 FAX: 510-450-3773
                                                                 cehn@aimnet.com

Children's Health Fund 212-535-9400
317 E. 64th Street   FAX: 212-535-7488
New York, NY 10021

Department of Health and Human Services, U.S. .202-619-0257

National Health Council 202-785-3910
1730 M Street, NW, Suite 500
Washington, DC 20036
    nonprofit association of more than 100 national health organizations;
    paperback with 44 health agencies that can provide health information

National Institute of Child Health and Human Development 301-496-5133
National Institutes of Health
9000 Rockville Pike, Blg 31, Rm 2A-32
Bethesda, MD 20892
    free government publications on topics such as Down's Syndrome, nutri-
    tion, and developmental disabilities

Parents 1-900-680-KIDS
    child care information sponsored by *Parents* magazine; many health-related
    topics; 95 cents per minute

Reaching Out 703-821-8955
National Maternal and Child Health Clearinghouse   ext. 254 or 265
8205 Greensboro Drive, Suite 600   FAX: 703-821-2098
McLean, VA 22102
    free 180 page directory of over 400 national organizations related to
    maternal and child health

METRO AREA

Health Information Center (HIC) 301-929-5520
Wheaton Regional Library   TTY: 301-929-5524
11701 Georgia Avenue
Wheaton, MD 20902
free telephone research for medical issues through MEDLINE;
free book referral research for medical issues

Health Source Bookstore 1-800-713-7122
1404 K Street, NW   202-789-7303
Washington, DC 20005   FAX: 202-789-7899
health books for children and parents

Poison Control Center 202-625-3333
National Capital Poison Center
3201 New Mexico Avenue, Suite 310
Washington, DC 20016

DISTRICT OF COLUMBIA

Department of Health 202-727-8500

Department of Human Services 202-724-5466

Department of Public Health 202-673-7700

Health Services for Children with Special Needs 202-675-5214
D.C. General Hospital, Bldg. 10
19th and Massachusetts Avenue, SE
Washington, DC 20003

Poison Control Center 202-625-3333
National Capital Poison Center
3201 New Mexico Avenue, Suite 310
Washington, DC 20016

MARYLAND

Department of Health and Human Services
Montgomery County 301-217-3500
Prince George's County 301-986-0300

Department of Health and Mental Hygiene
Mental Hygiene Administration 410-225-6860
Division of Child and Adolescent Services 410-767-6649
Programs for Children with Special Health Care Needs 410-225-5580
Children's Medical Services, Unit 50
201 West Preston Street
Baltimore, MD 21201

Poison Control Center 1-800-492-2414
outside of Maryland 301-528-7701
University of Maryland Pharmacy School
20 N. Pine Street
Baltimore, MD 21201

Special Needs Library 301-897-2212
6400 Democracy Boulevard   TTY: 301-897-2217
Bethesda, MD 20817
special format reading materials, information on disabling conditions

Young Children's Health and Safety Fair 301-217-3500
Montgomery County Health and Human Services
Montgomery County Adult Education
annual spring fair held at Montgomery Mall; car seats checked

VIRGINIA

Department of Health
Alexandria 703-838-4400
    Alexandria Health Information and Referral 703-548-3810
    Alexandria Health-Line 703-845-1243
Arlington County 703-358-4992
    Arlington County Health Center Commission 703-358-5030
Fairfax County 703-246-2411
    Fairfax City 703-246-7100
    Falls Church 703-534-8343
    Herndon 703-481-4242
    Mount Vernon 703-660-7100
    Springfield 703-569-1031

Department of Health, Virginia
Division of Children's Specialty Services 804-786-3691
P.O. Box 2448
Richmond, VA 23218
    programs for children with special health care needs

Department of Health and Human Services 703-838-0710
Alexandria 703-838-0900
Arlington County 703-358-5300
Fairfax County 703-222-0880

Poison Control Center, Tidewater Virginia 1-800-552-6337
Medical College, Pediatric Unit
P.O. Box 980522
Virginia Commonwealth University
Richmond, VA 23298

Public Health Nurses, Alexandria 703-838-4884
    home visits for health and wellness teaching and health care supervision

HEALTH CARE RESOURCES

Hospitals and Clinics

HOSPITALIZATION RESOURCES

See also **PARENT RESOURCES: Parent Info, Disabled/Chronically Ill Children**

National

Association for the Care of Children's Health 1-800-808-2224
7910 Woodmont Avenue, Suite 300   301-654-6549
Bethesda, MD 20814
> publications for helping children and families cope with hospitalization;
> some coloring books for ages 2 to 5

Pediatric Projects, Inc. 818-705-3660
P.O. Box 571555
Tarzana, CA 91357
> medically-oriented therapeutic toys and books for children coping with
> illness, hospitalization, and disability

Sick Kids Need Involved People (SKIP) 301-261-2602
216 Newport Drive
Severna Park, MD 21146
> information and education for families coping with a child's special
> medical care

Metro Area

Coordination Center for Home and Community Care, Inc. 301-621-7830
P.O. Box 613, Brightview Business Center
Millersville, MD 21108
> helps monitor home care for chronically ill children in Baltimore,
> Washington area

United Cerebral Palsy of Washington and Northern Virginia
Family Support Services 202-269-1500
3135 8th Street, NE
Washington, DC 20017
> short term loans of donated wheelchairs, walkers, etc.

DISTRICT OF COLUMBIA

Children's Hospital Information and Referral Line 202-884-BEAR
Children's Hospital 202-884-5000
    111 Michigan Avenue, NW
Children's Hospital at Spring Valley 202-745-8860
    4900 Massachusetts Ave, NW, #320

DC General Hospital 202-675-5000
    1900 Massachusetts Avenue, SE
    Washington, DC 20003

George Washington University Hospital 202-994-1000
    2121 I Street, NW
    Washington, DC 20037

Georgetown University Hospital 202-784-2000
    3800 Reservoir Road, NW
    Washington, DC 20007

Greater SE Community Hospital 202-574-6000
    1310 Southern Avenue, SE
    Washington, DC 20032

Hadley Memorial Hospital 202-574-5700
    4601 Martin Luther King Avenue, SW
    Washington, DC 20032

Hospital for Sick Children 202-832-4400
    1731 Bunker Hill Road, NE
    Washington, DC 20017

Howard University Hospital 202-865-1267
    2041 Georgia Avenue, NW
    Washington, DC 20060

Pediatrics AIDS/HIV Care, Inc. 202-328-1421
    Stephen Kosk, M.Div., Residential Program Director
    1317 G Street, NW
    Washington, DC 20005

Providence Hospital 202-269-7000
    1150 Varnum Street, NE
    Washington, DC 20017

Sibley Memorial Hospital 202-537-4058
    5255 Loughboro Road, NW
    Washington, DC 20016

Washington Clinic Medical Center, The 202-244-9270
    5401 Western Avenue, NW
    Washington, DC 20015
        physicians on call 24 hours a day

Washington Hospital Center 202-877-7000
    110 Irving Street, NW
    Washington, DC 20010

Yater Medical Group 202-785-2385
    1780 Massachusetts Avenue, NW
    Washington, DC 20036
        physicians on call 24 hours a day

HEALTH CARE RESOURCES

MARYLAND

After Hours Pediatric Care 301-369-0500
13922 Baltimore Avenue
Laurel, MD
M-F 5:30pm-11:00pm; Saturdays, Sundays, and holidays 1:30pm-9:00pm

Bowie Health Center Emergency Medical Care 301-262-5511
15001 Health Center Drive
Bowie, MD 20716

Children's Hospital Information and Referral Line. 1-888-884-BEAR
Children's Hospital at Laurel Lakes 301-369-4100
13922 Baltimore Avenue, Unit 4a, Laurel
Children's Hospital of Montgomery County 301-424-1755
14804 Physician's Lane, Suite 122, Rockville
Children's Hospital of Southern Maryland 301-868-5777
9440 Pennsylvania Ave, Upper Marlboro
over 40 specialties at consultative centers throughout the area

Greater Laurel Beltsville Hospital 301-470-3695
7100 Contee Road
Laurel, MD 20707

Holy Cross Hospital 301-905-0100
1500 Forest Glen Road
Silver Spring, MD 20910

Laurel Regional Hospital 301-725-4300
7300 Van Dusen Road
Laurel, MD 20707

Montgomery General Hospital 301-774-8882
18101 Prince Philip Drive
Olney, MD 20832

Prince George's Hospital Center 301-618-2000
3001 Hospital Drive
Cheverly, MD 20785

Shady Grove Adventist Hospital 301-279-6000
9901 Medical Center Drive
Rockville, MD 20850

Southern Maryland Hospital 301-868-8000
7503 Surratts Road
Clinton, MD 20735

Suburban Hospital 301-896-3100
8600 Old Georgetown Road
Bethesda, MD 20814

Washington Adventist Hospital 301-891-7600
7600 Carroll Avenue
Takoma Park, MD 20912

HEALTH CARE RESOURCES

VIRGINIA

Alexandria Child Health Clinic 703-838-4414
517 N. St. Asaph Street
Alexandria, VA 22314
physical exams for children ages 3 to 11; children with Medicaid

Alexandria Hospital 703-504-3000
4320 Seminary Road
Alexandria, VA 22205

Arlington Hospital 703-558-5000
1701 N. George Mason Drive
Arlington, VA 22205

Arlington County Child Health (Well Child) Clinic 703-358-5610
800 S. Walter Reed Drive
Arlington, VA 22204

Children's Hospital Information and Referral Line 1-888-884-BEAR
Children's Hospital of Northern Virginia .703-573-9383
3022 Williams Drive, Suite 100
Fairfax, VA
over 40 specialties at consultative centers throughout the area

Dominion Hospital 703-538-2872
2960 Sleepy Hollow Road
Falls Church, VA 22044

Fairfax Hospital 703-698-1110
3300 Gallows Road
Falls Church, VA 22042

Fair Oaks Hospital 703-391-3124
3600 Joseph Siewick Drive   703-391-3600
Fairfax, VA 22033

Flora Krause Casey Health Center 703-823-7333
1200 N. Howard Street
Alexandria, VA
diagnostic and treatment services, including pediatric sick care

Mount Vernon Hospital 703-664-7000
2501 Parkers Lane
Alexandria, VA 22306

Potomac Hospital 703-670-1313
2300 Opitz Blvd
Woodbridge, VA 22191

Prince William Hospital 703-369-8000
8700 Spring Valley Road
Manassas, VA 22110

Reston Hospital Center 703-689-9000
1850 Town Center Parkway
Reston, VA 22090

HEALTH CARE RESOURCES

Nutritionists and Nutritional Resources, Pediatric

See also **PARENT RESOURCES: Parent Info, Allergy and Asthma**

NATIONAL

American Dietetic Association Consumer Hotline 1-800-366-1655

Center for Science in the Public Interest 202-232-9110
1875 Connecticut Avenue, NW, Suite 300   FAX: 202-265-4954
Washington, DC 20009
   nutritional research and dietary information resource

Feingold Association of the United States 703-768-FAUS
P.O. Box 6550
Alexandria, VA 22306
   information on food additives and possible effects on child behavior, such as
   overactivity, attention deficit, anxiety, aggression, sleep disturbances and
   learning disabilities

Food Allergy Network 703-691-3179
10400 Eaton Place, Suite 107   FAX: 703-691-2713
Fairfax, VA 22030   fan@worldweb.net
http://www.foodallergy.org
   non-profit organization providing education and support to families dealing
   with food allergies

International Food Information Council 202-296-6540
1100 Connecticut Avenue, NW, Suite 430
Washington, DC 20036

METRO AREA

Children's Hospital Information and Referral Line 1-888-884-BEAR

Children's Hospital 202-884-3031
Gastroentrology/Nutrition Department

Consulting Nutritionists of the Chesapeake Bay Area and District of Columbia
Metropolitan Area Dietetic Association 202-289-4215
family nutrition planning, special diets

Developmental Delay Registry 301-652-2263
Kelly Dorfman, nutritionist, co-founder
Patricia Lemer, counselor, co-founder
6701 Fairfax Road
Chevy Chase, MD 20815
non-profit organization promoting healthy options for children with
developmental delays; counseling on nutrition and behavior; workshops on
nutrition issues

Dorfman, Kelly 301-340-2239
Gaithersburg, MD
consultative nutritionist for children

Feingold Association of the Washington Area 703-524-5566
P.O. Box 6550
Alexandria, VA 22306
information on food additives and possible effects on child behavior, such as
overactivity, attention deficit, anxiety, aggression, sleep disturbances and
learning disabilities

Food Research and Action Center (FRAC) .202-986-2200
1875 Connecticut Avenue, NW, Suite 540
Washington, DC 20009
nutritional counseling for parents

Health Source Bookstore 1-800-713-7122
1404 K Street, NW   202-789-7303
Washington, DC 20005   FAX: 202-789-7899
health books for children and parents

HEALTH CARE RESOURCES

Optometrists and
Visual Training, Pediatric

See also   HEALTH CARE RESOURCES: Pediatricians, Ophthalmologists
MENTAL HEALTH RESOURCES: Testing and Assessment, CHILDFIND
PARENT RESOURCES: Parent Info, Visually-Impaired
EC PROFESSIONAL RESOURCES: Child Care: Educational, Assessments,
Vision and Hearing Testing

REFERRALS AND INFORMATION

VISION USA 1-800-766-4466
243 North Lindbergh Boulevard
St. Louis, MO 63141
referrals to local free eye care offered for low-income children; sponsored
by the American Optometric Association; screening in January

WISER, Directory of Educational Services in the Washington Area
11140 Rockville Pike, #105 301-816-0432
Rockville, MD 20852
referrals to local optometrists

DISTRICT OF COLUMBIA

Kraskin, Jeffrey L., O.D 202-363-4450
Kraskin, Robert A., O.D.
4600 Massachusetts Avenue, NW
Washington, DC 20016
general optometric practice, including visual training therapy

Vision and Conceptual Development Center, The 202-862-0749
2440 Virginia Avenue, NW, Suite D-102   FAX: 202-862-4988
Washington, DC 20037
pre-school readiness evaluation

MARYLAND

Appelbaum, Stanley, OD 301-897-8484
6509 Democracy Blvd.
Bethesda, MD 20817
pediatric behavioral optometrist

Davis, Dr. Morton
4905 West Cedar Lane, Bethesda 301-530-6300
9100 Old Annapolis Road, Columbia 410-730-5808
308 South Main Street, Mt. Airy 301-829-1910
optometrist specializing in neural organization and integration of the
visual system

Frenkel, Dr. Debra S. 301-681-3767
647 Concerto Lane
Silver Spring, MD 20901

Friedman, Dr. Henry M. 301-897-5210
6509 Democracy Blvd.
Bethesda, MD 20817
    evaluation and treatment of visual dysfunctions, including low vision and
    learning-related vision problems

Glazier, Harold S., O.D. 301-670-1212
16003 Comprint Circle, Comprint Professional Center
Gaithersburg, MD 20877
    general optometric practice with specialty in behavioral optometry; learning
    related vision problems

Kaplan, Walter 301-977-7879
20 Summit Avenue
Gaithersburg, MD 20877

Kotlicky, Dr. Marsha
Kotlicky, Dr. Michael
    4905 West Cedar Lane, Bethesda 301-530-6300
    9100 Old Annapolis Road, Columbia 410-730-5808
    308 South Main Street, Mt. Airy 301-829-1910

Lewis, Nancy B., O.D. 301-589-7472
9215 Colesville Road
Silver Spring, MD 20910
    general optometric practice specializing in learning related visual disorders
    and visual therapy

VIRGINIA

Cantwell, Dennis R., O.D. 703-941-3937
7611 Little River Turnpike, 303W
Annandale, VA 22003

Garson, Dr. Wendy C. 703-442-0522
6849 Old Dominion Drive
McLean, VA 22101

Greenburg, Robert M., O.D. 703-471-4600
Sunset Hills Professional Center
11365 Sunset Hills Road
Reston, VA 22090
    optometry services and visual training

Optometric Eye Care Associates, P.C.
    3800 North Fairfax Drive, Arlington, 22203 703-522-3454
    5765-L Burke Center Parkway, Burke, 22015 703-250-2000
    14245-E Centreville Square, Centreville, 22020 703-830-2010

Sikes, Alan L., O.D. 703-978-5010
Burke Professional Center
9002 Fern Park Drive
Burke, VA 22015
    developmental-behavioral optometrist

HEALTH CARE RESOURCES

Pediatricians

See also **MENTAL HEALTH RESOURCES: Testing and Assessment**

REFERRALS AND INFORMATION

National

American Academy of Pediatrics 202-347-8600
Pediatrician Referral Source   FAX: 202-393-6137
141 Northwest Point Blvd   kids1st@aap.org
P.O. Box 927
Elk Grove Village, IL 60009
> for help in finding a qualified pediatrician or pediatric subspecialist, send
> the name of the desired specialty and a self-addressed, stamped envelope to
> the above address

American Medical Association 312-464-5000
Department of Physician Data Services
515 North State Street
Chicago, IL 60610

Metro Area

Children's Hospital Information and Referral Line 1-888-884-BEAR
over 40 specialties at consultative centers throughout the area

Johns Hopkins University Hospital Referral Line 1-800-45-JOHNS

WISER, Directory of Educational Services in the Washington Area
11140 Rockville Pike, #105 301-816-0432
Rockville, MD 20852
> referrals to local pediatricians

District of Columbia

Children's Hospital Information and Referral Line 202-884-BEAR

Sibley Memorial Hospital Physician Referral Service 202-966-6500
Monday through Friday, 9 am - 4 pm

Maryland

Children's Hospital Information and Referral Line 1-888-884-BEAR

Ferguson, Carolyn 410-550-8097
Developmental Pediatric Clinic
Kennedy Krieger Institute
707 North Broadway
Baltimore, MD 21205
referrals to developmental pediatricians at Kennedy Krieger Institute

Holy Cross Hospital 301-905-1214
Cross Connect Physicians Referral Service
1500 Forest Glen Road
Silver Spring, MD 20910

Montgomery County Medical Society
Patient Advocacy Referral Service 301-963-3100
P.O. Box 5689
Rockville, MD 20855

Prince George's County Medical Society
Physician Referral Service 301-341-7758
6307 Landover Road
Cheverly, MD 20785

Virginia

Alexandria Medical Society
Physicians Referral Service 703-356-6940
8227 Old Courthouse Road
Vienna, VA 22182

Children's Hospital Information and Referral Line 1-888-884-BEAR

First Call 703-845-4848
pediatrician referrals for Alexandria, Arlington, Reston

Prologue-Dial Doctors 1-800PROLOGU
901 N. Washington Street, Suite 500
Alexandria, VA 22314

ADD/ADHD SPECIALISTS

See also **MENTAL HEALTH RESOURCES: Testing and Assessment**
CHILD CARE AND SCHOOL RESOURCES: Private Preschools, Special Needs
CHILD CARE AND SCHOOL RESOURCES: Public Preschools, Special Programs
PARENT RESOURCES: Parent Info, Special Needs

Castellanos, Francisco Xavier, M.D. 301-496-4319
Child Psychiatry Branch
National Institutes of Health
9000 Rockville Pike
Bethesda, MD
ADHD, Tourette's Syndrome, learning disabilities, and other associated
disorders

Children's Hospital Information and Referral Line 1-888-884-BEAR
over forty specialties to treat children's medical needs at consultative
centers throughout the area

Denckla, Martha B., M.D. 410-550-9420
Developmental Cognitive Neurology Clinic
Kennedy Krieger Institute
707 North Broadway
Baltimore, MD 21205
pediatrician and psychiatrist specializing in ADHD

Einbinder, Lawrence, M.D. 301-897-3355
10215 Fernwood Road
Bethesda, MD 20817
neurologist specializing in ADD, Tourette's Syndrome, and migraines

Ferguson, Carolyn 410-550-8097
Developmental Pediatric Clinic
Kennedy Krieger Institute
707 Broadway
Baltimore, MD 21205
referrals to developmental pediatricians at Kennedy Krieger Institute

Fusner, June, M.D. 301-907-3690
Capitol Medical Group
5530 Wisconsin Avenue, Suite 1125
Chevy Chase, MD 20815
ADHD, LD, chronic diseases

Virginia Pediatric Group
8316 Arlington Blvd., Suite 502, Fairfax 703-573-2432
1311 Elden Street, Suite 312, Herndon 703-435-5202
ADHD/LD Counseling Services Helpline 703-849-9476
pediatricians specializing in ADD/LD

ALLERGISTS

See also HEALTH CARE RESOURCES: Nutritionists
PARENT RESOURCES: Parent Info, Allergy/Asthma

Metro Area

Children's Hospital 202-884-3440
Department of Allergy and Immunology

Maryland

Barbera, Jeanne M., M.D.
19519 Doctors Drive, Germantown 301-972-9433
50 W. Edmonston Dr., Suite 301, Rockville 301-251-3704

Lampl, Kathy, M.D.
10301 Georgia Avenue, Silver Spring 301-681-6055
9711 Medical Center Drive, Rockville 301-251-0880

Layton, Richard E., M.D. 410-337-2706
901 Dulaney Valley Rd, Dulaney Center II, Suite 602   info@allergyconnection.com
Towson, MD 21204   http://www.allergyconnection.com/layton/

Shapiro & Perez, M.D., P.A.
Melvyn F. Shapiro, M.D., F.A.A.P.
Aurora A. Perez, M.D., F.A.A.P.
10801 Lockwood Drive #260, Silver Spring 301-593-5566
2 Professional Park, Ste 215, Gaithersburg 301-330-5100
bi-lingual

Shier, Jerry, M.D.
10301 Georgia Avenue, Silver Spring 301-681-6055
9711 Medical Center Drive, Rockville 301-251-0880

Vaghia, Vincent, J., M.D.
19519 Doctors Drive, Germantown 301-972-9433
50 W. Edmonston Dr., Suite 301, Rockville 301-251-3704

Wolfe, Stanley, M.D.
10301 Georgia Avenue, Silver Spring 301-681-6055
9711 Medical Center Drive, Rockville 301-251-0880

Virginia

Inglefield, Joseph, M.D. 703-532-1131
107 N. Virginia Avenue   FAX: 703-532-1984
Falls Church, VA 22043

Murphy, Laurence J., M.D. 703-503-9100
5212 Lyngate Court
Burke, VA 22015

Staats, Stacey H., M.D. 703-503-9100
5212 Lyngate Court
Burke, VA 22015

HEALTH CARE RESOURCES

DERMATOLOGISTS

American Academy of Dermatology . . . . .http://www.aad.org
930 N. Meacham
Schaumburg, IL 60173

Children's Hospital 202-884-3440
Department of Dermatology

EAR, NOSE, AND THROAT SPECIALISTS

Children's Hospital 202-884-5000

McBride, Timothy, M.D. 703-573-7600
Otolaryngology Associates   FAX: 703-560-3608
8316 Arlington Blvd, Suite 300
Fairfax, VA

Shimoura, Steven, M.D. 301-570-1333
3416 Olandwood Court, Suite 207
Olney, MD 20832

GASTROENTEROLOGISTS

Bader, Ali, M.D. 202-884-3031
Department of Gastroenterology and Nutrition
Children's National Medical Center, Washington, DC
Shady Grove Hospital, Rockville, MD

Capital Area Pediatric Heartburn and Reflux Assn 301-972-6128
information and support to parents of children with gastroesophageal
reflux

Children's Hospital 202-884-3031
Department of Gastroenterology and Nutrition

NEPHROLOGISTS

Children's Hospital 202-884-3440
Department of Nephrology

Northern Virginia Pediatric Associates, P.C. .703-532-4446
107 North Virginia Avenue
Falls Church, VA
specialists in kidney disorders

NEUROLOGISTS

Children's Hospital Information and Referral Line 1-888-884-BEAR
Children's National Medical Center 202-884-5000
    111 Michigan Avenue, NW, DC 202-884-5000
    Spring Valley, 4900 Mass. Ave., NW, DC 202-745-8860
    13922 Baltimore Avenue, Unit 4a, Laurel, MD 301-369-4100
    14804 Physician's Lane, #122, Rockville, MD 301-424-1755
    3022 Williams Drive, Suite 100, Fairfax, VA 703-573-9383
        neuropsychological evaluations

Einbinder, Lawrence, M.D. 301-897-3355
    10215 Fernwood Road
    Bethesda, MD 20817
        neurologist specializing in Tourette's Syndrome, ADD, and migraines

Hyde, Thomas, M.D., Ph.D. 301-588-2011
    4701 Willard Avenue
    Chevy Chase, MD
        behavioral neurologist

OPHTHALMOLOGISTS

See also **HEALTH CARE RESOURCES: Optometrists and Visual Training**

Children's Hospital 202-884-3015
    Department of Ophthalmology

Hutcheon, Marcia, M.D. 301-997-0167
    Shady Grove Adventist Hospital
    Rockville, MD 20850

ORTHOPEDISTS

Abend, Jeffrey, M.D. 301-681-5400
    2102 Medical Park Drive, Suite 110
    Silver Spring, MD 20902

Children's Hospital 202-884-2112
    Department of Orthopedics

Gabriel, Shari, M.D. 703-435-6604
    1800 Town Center Drive
    Reston, VA 20190

Reff, Richard, M.D. 301-571-1951
    6500 Rock Spring Drive
    Bethesda, MD 20817

SPECIAL NEEDS

See also HEALTH CARE RESOURCES: Pediatricians, ADD/ADHD

Children's Hospital Information and Referral Line 1-888-884-BEAR
over 40 specialties at consultative centers throughout the area

Ferguson, Carolyn 410-550-8097
Developmental Pediatric Clinic
Kennedy Krieger Institute
707 Broadway
Baltimore, MD 21205
referrals to developmental pediatricians at Kennedy Krieger Institute

Koch, Barbara M., M.D.
6200 Montrose Road, Rockville, MD 301-231-5436
8348 Traford Lane, #203, Springfield, VA 703-644-6901
physical medicine and rehabilitation; diagnosis and treatment of cerebral
palsy, hypotonia, developmental delays, chronic pain, nerve and muscle
disorders

"How Can I Help My Child?"   Early Childhood Resource Directory

101

Physical and Occupational Therapists, Pediatric

See also MENTAL HEALTH RESOURCES: Testing and Assessment

REFERRALS AND INFORMATION

American Occupational Therapy Association, Inc. 301-652-9986
4720 Montgomery Lane
P.O. Box 31220
Bethesda, MD 20824

American Physical Therapy Association 703-684-2782
1111 North Fairfax Street
Alexandria, VA 22314

Developmental Delay Registry (DDR) 301-652-2263
Patricia Lemer
6701 Fairfax Road
Chevy Chase, MD 20815
referrals to occupational therapists

Neurodevelopmental Treatment Association 1-800-869-9295
referrals to physical and occupational therapists

Sensory Integration International 1-310-320-9986
1602 Cabrillo Avenue
Torrance, CA 90501
$3 for list of certified therapists; list by zip or area code; *A Parents' Guide to Understanding Sensory Integration* book available for $2.59;
Dr. Stanley Appelbaum, local Board Member 301-897-8484
list of area occupational therapists certified for evaluation and testing

WISER, *Directory of Educational Services in the Washington Area*
11140 Rockville Pike, #105 301-816-0432
Rockville, MD 20852
referrals to physical therapists

DISTRICT OF COLUMBIA

Israel, Lynne C., & Associates, Inc. 202-986-9896
1700 Kalorama Road, NW, Suite 106
Washington, DC 20009
sensory integration; evaluation and treatment; comprehensive services

Peters Pediatric Nursing Team, Inc. 202-291-0062
6856 Eastern Avenue, NW, Suite 210
Washington, DC 20012
licensed home health agency

MARYLAND

Balzer-Martin, Lynn, Ph.D., OTR 301-654-1828
6648 Hillandale Road
Chevy Chase, MD 20815
      sensory integration; Balzer-Martin Preschool Screening Program (BAPS):
      method for identifying possible developmental problems in young children;
      on-site screening $60 manual available from St. Columba's Nursery School,
      4201 Albemarle Street, NW, Washington, DC 20016

Bassin, Barbara S., OTR, B.C.P. 301-897-8484
6509 Democracy Blvd.
Bethesda, MD 20817
      evaluation and treatment of children with learning, coordination, and/or
      behavioral problems related to sensory integrative dysfunction

Cappuccilli, Judith, P.T. 301-952-0336
Upper Marlboro, MD

Chesapeake Center, The 301-942-6766
10400 Connecticut Avenue, suite 206
Kensington, MD 20895
      screenings, consultation, therapy

Early Intervention Associates 301-468-9343
Jill Kider, OTR
Rebecca Leonard, M.S., P.T.
6262 Montrose Road
Rockville, MD 20852

Ivymount School, The 301-469-0223
11614 Seven Locks Road
Rockville, MD 20854
      evaluation and treatment for children experiencing motor, sensory, and
      speech/language difficulties

Newman, Joyce, M.A. 301-656-1543
7475 Wisconsin Avenue
Bethesda, MD 20814
      provides remedial work with gross and fine motor and visual perception
      problems; balance, body awareness, spatial awareness, dexterity, visual motor
      coordination

Nolan, Linda 301-585-3983
1903 Seminary Road
Silver Spring, MD 20910
      sensory integration, postural and coordination disorders

Pediatric Therapy Associates 301-942-6006
Donna Klem
Kathleen Rodriguez
11302 Veirs Mill Road
Wheaton, MD 20902
      pediatric therapy and developmental services for children with special
      needs

Peters Pediatric Nursing Team, Inc. 410-486-3800
1700 Reistertown Road
Baltimore, MD 20012
licensed home health agency

Rehabilitation Services, Inc.
9811 Mallard Drive, Suite 109, Laurel 301-498-8100
5650 Shields Drive, Bethesda 301-530-8100
physical therapy, occupational therapy, speech language pathology; free
screenings; free parent seminars

Scheiner, Nancy, M.S., OTR 301-654-1297
5520 Uppingham Street
Chevy Chase, MD 20815
developmental delays, sensory integration dysfunction

Treatment and Learning Centers 301-424-5200
9975 Medical Center Drive   TDD 301-424-5203
Rockville, MD 20850
occupational and physical therapy provided at home, school

TRI Rehab of Germantown, Inc. 301-540-4700
19733 Executive Park Circle   FAX: 301-540-4721
Germantown, MD 20874
gross and fine motor delays, perceptual delays, language and oral motor
disorders

Washington Developmental Center, Inc., The .301-585-3983
1903 Seminary Road
Silver Spring, MD
occupational and physical therapy, parent support groups

VIRGINIA

Chesapeake Center, The 703-924-4100
6506 Loisdale Road, Suite 300
Springfield, VA 22150
screenings, consultation, therapy

Child Development Center of Northern Virginia .703-534-5353
111 North Cherry Street
Falls Church, VA 22046
sliding fee, developmental evaluations; preschool program

Ganz, Lynne J., OTR and Associates 703-689-4451
11501 Sunset Hills Road
Reston, VA
evaluation, consultation and treatment; sensory integration, neurodevelopmental treatment

Hannah, Jean, M.A., OTR 703-750-0414
5031 Backlick Road
Annandale, VA 22003
evaluation and treatment of motor impairments, developmental delay,
sensory-motor deficits, cerebral palsy

Kane, Virginia, M.S., OTR 703-750-2443
Skill Builders, Inc.
7617 Little River Turnpike, Suite 310
Annandale, VA 22003
sensory integration and neurodevelopmental approach

Mitchell, Francie 703-689-4451
serving Fairfax, Loudoun, and Prince William Counties

Moses, Myania, OTR 703-527-2166
4731 N. 23rd Street
Arlington, VA 22207
evaluation and treatment of fine, visual, and perceptual motor development
and sensory integration

Pediatric Therapy Offices 703-242-1921
407 Church Street, Suite D
Vienna, VA 22180
evaluation and treatment; neurodevelopmental treatment and sensory
integration

Peters Pediatric Nursing Team, Inc. 703-941-8600
5501 Backlick Road
Springfield, VA 22151
licensed home health agency

SKILLBUILDERS 703-750-2443
7617 Little River Turnpike, Suite 310, Annandale
6845 Elm Street, Suite 711, McLean
evaluation and treatment; sensory integration, fine motor, visual motor and
perceptual motor activities

Syron, Suzan C., and Associates 703-569-7500
8348 Traford Lane, Suite 200
Springfield, VA 22152
pediatric physical and occupational therapy services

Wilson, Peg, M.S., OTR 703-683-0259
335 S. Patrick Street
Alexandria, VA
sensory integration; neurodevelopmental treatment; serving the
metropolitan area

Speech and Hearing Specialists, Pediatric

See also PARENT RESOURCES: Parent Info, Hearing-Impaired
PARENT RESOURCES: Parent Info, Stuttering
EC PROFESSIONAL RESOURCES: Child Care: Educational, Assessments,
Vision and Hearing Tests

REFERRALS AND INFORMATION

National

American Speech-Language-Hearing Association 1-800-638-8255
National Association for Hearing and Speech Action 1-800-638-8255
10801 Rockville Pike
Rockville, MD 20852
referrals to speech pathologists

Neurodevelopmental Treatment Association 1-800-869-9295
referrals to speech therapists

Metro Area

WISER, Directory of Educational Services in the Washington Area
11140 Rockville Pike, #105 301-816-0432
Rockville, MD 20852
referrals to speech therapists

District of Columbia

DC Speech-Language-Hearing Association 202-651-5378
Robin Goffen, President
P.O. Box 91016
Washington, DC 20090

Washington Hearing and Speech Society 202-244-4420

Virginia

Northern Virginia Resource Center for Deaf and Hard-of-Hearing Persons 703-352-9055
10359 Democracy Lane   TTY 703-352-9057
Fairfax, VA
information on audiologists, support groups, programs, videos, etc. for
families with hearing-impaired children

Speech-Language-Hearing Association of Virginia, Inc. 804-379-8441
Karen Corso
P.O. Box 35653
Richmond, VA 23235

DISTRICT OF COLUMBIA

CHILDFIND 202-727-8300
> free testing and treatment of children 2yrs 9 mos through 4;
> children 0 to 2 yrs 9 mos., ask for Infant & Toddler Program; multi-lingual

Children's Hearing and Speech Center .202-884-5600
Children's Hospital National Medical Center
Washington, DC 20010

MARYLAND

Chesapeake Center, The 301-942-6766
10400 Connecticut Avenue, #206
Kensington, MD
> assessment and treatment of language and reading difficulties

CHILDFIND:
Anne Arundel County 410-956-0741
Baltimore City 410-396-6227
Baltimore County 410-887-3017
Calvert County 410-535-7380
Caroline County 410-479-3246
Cecil County 410-996-5444
Dorchester County 410-221-0837
Harford County 410-638-3814
Howard County 410-313-7046
Kent County 410-778-3483
Montgomery County 301-279-FIND
Prince George's County 301-952-6341
Somerset County 410-651-1485
Talbot County 410-820-8263
Wicomico County 410-749-5176
Worcester County . . . . .410-632-2582 ext. 233
> free testing and treatment of children 2yrs 9 mos through 4;
> children 0 to 2 yrs 9 mos, ask for Infant & Toddler Program; multi-lingual

Children's Hearing and Speech Center .301-217-5439
Children's National Medical Center, Shady Grove   301-424-1755
14804 Physicians Lane
Rockville, MD 20850

Communication Enrichment Services 301-652-2200
Diane Lewis, M.A., CCC-SLP
5109 Battery Lane
Bethesda, MD
> communication delays, including dyspraxia-oral motor, LD, autism,
> Down's Syndrome

Cowan Communications Services 301-460-0220
13817 Congress Drive
Rockville, MD
> comprehensive services for speech, learning disabilities, feeding and
> swallowing disorders, myofunctional therapy, home visits

Early Intervention Associates 301-468-9343
Susan Abrams, MA CCC-SP
6262 Montrose Road
Rockville, MD

Family Hearing Center, The 301-424-5200
9975 Medical Center Drive   TDD 301-424-5203
Rockville, MD
hearing specialists

Hearing and Speech Center 301-949-8070
11160 Veirs Mill Road, Suite 310   www.hearingcenter.com
Wheaton, MD 20902
testing and treatment

Hearing Health Care, Inc. 301-946-2434
3913 Ferrera Avenue
Wheaton, MD 20906
testing and treatment

Ivymount School 301-469-0223
11614 Seven Locks Road
Rockville, MD 20854
evaluation and treatment for children experiencing motor, sensory, and
speech and language difficulties

Language Experience, The 301-365-1232
Leslie Kessler
6747 Surreywood Lane
Bethesda, MD 20817
speech evaluations and therapy

Maryland Vision and Hearing Testing, Inc.
Wendy Chansky 301-474-4198
Patty Reeley 301-439-2536
8009 Brett Place
Greenbelt, MD 20770
private testing service that screens all children ages 3 and up for vision and
hearing; on-site at schools

Meisler, Barbara Altman, LSP, CCC 301-649-5333
11411 Monticello Avenue
Silver Spring, MD

Montgomery County Infants & Toddlers Program 301-279-1250
free testing and services for children from birth to 2 yrs 9 mos.;
multi-lingual; see CHILDFIND

Pediatric Speech-Language Clinic 301-774-8881
Montgomery General Hospital
18101 Prince Philip Drive
Olney, MD

Rehabilitation Services, Inc.
9811 Mallard Drive, Suite 109, Laurel 301-498-8100
5650 Shields Drive, Bethesda 301-530-8100
speech language pathology; free screenings; free parent seminars

Ridley & Fill Speech & Language Associates, Chtd. 301-652-8997
4909 Hampden Lane, Suite One
Bethesda, MD 20814
diagnostic and treatment for full range of speech and language disorders;
home visits available

Rubinoff, Laura, and Associates 301-493-4695
6505 Democracy Blvd.
Bethesda, MD 20817
diagnostic and therapeutic services with speech delays and disorders

Shevitz, Stephen 301-345-9191
Communication Associates
800 Brett Place
Greenbelt, MD

Speech-Language Center of Olney 301-774-2247
Joanne Sabin, MA, CCC-SLP
19504 DuBarry Drive
Brookville, MD 20833

Therapeutic Intervention Services 301-942-6002
Susan M. Porgess, MS, CCC, Sp.
11302 Veirs Mill Road
Wheaton, MD

Treatment and Learning Centers 301-424-5200
9975 Medical Center Drive   TDD 301-424-5203
Rockville, MD 20850
speech evaluation and therapy provided at home, school

University of Maryland Hearing and Speech Clinic 301-405-4218
Colleen Worthington, Clinic Director
Lefrak Hall
College Park, MD 20742
hearing and speech clinic; also, clinic sponsors a preschool program
for language-delayed children

VIRGINIA

Blue Ridge Speech and Hearing Center
2 Cardinal Park Drive, #201B, Leesburg 703-777-5050
2 Pidgeon Hill Drive, #430, Sterling 703-430-5454

Calvert, Mary Balfour, M.A., C.C.C. 703-549-5432
217 Wolfe Street, Old Town
Alexandria, VA

Chesapeake Center, The 703-765-6200
6911 Richmond Highway, Suite 415
Alexandria, VA

Child Development Center of Northern Virginia 703-534-5353
111 North Cherry Street
Falls Church, VA
sliding fee, developmental evaluations; preschool program

CHILDFIND:
Alexandria 703-824-6708
Arlington 703-358-6042
Falls Church 703-241-7695
Fairfax County 703-876-5244
Lorton 703-446-2100
Loudoun County 703-771-6430
Manassas Park 703-631-0455
free testing and treatment of children 2yrs 9 mos through 4;
children 0 to 2 yrs 9 mos, ask for Infant & Toddler Program; multi-lingual

Children's Speech and Language Services
626-J Grant Street, Herndon 703-435-0488
939 South Wakefield Street, Suite 101, Arlington 703-685-1070
testing, evaluation and therapy

Falck-Muten, Susan, M.A., CCC-SLP and Associates 703-707-0090
11501 Sunset Hills Road, Suite 300
Reston, VA
evaluation and treatment of speech and language

Hodapp, Mary, M.A., C.C.C. 703-534-6822
5510 N. 17th Street
Arlington, VA 22205
evaluation and treatment of young children

Nelson Center, The 703-941-7544
5103-E Backlick Road
Annandale, VA
speech and language, motor speech disorders, stuttering

Newman Speech and Language Services 703-256-2554
7117 Falcon Street
Annandale, VA
language disorders; English as a second language

Old Dominion Speech Therapy Services 703-378-1012
P.O. Box 220252
Chantilly, VA 22022
speech and language evaluation and treatment at home or school

Person, Cheryl L. and Associates
8348 Traford Lane, Suite 202, Springfield 703-541-5880
100 Carpenter Drive, Suite 201, Sterling 703-709-9090
evaluation and treatment of speech and language

Pilberg, Shelley, M.S., C.C.C. 703-978-7894
8243 Toll House Road
Annandale, VA

Mental Health Resources

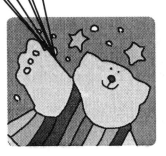

Resources Concerning the Emotional, Social, Behavioral and Cognitive Growth and Development of Young Children

MENTAL HEALTH RESOURCES includes:

- **Counseling Centers:** includes centers whose main service is counseling

- **Mental Health Information and Resources:** includes mental health agencies, associations, centers and organizations providing a broad spectrum of family and comunity services and support and information

- **Mental Health Practitioners, Child and Family:** includes . . .
  Psychiatrists: M.D.s who provide therapy and prescribe medication
  Psychologists: Ph.D.s or Psy.D.s who provide therapy and perform diagnostic testing
  Social Workers: M.S.W.s or L.C.S.W.s who provide therapy
  Specialists in Art, Movement, and Music Therapy
  Specialists in Special Needs

- **Testing and Assessment, Pediatric:** for social, emotional, behavioral, and cognitive concerns

The Table of Contents on the next page provides a detailed listing of this section.

Notes:

1. <u>**Be sure to look in "Metro Area" when available.**</u> <u>Metro Area</u> resources are available throughout the entire Washington metropolitan area. These resources are not repeated in the separate <u>District of Columbia</u>, <u>Maryland</u>, and <u>Virginia</u> listings.

2. Testing and assessment for health care concerns are performed by the health care specialists listed in HEALTH CARE RESOURCES.

Mental Health Resources
Table of Contents

Counseling Centers 113
   District of Columbia 113
   Maryland 114
   Virginia 116
   Multi-cultural Counseling Centers 119
Mental Health Information and Resources 121
   National 121
   District of Columbia 121
   Maryland 122
   Virginia 123
Mental Health Practitioners, Child and Family 124
   Referrals and Information 124
   Psychiatrists 126
      Metro Area 126
      District of Columbia 126
      Maryland 126
      Virginia 126
   Psychologists 127
      Metro Area 127
      District of Columbia 127
      Maryland 128
      Virginia 131
   Social Workers 132
      District of Columbia 132
      Maryland 132
      Virginia 134
   Specialists 135
      Art Therapists 135
      Movement/Dance Therapists 136
      Music Therapists 137
      Special Needs 139
Testing and Assessment, Pediatric 141
   District of Columbia 141
   Maryland 142
   Virginia 144

MENTAL HEALTH RESOURCES

Counseling Centers

See also GENERAL RESOURCES: Helplines, HOTLINES
MENTAL HEALTH RESOURCES: Mental Health Information
MENTAL HEALTH RESOURCES: Mental Health Practitioners
PARENT RESOURCES: Parent Resource Centers

DISTRICT OF COLUMBIA

Adoption and Infertility Counseling 202-234-6483
3000 Connecticut Avenue, N.W.
Washington, D.C.
family issues with adoption

Afro-American Counseling 202-723-0030
2911 Georgia Avenue, NW
Washington, DC 20910
counseling, psychotherapy; children ages 2-5 and adults

Catholic Charities Social Services 202-526-4100
1438 Rhode Island Avenue, NE
Washington, DC 20018
counseling families and children in need, regardless of race, creed, or origin

Children's Hospital 202-884-5000
111 Michigan Avenue, NW, Washington, DC
Children's Hospital of Spring Valley 202-745-8860
4900 Massachusetts Avenue, NW, 320, Washington, DC
counseling professionals on staff

Counseling and Psychotherapy Services 202-244-8855
FAX: 202-244-8855

family issues, including parenting; several locations, call for closest address

DC Mental Health Centers
North Community Mental Health Center 202-576-7253
1125 Spring Road, NW
Region 4 Mental Health Center 202-373-7083
St. Elizabeth's Hospital, 2700 MLK, Jr, Avenue, SE
South Community Mental Health Center 202-673-9000
DC General Hospital, 1905 E Street, SE

d'Alelio, William A., Ph.D. and Associates 202-362-3331
Psychological Services
4545 42nd Street, NW, #200
Washington, DC 20016
social skills groups for children ages 4 and up

Jewish Social Service Agency 202-887-1644
B'nai B'rith Building, Suite 534
1640 Rhode Island Avenue, NW
Washington, DC 20036
sliding fee scale services for children and parents; non-sectarian; parent
counseling; ADD

Kingsbury Center 202-232-5878
Carolyn Atkinson Thornell, Director 202-232-5989
2138 Bancroft Place, NW FAX: 202-667-2290
Washington, DC 20008
multidisciplinary psychological evaluations; also psychotherapy, school
consultation, and parent education

Psychiatric Institute of Washington 202-965-8200
4228 Wisconsin Avenue, NW
Washington, DC 20016

MARYLAND

Affiliated Community Counselors, Inc. 301-251-8965
50 West Montgomery Avenue, Suite 110
Rockville, MD 20850

Afro-American Counseling 301-589-5707
8121 Georgia Avenue
Silver Spring, MD 20901
counseling, psychotherapy; children 2-5 and up and adults

Catholic Charities Social Services 301-434-2550
1504 St. Camillus Drive
Silver Spring, MD 20903
counseling families and children in need, regardless of race, creed, or origin

Center for Children and Adolescents 410-281-2070
405 Frederick Road
Baltimore, MD 21228
psychological testing, evaluation and treatment for ages 4 and up;
psychiatrists, psychologists, and therapists

Child Center and Adult Services 301-279-5866
611 Rockville Pike FAX: 301-279-2155
Rockville, MD 20852
child therapy, play therapy, family therapy; private, non-profit mental health
agency since 1978; Spanish and Mandarin Chinese speaking therapists available

Children's Hospital at Laurel Lakes 1-800-787-0006
13922 Baltimore Avenue, Unit 4a 301-369-4100
Children's Hospital of Montgomery County 1-800-787-0243
14804 Physician's Lane, Suite 122, Rockville 301-424-1755
counseling professionals on staff

Community Psychiatric Center
8311 Wisconsin Avenue, Bethesda 301-933-2402
2424 Reedie Drive, Wheaton 301-656-5220
parenting groups, separation workshops, counseling; private, nonprofit

Family Center for Mediation and Counseling 301-946-3400
3514 Plyers Mill Road
Kensington, MD

MENTAL HEALTH RESOURCES

Family Counseling Center, The 301-840-2000
Family Services Agency, Inc.
640 E. Diamond Avenue
Gaithersburg, MD 20895
family counseling, parenting classes; fees based on a sliding scale

Family Life Center 410-997-3557
10451 Twin Rivers Road
Columbia, MD 21044
counseling center for young children and families

Family Services Agency 301-840-2000
640 East Diamond Avenue
Gaithersburg, MD 20895
individual and family support, parenting classes; sliding scale fee

Frost Counseling Center 301-933-9033
4915 Aspen Hill Road
Rockville, MD

Jewish Social Service Agency
6123 Montrose Road, Rockville .301-881-3700
TDD 301-984-5662
22 Montgomery Village Avenue, Gaithersburg 301-990-6880
TDD 301-990-7215
sliding fee scale services for children and parents; non-sectarian; parent
counseling; ADD

Lourie Center, Reginald S., for Infants and Young Children 301-984-4444
11710 Hunters Lane
Rockville, MD 20852
assessment and treatment of emotional and developmental disorders;
parent-child groups; social skills groups for children ages 4-8

Montgomery County Mental Health Centers
Colesville MHC, 14015 New Hampshire Ave, Silver Spring 301-989-1910
Germantown MHC, 12900 Middlebrook Rd, Germantown 301-217-3340
Rockville MHC, 401 Hungerford Drive, Rockville 301-217-1350
Silver Spring MHC, 8818 Georgia Ave, SilverSpring 301-217-3200
Wheaton MHC, 2424 Reedie Drive, Wheaton 301-217-4820

Montgomery County Public Schools
Counseling Center 301-230-0675
Parent Center 301-230-0674
counseling services in Spanish, Chinese, Vietnamese, Cambodian, Russian,
French, Yiddish, Hindi, and Korean

Mustafa Counseling Services 1-800-876-1123
Diana Z. Mustafa, M.A.   301-890-7416
3009 Memory Lane
Silver Spring, MD 20904
family counseling

National Institute of Relationship Enhancement (NIRE) .301-986-1479
William Nordling, Ph.D., Clinical Director   FAX: 301-699-8835
4400 East-West Highway, Suite 28
Bethesda, MD 20814
counseling center for children, couples, and families; non-profit

Parent Care, Inc. 1-800-224-3893
Scott Buehler, Director   301-770-CARE
6239 Executive Boulevard   drscott@parentcare.com
Rockville, MD 20852   www.parentcare.com
family counseling

Pediatric Psychology Association 301-657-8708
Mary Ann B. Caruso, Ph.D.
Amy B. Livingood, Ph.D.
4405 East-West Hwy, Suite 409
Bethesda, MD 20854
evaluation for LD, ADD, school readiness; family counseling

**Pediatric Therapy and Developmental Services for
Children with Special Needs** 301-942-6006
11302 Veirs Mill Road
Wheaton, MD 20902

Prince George's County Family Home Intervention 301-817-3235
in-home services to children and families with serious psychiatric problems

Prince George's County Hispanic Outreach 301-986-0202
bi-lingual psychiatrists and social workers counsel Hispanic families

Prince George's County Mental Health Centers
Cheverly MHC, 3003 Hospital Drive, Cheverly 301-386-0202
Clinton MHC, 9314 Piscataway Road, Clinton 301-856-9550
Laurel MHC, 8101 Sandy Spring Road, Laurel 301-498-7500
Penn Silver MHC, 5408 Silver Hill Road, Forestville 301-817-3235

**University of Maryland Parent Consultation and
Child Evaluation Program** 301-314-7673
psychiatric evaluations and diagnostic testing; parent and family counseling

VIRGINIA

Alexandria Mental Health Center 703-836-5751
720 N. Asaph Street   703-838-6400
Alexandria, VA 22314

Alexandria Mediation 703-684-7677
counseling for family conflict, divorce, blended families, siblings

Annandale Counseling Center 703-750-0692
7008-B Little River Turnpike
Annandale, VA 22003
scaled fees; parent workshops, developmental issues, family conflict,
ADHD, LD

Arbor Center, The 703-352-8900
  10560 Main Street, Suite 410
  Fairfax, VA 22030
      emotional problems; parent-child conflict; separation, divorce

Arlington County Mental Health Center 703-358-5150
  1725 N. George Mason Drive
  Arlington, VA 22205

Catholic Charities Social Services
  Arlington 703-841-2531
  Burke 703-425-0100
  Fairfax County, Children's Services 703-425-0100
  Fairfax County, Family Services 703-841-2531
  Fredericksburg 540-371-1124
  Winchester 540-667-7940
      counseling families and children in need, regardless of race, creed, or origin

Center for Multicultural Human Services 703-533-3302
  701 W. Broad Street, Suite 305
  Falls Church, VA 22046
      serving children and families in 15 languages; counseling for young children;
      reduced fee or free services for eligible individuals

Center for Therapy and Education, The 703-442-7723
  7700 Leesburg Pike, Suite 113
  Falls Church, VA 22043
      family therapy, parenting skills, parent support groups

Centreville Counseling Center 703-817-0209
  5729 Centre Square Drive
  Centreville, VA 22020
      special needs children, family counseling

Chesapeake Psychological Services, P.C. 703-642-6697
  5041-A Backlick Road
  Annandale, VA

Children's Hospital of Northern VA 1-800-787-0467
  3022 Williams Drive, Suite 100   703-573-9383
  Fairfax, VA 22031
      counseling professionals on staff

Commonwealth Psychological Associates 703-734-0787
  1479 Chain Bridge Road
  McLean, VA 22182
      families; LD, ADD; parent and child conflicts

Cornerstone Family Counseling, P.C. 703-591-2551
  10366B Democracy Lane, Fairfax   FAX: 703-591-2563
  9832 Business Way, Manassas
      personal counseling from a Christian perspective

Jewish Social Service Agency
  7345 McWhorter Place, Annandale 703-750-5400
  12523 Lawyers Road, Herndon 703-750-5400
      sliding fee scale services for children and parents; non-sectarian; parent
      counseling; ADD

MENTAL HEALTH RESOURCES

MENTAL HEALTH RESOURCES

Fairfax County Mental Health Centers
Mt. Vernon Center for Community Mental Health 703-360-6910
   8119 Holland Road, Alexandria, VA 22306
Northwest Center for Community Mental Health 703-481-4100
   1850 Cameron Glen Drive, Reston, VA 22090
Woodburn Center for Community Mental Health 703-573-0523
   3340 Woodburn Road, Annandale, VA 22003

Kellar Center, The 703-218-8500
   10396 Democracy Lane
   Fairfax, VA 22030
      family therapy, ADD; therapeutic summer camp

Mental Health Solutions 703-471-6117
   offices throughout Northern Virginia

Northern Virginia Family Service
Alexandria 703-370-3223
Dale City 703-680-9358
Fairfax County 703-533-9727
Falls Church 703-533-9727
Herndon 703-689-0208
Leesburg 703-771-2595
TDD 1-800-828-1120
      counseling & psychotherapy, sliding fee scale

Pierss Family Services 703-359-8311
   9441 Silver King Court
   Fairfax, VA 22031
      family counseling; military families welcome

T.H.R.I.V.E., Incorporated 703-536-7921
   701 West Broad Street #202
   Falls Church, VA 22046
      counseling for families and children

Women's Center of Northern Virginia, The 703-281-2657
   133 Park Street, NE
   Vienna, VA 22180
      counseling, support groups for mothers

MULTI-CULTURAL COUNSELING CENTERS

Referrals and Information

Washington Area Counseling Alliance 1-800-731-3109
referrals to counseling and psychotherapy services for families; multi-lingual referrals

District of Columbia

Korean Community Service Center 202-882-8270
7720 Alaska Avenue, NW
Washington, DC 20012

Multicultural Clinical Center 202-659-5380
Daisy M. Pascualvaca, Ph.D.
3301 New Mexico Avenue, NW, Suite 322
Washington, DC 20016
neuropsychological evaluations of behavioral and/or emotional difficulties; ADD, LD; services also in Spanish

Naim Foundation 202-462-5715
3000 Connecticut Avenue, NW, Suite 136
Washington, DC 20008
multi-cultural counseling for Arabic speakers; family therapy; child therapy; psychological testing

Maryland

Child Center and Adult Services 301-279-5866
611 Rockville Pike   FAX: 301-279-2155
Rockville, MD
private, non-profit mental health agency since 1978; children, family, play therapy; Spanish and Mandarin Chinese speaking therapists available

Hispanic Outreach, Prince George's County 301-986-0202
bi-lingual psychiatrists and social workers counsel Hispanic families

Korean Family Counseling and Research Center 301-949-5902
10914 Georgia Avenue
Wheaton, MD 20902
counseling for young children and families; Koreans only

Montgomery County Public Schools
Counseling Center 301-230-0675
Parent Center 301-230-0674
counseling services in Spanish, Chinese, Vietnamese, Cambodian, Russian, French, Yiddish, Hindi, and Korean

Prince George's County Hispanic Outreach 301-986-0202
bi-lingual psychiatrists and social workers treat Hispanic families

---

Virginia

Center for Multicultural Human Services 703-533-3302
  Fairfax County Services
  701 W. Broad Street, Suite 305
  Falls Church, VA 22046
    serving children and families in fifteen languages; counseling for young children; reduced fee or free services for eligible individuals

Korean Community Service Center 703-354-6345
  7610 New Castle Drive
  Annandale, VA 22003

MENTAL HEALTH
RESOURCES

Mental Health Information and Resources

See also **GENERAL RESOURCES: Computer Online Services**
GENERAL RESOURCES: Helplines, HOTLINES
MENTAL HEALTH RESOURCES: Counseling Centers
MENTAL HEALTH RESOURCES: Mental Health Practitioners
PARENT RESOURCES: Parent Info, specific topics

NATIONAL

Center for Mental Health Services 301-443-2792
Office of Public Information
5600 Fishers Lane, Suite 13-103
Rockville, MD 20857
information and brochures on autism, LD, etc.

National Institute for Mental Health 301-443-4513
Information Resources and Inquiries Branch
5600 Fishers Lane, Room 7C02, MSC8030
Bethesda, MD 20892
information and brochures on mental health issue for young children

National Institute for Mental Health 301-443-5944
Child and Adolescent Disorder Research
5600 Fishers Lane, Room 18C17
Bethesda, MD 20892

National Mental Health Association Information Center 1-800-969-6642
1021 Prince Street   703-684-7722
Alexandria, VA 22314

DISTRICT OF COLUMBIA

DC Commission on Mental Health Services 202-576-7253
Child Youth Services Administration
2700 Martin Luther King Avenue, SE, #L Bldg
Washington, DC 20032

DC Mental Health Centers
North Community Mental Health Center, 1125 Spring Road, NW 202-576-7253
Region 4 Mental Health Center, St. Elizabeth's Hospital, 2700 MLK, Jr, Avenue, SE . . .202-373-7083
South Community Mental Health Center, D.C. General Hospital, 1905 E Street, SE . .202-673-9000

Department of Human Services 202-279-6000
Department of Social Services 202-727-5930
Early Childhood   202-727-1839

Mental Health Association of District of Columbia 202-262-6363
1628 16th Street, NW, 4th Floor
Washington, DC 20009

MARYLAND

Children and Youth with Serious Emotional Problems
A Guide for Families Seeking Help
Mental Health Association of Maryland 301-235-1178

Department of Health and Mental Hygiene 410-767-6649
Division of Child and Adolescent Services
201 West Preston Street
Baltimore, MD 21201

Department of Social Services
Montgomery County 301-217-6980
Prince George's County 301-808-5553

Mental Health Association of Maryland 410-235-1178
711 West 40th Street, Suite 428
Baltimore, MD 21211
Anne Arundel County 410-268-1363
Baltimore 410-235-1178
Charles County 410-283-2410
Frederick County 410-663-0011
Howard County 410-730-3773
Montgomery County 301-424-0656
Prince George's County 301-499-2107

Montgomery County Mental Health Centers
Colesville MHC, 14015 New Hampshire Ave, Silver Spring 301-989-1910
Germantown MHC, 12900 Middlebrook Road, Germantown 301-217-3340
Rockville MHC, 401 Hungerford Drive, Rockville 301-217-1350
Silver Spring MHC, 8818 Georgia Avenue, Silver Spring 301-217-3200
Wheaton MHC, 2424 Reedie Drive, Wheaton .301-217-4820

Prince George's County Division of Mental Health 301-883-7837
1701 McCormick Drive   FAX: 301-883-7881
Largo, MD 20774   TDD: 301-386-0257

Prince George's County Human Relations 301-883-6170

Prince George's County Mental Health Centers
Cheverly MHC, 3003 Hospital Drive, Cheverly .301-386-0202
Clinton MHC, 9314 Piscataway Road, Clinton .301-856-9550
Laurel MHC, 8101 Sandy Spring Road, Laurel .301-498-7500
Penn Silver MHC, 5408 Silver Hill Road, Forestville 301-817-3235

VIRGINIA

Alexandria Community Mental Health Center 703-836-5751
720 N. Asaph Street 703-838-6400
Alexandria, VA 22314

Arlington Mental Health Center 703-358-5150
1725 N. George Mason Drive
Arlington, VA 22205

Department of Health and Human Services, Virginia 703-838-0710
Alexandria 703-838-0900
Alexandria, Early Childhood Services 703-838-0785
Arlington County, Human Services 703-358-5300
Fairfax County 703-222-0880

Department of Mental Health, Mental Retardation, and Substance Abuse:
Child and Adolescent Mental Health 804-371-2177
P.O. Box 1797
Richmond, VA 23214

Department of Family Services
Alexandria 703-838-0750
Arlington County 703-358-4994
Fairfax County 703-324-7800
Fairfax County, Early Childhood 703-324-8100

Department of Social Services
Alexandria 703-838-0750
Arlington County 703-358-5108
Falls Church 703-241-5005
Fairfax County 703-324-7500
Loudoun County 703-777-0360
Prince William County 703-792-7500

Department of Mental Health
Alexandria 703-838-6400
Arlington County 703-358-5150
Fairfax County 703-324-7095

Fairfax County Mental Health Centers
Mt. Vernon Center, 8119 Holland Road, Alexandria 703-360-6910
Northwest Center, 1850 Cameron Glen Drive, Reston 703-481-4100
Woodburn Center, 3340 Woodburn Road, Annandale 703-573-0523

Fairfax County Office for Children 703-449-9555

Mental Health Association of Virginia 804-649-8481
Jane Weirich, Executive Director
201 West Broad Street, Suite 503
Richmond, VA 23215

Mental Health Association of Alexandria 703-212-0010

Mental Health Practitioners, Child and Family

REFERRALS AND INFORMATION

Metro Area

American Association for Marriage and Family Therapy .1-800-374-2638
1100 17th Street, NW, 10th Floor   202-452-0109
Washington, DC 20036   301-279-8755
referrals for family counseling; publishes *Consumers' Guide to Marriage and Family Therapy*

American Psychiatric Association, The 202-682-6270
referral services

American Psychological Association, The 202-336-5800
referral services

Children's Hospital
Department of Psychiatry 202-884-5386
Department of Psychology 202-884-5995
Referral Line 1-888-884-BEAR
referrals to psychiatrists and psychologists in consultative centers in DC, MD, and VA

Greater Washington Society for Clinical Social Workers, The 301-530-4765
free referrals to qualified clinical social workers licensed to practice in the Washington area

Coalition for Marriage, Family and Couples Education Practitioners Directory
Diane Sollee, Director, CMFCE, L.L.C 202-966-5376
5310 Belt Road, NW   FAX: 202-362-0973
Washington, DC 20015   CMFCE @his.com
directory of mental health practitioners for families   http://www.his.com/~CMFCE

Washington Area Counseling Alliance 1-800-731-3109
referrals to counseling and psychotherapy services for families; multi-lingual referrals

Washington Metropolitan Area Guide to Therapy Groups for Children, Adolescents, and Parents 202-686-4084
Sylvia Stultz, Ph.D.   FAX: 202-686-4889
5153 34th Street, NW   WWW.DN.NET/Stultz
Washington, DC 20008
free brochure includes listings of groups for parents

WISER, Directory of Educational Services in the Washington Area 301-816-0432
11140 Rockville Pike, #105
Rockville, MD 20852
referrals to local mental health practitioners

District of Columbia

American Academy of Child and Adolescent Psychiatry 202-955-7025
    Frederick Solomon, DC Delegate for Referrals 202-363-4204
    3615 Wisconsin Avenue, NW
    Washington, DC 20016

Children's Hospital Referral Line 202-884-BEAR

DC Crisis and Referral Hotline 202-223-2255

Department of Human Services Information and Referral Line 202-724-5466

District of Columbia Psychological Association, The 202-336-5557
    750 1st Street, NE, #6124
    Washington, DC 20002
        referrals to child psychologists in DC

Maryland

American Academy of Child and Adolescent Psychiatry .202-955-7025
    Parnjit Joshi, Maryland Delegate for Referrals 410-955-7025
    3615 Wisconsin Avenue, NW
    Washington, DC 20016

Child Care Connection 301-942-5374
    Montgomery County Public Schools
        referrals to professionals as necessary

Children's Hospital Referral Line 1-888-884-BEAR

Maryland Psychological Association, The 301-953-1371
                                      301-596-3999
    Baltimore 410-995-0499
        referral service for child psychologists in Maryland

Therapistline 301-738-7176
    Wednesdays and Fridays only; Montgomery County referral helpline for
    individuals who have limited or no financial resources for therapy; links
    people with mental health professionals who accept a sliding scale fee

Virginia

American Academy of Child and Adolescent Psychiatry .202-955-7025
    Charles Devitt, Virginia Delegate for Referrals   804-455-6100
    3615 Wisconsin Avenue, NW
    Washington, DC 20016

Child Developmental Clinic, Arlington County 703-358-4930
    referrals for behavioral and emotional problems

Children's Hospital Referral Line 1-888-884-BEAR

Virginia Psychological Association, The 703-379-9520
    referral services for child psychologists in Virginia

MENTAL HEALTH RESOURCES

PSYCHIATRISTS

Metro Area

Children's Hospital, Department of Psychiatry 202-884-5386
consultative centers throughout the area

District of Columbia

Tobin, Kenneth, M.D. 202-884-5240
Children's Hospital
child psychiatrist

Maryland

Castellanos, Francisco Xavier, M.D. 301-496-4319
Child Psychiatry Branch
National Institutes of Health
9000 Rockville Pike
Bethesda, MD
neuropsychiatrist specializing in ADHD, Tourette's Syndrome, learning
disabilities, and other associated disorders

Denckla, Martha B., M.D. 410-550-9420
Developmental Cognitive Neurology Clinic
Kennedy Krieger Institute
707 Broadway
Baltimore, MD 21205
ADHD specialist

Greenspan, Stanley, M.D. 301-657-2348
7201 Glenbrook Road
Bethesda, MD
child play therapy; family issues; video *Floor Time: Tuning in to Each Child*
on the importance of adults engaging children in meaningful play
(see GENERAL RESOURCES: Videos)

Trashinsky, Charles, M.D. 301-530-8877
6300 Carnegie Drive
Bethesda, MD
child psychiatry

Zwerdling, Timothy, M.D. 301-587-5378
2907 Woodstock Avenue
Silver Spring, MD 20910
family therapy

Virginia

A. Bradley Chapman, M.D. 703-960-4901
Frank Michner, M.D.
2059 Huntington Avenue, Suite 108
Alexandria, VA 22303
specialists in ADD/ADHD, LD

PSYCHOLOGISTS

Metro Area

Children's Hospital, Department of Psychology 202-884-5995
consultative centers throughout the area

District of Columbia

Cohen, Douglas L., Ph.D. 202-298-8585
1206 Potomac Street, NW
Washington, DC 20007
couples therapy for parents; fathering issues

Koenig, Ronnie, Ph.D. 202-234-6483
Adoption and Infertility Counseling
3000 Connecticut Avenue, NW
Washington, DC 20008
family issues concerning adoption

Lytle, Linda, Ph.D. 202-298-8514
2000 P Street, NW   TTY: 202-298-8515
Washington, DC 20030
couples therapy for families with hearing-impaired issues

Raphael-Howell, Frances, Ph.D. 202-583-0316
3010 W Street, SE
Washington, DC 20020
pediatric clinical psychologist; registered child play therapist and
supervisor; board-certified forensic examiner

Reynolds, Ruth Shereshefsky, Ph.D. 202-244-0307
4501 Connecticut Avenue, NW, Suite 217
Washington, DC 20008
therapy with young children; parent counseling; school consultation; evaluations

Shere, Stephen H., Ph.D. 202-833-1447
1224 29th Street, NW
Washington, DC 20007
couples therapy for parents

Stultz, Sylvia, Ph.D. 202-686-4084
5153 34th Street, NW
Washington, DC 20008
psychotherapy with children and families; special needs

Turetsky, Daniel, Psy.D. 202-210-5947
3222 N Street, NW
Washington, DC 20007
family therapy; child play therapy; parent consultation; psychological evaluations

Wake, Kendall, Spring, Isenman, and Associates 202-686-7699
5247 Wisconsin Avenue, NW
Washington, DC 20015
child psychologists

Maryland

Avigan, Helen, Ph.D. 301-681-5657
502 Hermleigh Road
Silver Spring, MD 20902
psychoevaluation; therapy

Ben-Ami, Uzi, Ph.D. 301-424-1941
205 Watts Branch Parkway
Rockville, MD 20850
ADD, LD specialist

Beuse, Eileen, Ph.D. 301-365-4375
8608 Ridge Road   FAX: 301-365-3438
Bethesda, MD 20817
child play therapy; parent therapy; parent consultant

Blum, Karen, Ph.D. 301-907-0941
4933 Auburn Avenue
Bethesda, MD 20814
child psychologist

Caruso, Mary Ann, Ph.D. 301-656-9595
4405 East West Highway, Suite 409
Bethesda, MD 20814
psychological evaluations; diagnosis; psychotherapy; counseling

Celotta, Beverly, Ph.D. 301-330-8803
13517 Haddonfield Lane
Gaithersburg, MD 20878

Ciardi, Charmaine, Ph.D. 301-365-5929
Parent-Child Development Services
8203 Woodhaven Blvd.
Bethesda, MD 20817
child psychologist

Edelstein, Terry, Ph.D. 301-965-4097
4909 Hampden Lane
Bethesda, MD 20814
child play therapy; groups for parents of children with speech and language
problems

Emmanuel, Gary, Ph.D. 301-986-8020
4933 Auburn Avenue, Suite 202
Bethesda, MD 20814
family therapy

Grobel, Anna, Ph.D. 301-229-0044
Brookmont Associates   FAX: 301-229-0151
6109 Broad Street
Bethesda, MD 20816
child and family psychotherapy; emotional problems; learning disabilities;
educational consultant

Guerney, Bernard, Ph.D. 301-986-1479
    The National Institute of Relationship Enhancement
    4400 East-West Hwy, Suite 28
    Bethesda, MD 20814
        family therapy; couples counseling

Guerney, Louise, Ph.D. 301-986-1479
    The National Institute of Relationship Enhancement
    4400 East-West Hwy, Suite 28
    Bethesda, MD 20814
        child play therapist; family therapy; parent education

Hazen, Sharlie, Ph.D. 301-858-7023
    1509 Richie Highway, Suite F
    Arnold, MD 21012
        assessment and behavioral problems, birth through age 5; family counseling

Hoffmeyer, Lisa, Ph.D. 410-788-2686
    2324 West Joppa Road, Suite 420, Lutherville   FAX: 410-321-9537
    9650 Santiago Road, Suite 103, Columbia
        developmental psychologist; attachment issues, adoption and foster care
        issues, divorce, sleeping and eating disorders; birth through age 5

Hyde, Thomas, M.D., Ph.D. 301-588-2011
    4701 Willard Avenue
    Chevy Chase, MD 20813
        behavioral psychologist and neurologist

Ladkin, Jean, Ph.D. 301-594-9765
    19945 Pratt Place
    Silver Spring, MD 20901
        child play therapist for children ages 3 through 5

Livingood, Amy B., Ph.D. 301-657-8708
    4405 East-West Hwy, Suite 409
    Bethesda, MD 20854
        evaluation for LD, ADD, school readiness; family counseling

Nordling, William, Ph.D. 301-986-1479
    Director, Play Therapy and Filial Therapy Certification Programs   FAX: 301-986-1479
    The National Institute of Relationship Enhancement
    4400 East-West Hwy, Suite 28
    Bethesda, MD 20814
        child play therapy; parent education

O'Brien, Dana E., Ph.D. 301-593-6554
    Silver Spring, MD 20904
        groups for parents to learn management techniques for a variety of behavior
        problems, including ADD

Parks, Charles, Ph.D. 301-320-3266
    6505 Wiscasset Road
    Bethesda, MD 20816
        psychotherapy; parent counseling

MENTAL HEALTH RESOURCES

Ruth, Richard, Ph.D. 301-933-3072
11303 Amherst Avenue, Suite 1
Wheaton, MD 20902
cross-cultural therapy; physical disability; services also in Spanish

Smith, Lawrence, L.C.S.W.-C. 301-565-8225
8720 Georgia Avenue, Suite 802
Silver Spring, MD 20910
family therapy; parent consultation and education

Turetsky, Daniel, Psy.D. 301-913-5947
4809 St. Elmo Avenue
Bethesda, MD 20815
family therapy; child play therapy; parent consultation; evaluations

Tynan, Douglas, Ph.D. 301-217-5449
Rockville, MD
groups for parents of children with oppositional/defiant disorder or ADD;
child therapy

Webbink, Dr. Patricia, & Associates, P.A. 301-229-0044
Brookmont Associates   FAX: 301-229-0151
6109 Broad Street
Bethesda, MD 20816
child and family therapy

Zinner, Ellen, Psy.D. 301-942-6440
Center for Loss and Grief Therapy
10400 Connecticut Avenue, Suite 514
Kensington, MD 20895
grief and loss therapy with parents and children

Virginia

Burt, Charles E., Ph.D. 703-471-4123
11741 Bowman Green Drive
Reston, VA 20190
evaluation and treatment for children; parenting problems

Davidow, Sharon, Ph.D. 703-760-0910
7700 Leesburg Pike, Suite 302
Tysons Corner, VA

Doherty, Susan, Ph.D. 703-836-8340
629 S. Washington Street
Alexandria, VA 22314
psychological evaluations; developmental disabilities; play therapy and
family therapy

Farber, Edward, Ph.D. 703-437-3236
Reston Psychological Center
1800 Town Center Parkway, Suite 411
Reston, VA 22090
psychotherapy and psychodiagnostic services

Federici, Ronald S., Psy.D., and Associates, P.C.
400 S. Washington Street, Alexandria 703-548-0721
2200 Opitz Blvd., Suite 340, Woodbridge 703-491-4329
neuropsychologist; specializes in children adopted from East European
countries

Heitin, Ruth C., Ph.D. 703-519-7181
Educational Consulting Services of Northern Virginia
100 West Howell Avenue
Alexandria, VA 22301
psychoeducational evaluation; ADD, LD; deaf children

Hoar, Barbara, Ph.D. 703-548-4333
228 S. Washington Street
Alexandria, VA 22314

Rosenfeld, Richard U., Ph.D. 703-425-9080
8992 Fern Park Drive
Burke, VA

Ross-Kidder, Kathleen, Ph.D. 703-255-2133
521 Maple Avenue, NW   202-994-6697
Vienna, VA 22180
diagnosis; psychotherapy and testing; counseling

Stusnick, Madeline S., Ph.D. 703-425-9080
8992 Fern Park Drive
Burke, VA
family therapy; ADD, LD, special needs

MENTAL HEALTH RESOURCES

SOCIAL WORKERS

District of Columbia

Caldwell, David, M.S.W. 202-298-8311
1210 Elton Court, NW
Washington, DC 20007
  child play therapy; family therapy

Dranitzke, Susan, M.E., M.S.W., L.C.S.W. .202-544-5222
Resources for Children
124 12th Street, SE
Washington, DC 20003
  family therapy; play therapy; educational consultant

Maryland

Bangert, Jill, L.C.S.W. 301-229-0044
Brookmont Associates   FAX: 301-229-0151
6109 Broad Street
Bethesda, MD 20816
  child and family therapy

Bauman, Susan, L.C.S.W. 301-933-9890
10400 Connecticut Avenue, Suite 600
Kensington, MD 20895
  parent guidance; psychotherapy; evaluations

Caldwell, David, M.S.W. 703-912-5913
4933 Auburn Avenue
Bethesda, MD 20814
  child play therapy; family therapy

Goldman, Linda, M.S.W. 301-942-6440
Center for Loss and Grief Therapy
10400 Connecticut Avenue, Suite 514
Kensington, MD 20895
  grief and loss therapy for children and parents

Hausen, Carrie, L.C.S.W.-C. 301-986-1479
The National Institute of Relationship Enhancement
4400 East-West Hwy, Suite 28
Bethesda, MD 20814
  child play therapist; family therapy; parent education

Kelner, Paul, M.S.W. 301-681-9257
11401 Encore Drive   pkelner@us.net
Silver Spring, MD 20901
  adoption social worker; adoption home studies, counseling

Miller, Elizabeth, L.C.S.W. 301-656-7014
2 Wisconsin Circle, Suite 210
Chevy Chase, MD 20815
evaluation and therapy with young children and parents

Neuberger, Sally, L.C.S.W. 301-424-5200
Rockville, MD
workshops and consultations offered on coping and advocacy for caretakers
of children who have special needs

Poland, Janice, L.C.S.W. 301-229-0044
Brookmont Associates   FAX: 301-229-0151
6109 Broad Street
Bethesda, MD 20816
child therapy and family therapy

Salzman, Melinda C., M.S.W. 301-588-3225
Silver Spring, MD
support groups for mothers of children ages 6 months to 6 years

Scuka, Robert F., Ph.D., L.C.S.W.-C. 301-986-1479
The National Institute of Relationship Enhancement
4400 East-West Hwy, Suite 28
Bethesda, MD 20814
child play therapy; family therapy; parent education

Spranger, Patricia, L.C.S.W.-C. 301-587-5495
Psychotherapy Services
204 Parkside Road
Silver Spring, MD 20910
family therapy; parenting skills; stepfamilies

Stein, Eliot, M.S.W. 301-986-1479
The National Institute of Relationship Enhancement
4400 East-West Hwy, Suite 28
Bethesda, MD 20814
child play therapist; family therapy; parent education

Turner, Edward, M.S.W., L.C.S.W. 301-654-4029
4848 Battery Lane, Suite 101
Bethesda, MD 20814
psychotherapy for children and families; family consultation

Wear, Robert, L.C.S.W.-C. 301-652-1582
Bethesda, MD
fathers' groups that offer tools to help reestablish positive connections
between fathers and sons

MENTAL HEALTH RESOURCES

Virginia

Beck, Patricia C., L.C.S.W. 703-569-6492
6129 Brandon Avenue, Suite 116
Springfield, VA 22150

Caldwell, David, M.S.W. 703-912-5913
5711 Guy Place
Springfield, VA 22151
    child play therapy; family therapy

Donner, Goldye P., L.C.S.W. 703-569-6492
6129 Brandon Avenue, Suite 116
Springfield, VA 22150

Marks, Susan, L.C.S.W. 703-827-8815
7700 Leesburg Pike, Suite 221
Falls Church, VA 22043
    family counseling; ADD; Tourette's Syndrome; separation and divorce; grief
    work; multi-cultural concerns; autism; obsessive compulsive disorder

Sternberg, Abby M., L.C.S.W., BCD 703-978-2198
5206-B Rolling Road, Burke
3700 Joseph Siewick Drive, #304, Fairfax
    child and family therapy; parent education; families with handicapped
    children

SPECIALISTS: ART THERAPISTS

Referrals and Information

Art Therapy Association of Maryland 410-244-0836
P.O. Box 32364
Baltimore, MD 21282
lists of local art therapists

District of Columbia

DiMaria, Audrey 202-576-7154
Northwest Washington
art therapy with ages 5 and up, specializing in severely emotionally
disturbed children

Maiorana, Wendy 202-686-5471
4318 Fessenden Street, NW
Washington, DC 20016
art therapy with ages 4 and up

Maryland

Bass-Feld, Eena, A.T.R. 410-998-9520
10806 Reisterstown Road, Suite 3-C
Owings Mills, MD 21117
art therapy with ages 2-5, specializing in children of separated and divorced
families, sexually abused children, and children of domestic violence

Kolodny, Peggy L., M.A., A.T.R., C.P.C. 410-998-9520
10806 Reisterstown Road, Suite 3-C
Owings Mills, MD 21117
preschooler and adult therapy; child trauma

Ross, Ruth, A.T.R. 410-484-6604
17 Warren Road, Suite 5B
Baltimore, MD 21208
art therapy with children ages 2-5 and their families

Smitheman-Brown, Valerie, A.T.R. 410-494-1440
750 E. Fairmount Avenue
Baltimore, MD 21231
art therapist specializing in special needs, especially autism

Highto, Gwen, A.T.R-B.C. 410-252-4000
Timonium, MD
board certified art therapist, children ages 2-5, families, sexual abuse

Virginia

Power, Helen 703-876-8480
8320 Professional Hill Drive
Fairfax, VA 22031
art therapist, children ages 2-5

MENTAL HEALTH RESOURCES

SPECIALISTS: MOVEMENT/DANCE THERAPISTS

Referrals and Information

American Dance Therapy Association 410-997-4040
Karen Martin, Coordinator for MD,DC,VA   301-428-3218
2000 Century Plaza, Suite 230
10632 Patuxent Parkway
Columbia, MD 21044

Metro Area

Bannon, Veronica, A.D.T.R. 410-368-7963
dance/movement therapist; special needs children

Cook-Auerbach, Cheryl, C.M.A., A.D.T.R. 301-236-4743
dance therapist

Cupers, Freddie 410-484-0586
1207 Pine Ridge Lane
Baltimore, MD 21208
consultant on dance therapy

Given, Judy 410-367-6447
Baltimore, MD
movement/dance therapy with children ages 0-8; speeches and workshops
on movement therapy techniques

McGeehan, Theresa 410-527-0516
14201 Sagewood Road
Phoenix, MD 21131
practicing dance therapist with children ages 2-5

Sing, Mary 301-571-0151
Kensington, MD
dance/movement therapy; consultant on dance therapy

SPECIALISTS: MUSIC THERAPISTS

Referrals and Information

National Association for Music Therapy 301-589-3300
8455 Colesville Road, Suite 930
Silver Spring, MD 20910
 information for parents and professionals on music therapy; list of local
 music therapists

District of Columbia

Cherrie, Dave 301-497-8280
Washington, DC 20009

Hughes, Frances 202-727-3850
Washington, DC 20024

Maryland

Adler, Ruthlee 301-569-0223
Bethesda, MD 20817

Bidus, Kimberly 301-496-9365
Chevy Chase, MD 20815

Davis, Maryalice 410-987-6200
Bowie, MD 20716   ext. 507

Eaton, James 301-918-8542
Silver Spring, MD 20902

Edelson, Dora 410-986-6200
Wheaton, MD 20906   ext. 518

Eisenhower, Diane 202-363-1333
Rockville, MD 20851

Gangler, Roberta 301-365-3080
Silver Spring, MD 20906

Lane, Sean 301-405-6475
Upper Marlboro, MD 20772

Mollard, Kathryn 301-770-8320
Germantown, MD 20874

Nicholas, Joan 301-372-1840
Springfield, VA 22152

Portis-Joyner, Jacqueline 703-358-5779
Landover, MD 20785

Sobczak, Angie 301-497-8264
Laurel, MD 20724

Spector, Anne 301-251-6800
Derwood, MD 20855

Washington, Donna 202-373-7251
Greenbelt, MD 20770

Wobus, Nadine 301-249-1703
Bowie, MD 20716

Worsley, Crystal 202-373-7251
Hyattsville, MD 20781

Virginia

Allain, Gayle 301-933-0060
Reston, VA 21090

Dowdy, Ava 703-846-8900
Vienna, VA 22180

Miller, Gwendolyn 703-978-0757
Woodbridge, VA 22191

Verhagen, Gary 703-354-4042
Annandale, VA 22003

MENTAL HEALTH RESOURCES

SPECIALISTS: SPECIAL NEEDS

See also HEALTH CARE RESOURCES: Pediatricians, ADD/ADHD Specialists
MENTAL HEALTH RESOURCES: Mental Health Practitioners, Psychiatrists,
Psychologists, Social Workers

District of Columbia

ADHD Center 202-966-8806
4545 42nd Street, NW
Washington, DC 20007
diagnosis and interventions in ADHD

Multicultural Clinical Center 202-659-5380
Daisy M. Pascualvaca, Ph.D.
3301 New Mexico Avenue, NW, Suite 322
Washington, DC 20016
neuropsychological evaluations of behavioral and/or emotional difficulties;
ADD, LD; services also in Spanish

Maryland

Ivymount School 301-469-0223
11614 Seven Locks Road
Rockville, MD 20854
evaluation and treatment for children experiencing motor, sensory, and
speech/language difficulties

Kellar Center, The 703-218-8500
10396 Democracy Lane
Fairfax, VA
ADD, LD assessment and services

Kersting, Jeanne M. 301-951-3301
3712 Leland Street
Chevy Chase, MD 20815
hearing-impaired children; also, developmentally delayed

Lourie Center, Reginald S., for Infants and Young Children 301-984-4444
11710 Hunters Lane
Rockville, MD 20852
assessment and treatment of emotional and developmental disorders

Rabinowitz, Arlene, M.S. 301-585-3983
1903 Seminary Road
Silver Spring, MD 20910
diagnosis and treatment of learning disabilities

Stern, Judith, M.A. 301-424-1941
205 Watts Branch Parkway
Rockville, MD 20850
educational consultant specializing in ADD/LD

Virginia

Attention Disorder Treatment Center of Northern VA 703-960-4901
A. Bradley Chapman, M.D.
Frank Michner, M.D.
2059 Huntington Avenue, Suite 108
Alexandria, VA 22303
  specialists in treatment of concentration problems

Biopsych
5101-C Backlick Road, Annandale 703-354-1804
300 S. Washington Street, Alexandria 703-836-2666
  behavioral therapy and biofeedback treatment for ADD/ADHD

Chesapeake Psychological Services 703-642-6697
5041-A Backlick Road
Annandale, VA 22003
  diagnosis and treatment for ADD

Green Medical Center, Ltd. 703-883-0303
8230 Leesburg Pike, Suite 570
Vienna, VA
  comprehensive multi-disciplinary medical approach to ADD

PATHFINDERS, INC. 703-239-2750
Lori Carver-Johnson
  consultants to parents with ADD children

Testing and Assessment, Pediatric

See also **HEALTH CARE RESOURCES: Nutritionists**
HEALTH CARE RESOURCES: Optometrists and Visual Training
HEALTH CARE RESOURCES: Pediatricians
HEALTH CARE RESOURCES: Physical and Occupational Therapists
HEALTH CARE RESOURCES: Speech and Hearing Specialists
MENTAL HEALTH RESOURCES: Mental Health Practitioners

DISTRICT OF COLUMBIA

ADHD Center 202-966-8806
4545 42nd Street, NW
Washington, DC 20007
diagnosis and interventions in ADHD

CHILDFIND 202-727-8300
free testing and treatment of children 2yrs 9 mos through 4;
children birth to 2 yrs 9 mos, ask for Infant & Toddler Program;
developmental delays; multi-lingual

Children's Hospital
111 Michigan Avenue, NW 202-884-5000
Children's Hospital at Spring Valley
4900 Massachusetts Avenue, NW 202-745-8860
psychological testing, developmental evaluations

Georgetown University Child Development Center 202-687-8635
Tawara Taylor 202-687-8807
3307 M Street, NW
Washington, DC 20007
testing and assessment

Jeffries, Marcia, M.Ed. 202-686-7699
Wake, Kendall, Greene, Spring and Isenman
5247 Wisconsin Avenue, NW
Washington, DC 20015
educational diagnostician for learning problems and disabilities

Kingsbury Center 202-232-5878
Carolyn Atkinson Thornell, Director   202-232-5989
2138 Bancroft Place, NW   FAX: 202-667-2290
Washington, DC 20008
multidisciplinary psychological evaluations; LD; psychotherapy; school
consultation; parent education

Multicultural Clinical Center 202-659-5380
Daisy M. Pascualvaca
3301 New Mexico Avenue, NW, Suite 322
Washington, DC 20016
neuropsychological evaluations of behavioral and/or emotional difficulties;
ADD, LD; services also in Spanish

Naim Foundation 202-462-5715
3000 Connecticut Avenue, N.W., Suite 136
Washington, DC 20008
multi-cultural counseling for Arabic speakers; psychological testing; family
therapy; child therapy

Wake, Kendall, Springer, Isenman & Associates 202-686-7699
5247 Wisconsin Avenue, NW, Suite 4
Washington, DC 20015
comprehensive psychoeducational evaluations

MARYLAND

Balzer-Martin Preschool Screening Program (BAPS)
Lynn Balzer-Martin, Ph.D., O.T.R 301-654-1828
screening method for identifying possible developmental problems in
children ages 3, 4, and 5 years old; based upon a sensory integration model;
on-site screening available; $60 manual available from St. Columba's Nursery
School, 4201 Albemarle Street, NW, Washington, DC 20016

Bassin, Barbara S., O.T.R., B.C.P. 301-897-8484
6509 Democracy Blvd.
Bethesda, MD 20817
evaluation and treatment of children with learning, coordination, and/or
behavioral problems related to sensory integration dysfunction

Beardsley, Mary, M.Ed. 301-652-1947
5101 River Road, Suite 105
Bethesda, MD 20816
psychoeducational assessment and consultation

CHILDFIND:
Anne Arundel County 410-956-0741
Baltimore City 410-396-6227
Baltimore County 410-887-3017
Calvert County 410-535-7380
Caroline County 410-479-3246
Cecil County 410-996-5444
Dorchester County 410-221-0837
Harford County 410-638-3814
Howard County 410-313-7046
Kent County 410-778-3483
Montgomery County 301-279-FIND
Prince George's County 301-952-6341
Somerset County 410-651-1485
Talbot County 410-820-8263
Wicomico County 410-749-5176
free testing and treatment of children 2yrs 9 mos through 4;
children birth to 2 yrs 9 mos, ask for Infant & Toddler Program;
developmental delays; multi-lingual

Children's Hospital at Laurel Lakes
13922 Baltimore Avenue, Unit 4a, Laurel 301-369-4100
Children's Hospital of Montgomery County
14804 Physician's Lane, Suite 122, Rockville 301-424-1755
Children's Hospital of Southern Maryland
9440 Pennsylvania Ave, Upper Marlboro 301-868-5777
    psychological testing, developmental delays

Diagnostic Assessment Associates 301-657-2257
5101 River Road, Suite 106
Bethesda, Md 20816
    complete psychological and educational evaluations; specialize in
    LD, ADD

Ivymount School 301-469-0223
11614 Seven Locks Road
Rockville, MD 20854
    evaluation and treatment for children experiencing motor, sensory, and
    speech/language difficulties

Lourie Center, Reginald S., for Infants and Young Children 301-984-4444
11710 Hunters Lane
Rockville, MD 20852
    assessment and treatment of emotional and developmental disorders

Maryland Infants and Toddlers Program 1-800-535-0182
Baltimore 410-333-8100
    testing and early intervention services for children from birth through
    2 yrs 9 months

Slattery, Valerie G., Ph.D. 301-299-8085
10428 Masters Terrace
Potomac, MD 20854
    psychoeducational assessment

Spodak, Ruth, & Associates 301-770-7507
6155 Executive Boulevard
Rockville, MD 20852
    psychoeducational evaluations to diagnose LD and ADHD

Thompson, Anne B., Ph.D. 301-657-8314
5101 River Road, #106
Bethesda, MD 20816
    psychoeducational evaluations; LD, ADHD; kindergarten readiness

Treatment and Learning Centers 301-424-5200
9975 Medical Center Drive   TDD: 301-424-5203
Rockville, MD 20850
    psychoeducational testing for ADHD, LD

University of Maryland Parent Consultation and Child Evaluation Program 301-314-7673
    psychiatric evaluations and diagnostic testing

Wake, Anne Parker, Ph.D. 301-652-0204
5114 Wessling Lane
Bethesda, MD 20814
    psychoeducational evaluation

VIRGINIA

Child Developmental Clinic, Arlington County 703-358-4930
   testing and evaluation for behavioral and emotional issues

CHILDFIND:
  Alexandria 703-824-6708
  Arlington 703-358-6042
  Falls Church 703-241-7695
  Fairfax County, Devonshire Center 703-876-5244
  Fairfax County, Lorton 703-446-2100
  Loudoun County 703-771-6430
  Manassas Park 703-631-0455
    free testing and treatment of children 2yrs 9 mos through 4;
    children birth to 2 yrs 9 mos, ask for Infant & Toddler Program;
    developmental delays; multi-lingual

Children's Hospital of Northern Virginia 703-573-9383
  3022 Williams Drive, Suite 100
  Fairfax, VA 22031
    psychological testing; developmental evaluations

Heitin, Ruth C., Ph.D. 703-519-7181
  Educational Consulting Services of Northern Virginia
  100 West Howell Avenue
  Alexandria, VA 22301
    psychoeducational evaluations; ADD/LD; deaf children

Vienna Psycho-Educational Associates 703-255-2133
  521 Maple Avenue, NW
  Vienna, VA 22180
    diagnosis of LD, ADD, and emotional disturbance

MENTAL HEALTH RESOURCES

Child Care and School Resources

Resources About Child Care and Schools

The Child Care and School Resources section provides information <u>about</u> child care, including nannies, home care providers, daycare centers, and private and public preschools and kindergartens.

CHILD CARE AND SCHOOL RESOURCES includes:

- **Babysitting Referrals**

- **Child Care Referrals and Information:** includes referrals and information for home care providers and daycare centers

- **Child Care Special Resources:** includes
    Background checks and surveillance for child care providers
    Drop-in child care centers
    Scholarships and sliding fee child care
    Sick children child care, including general care and respite care

- **Consultants about Child Care and Schools:** includes educational consultants on multi-cultural issues and special needs

- **Educational Information and Resources**

- **Nannies:** includes support and information for nannies and employers

- **Private Preschools and Kindergartens:** includes referrals and information, including information on special preschools

- **Public Preschools and Kindergartens:** includes information on public schools, including Head Start, and special needs programs

The Table of Contents on the next page provides a detailed listing of this section.

Note:

<u>**Be sure to look in "Metro Area" when available.**</u> <u>Metro Area</u> resources are available throughout the entire Washington metropolitan area. These resources are not repeated in the separate <u>District of Columbia</u>, <u>Maryland</u>, and <u>Virginia</u> listings.

**CHILD CARE AND
SCHOOL RESOURCES**

Child Care and School Resources
Table of Contents

Babysitting Referrals 147
Child Care Referrals and Information 148
    Metro Area 148
    District of Columbia 148
    Maryland 149
    Virginia 150
Child Care Special Resources 151
    Background Checks and Surveillance 151
    Drop-In Child Care Centers 151
    Scholarships and Sliding Fee Child Care 152
    Sick Children Child Care 153
Consultants about Child Care and Schools 155
    Educational Consultants 155
    Multi-cultural Educational Consultants 157
    Special Needs Educational Consultants 157
Educational Information and Resources 159
Nannies 160
    Agencies 160
    Health Insurance for Nannies 162
    Hiring 162
    Newsletters and Publications 162
    Support and Training for Nannies 162
    Tax Guidance for Household Employers 162
Private Preschools and Kindergartens 163
    General School Referrals and Information 163
    Cooperative Preschool Information 165
    Montessori School Information 165
    Reggio Emilia Preschool Information 165
    Special Needs Schools Information 166
    Waldorf School Information 168
Public Preschools and Kindergartens 169
    National Information 169
    District of Columbia Public School Information 169
    Maryland Public School Information 170
    Virginia Public School Information 171
    Special Needs Programs 172

**CHILD CARE AND
SCHOOL RESOURCES**

Babysitting Referrals

See also **CHILD CARE AND SCHOOL RESOURCES: Child Care Special Resources, Drop-In Centers**
CHILD CARE AND SCHOOL RESOURCES: Nannies

Carriage Trade Nannies 703-534-6269
2946 Sleepy Hollow Road, Suite 2B
Falls Church, VA 22044
temporary childcare

Chevy Chase Babysitters 301-916-2694
serving MD and DC
providing short-term, temporary and occasional babysitting; days, evenings,
weekends

Georgetown University Employment Referral Service 202-687-4187
White Gravenor, Room G07   FAX: 202-687-6542
37th and O Streets, NW
Washington, DC 20007
lists hundreds of college students interested in babysitting in DC area

Mothers' Aides, Inc. 703-250-0700
temporary and emergency in-home child care since 1979;
serving metropolitan Washington area

WeeSIT Sitting Services 703-764-1542
serving Northern Virginia
temporary, short term child care

White House Nannies 301-652-8088
7200 Wisconsin Avenue, Suite 409
Bethesda, MD 20814
evening, weekend, temporary, and emergency childcare

CHILD CARE AND SCHOOL RESOURCES

Child Care Referrals and Information

See also **PARENT RESOURCES: Parent Info, Low Income Resources**
PARENT RESOURCES: Parent Resource Centers
EC PROFESSIONAL RESOURCES: Child Care, Licensing

METRO AREA

Child Care Bureau 301-330-8401
9055-D Gaither Road
Gaithersburg, MD 20877
child care directories

LifeWork Strategies, Inc. 1-800-777-1720
710 East Gude Drive, Suite A
Rockville, MD 20850
child care referral service for Greater Washington-Baltimore Metro area

Independent School Guide: Washington DC & Surrounding Area
Independent Schools Guides 301-986-5370
7315 Brookville Road   301-652-8635
Chevy Chase, MD 20815   301-986-0698
over 340 private schools from preschool up; includes summer programs, day
care LD, ED; area book stores or send $14.95 + $2.00 postage and handling

Metropolitan Washington Preschool and Day Care Guidebook
Merry Cavanaugh 202-338-7257
3833 Calvert Street, NW
Washington, DC 20007
1,000 listings in DC, MD, and VA; review of required licensing and
accreditation in DC, MD, and VA; available by phone or at Crown Books and
The Cheshire Cat Book Store

National Association of Child Care Resources & Referral Agencies 202-393-5501
1319 F Street, NW, Suite 606
Washington, DC 20004
nationwide service providing local child care referrals

SHARE Care 301-320-2321
5905 Namakagan Road
Bethesda, MD 20816
computer data base to match families for shared child care

DISTRICT OF COLUMBIA

DC Government Information and Referral 202-727-7226

Department of Consumer and Regulatory 202-727-7225

Washington Child Development Council 202-387-0002
referrals for daycare in DC

MARYLAND

General

Child Care Consortium 301-695-4508
22 South Market Street
Frederick, MD 21701

LOCATE: Child Care Statewide 410-625-1111
Maryland Committee for Children
608 Water Street
Baltimore, MD 21202
resource and referral service for parents in search of child care

Maryland State Department of Education
Nonpublic School Approval Branch 410-767-0408
Virginia Cieslicki   FAX: 410-333-8963
200 W. Baltimore Street   vcieslic@state.md.us
Baltimore, MD 21201
lists of approved schools, centers, and programs; approval agency for nursery
schools, daycare centers, and special needs programs for children ages 2,3,
and 4; preschoolers in Maryland may also attend nursery school programs
operated by churches or temples that are not approved by the State Board of
Education, but are registered with the State Department of Human Resources

Montgomery County

Child Care Connection 301-279-1773
Child Care Information and Referral   TDD thru MD relay:1-800-735-2258
332 West Edmonston Drive, B-6
Rockville, MD 20852
link to wide selection of child care programs in Montgomery County;
Montgomery County's only approved child care referral service;"Paying for
Child Care," info sheet for parents on the costs of care and payment options

Child Care Licensing & Regulation 301-294-0344

CONTACT Child Care Services 301-279-1260
Children's Resource Center   TDD: 301-217-1246
Department of Family Resources
332 West Edmonston Road
Rockville, MD 20852
focal point for coordination of child care services in Montgomery County

Family Day Care Association of Montgomery County 301-871-6810

Working Parents Assistance Program 301-217-1155
child care subsidies

Working Families Center 301-279-8497
Children's Resource Center
332 West Edmonston Road
Rockville, MD 20852
information, support and resources for parents and family day care providers

Prince George's County

Child Care Licensing and Regulation 301-808-1685

Prince George's County Child Care Information and Referral 301-772-8400
   Prince George's Child Care Resource Center 301-772-8420
   9475 Lottsford Road, Suite 202   FAX: 301-772-8410
   Landover, MD 20785   TDD: 301-772-8408
      LOCATE: program for child care referrals

VIRGINIA

General

Child Care Resource and Referral 703-358-5101

Family Care Solutions, Inc. 703-440-0213

Alexandria

Child Care Office, Department of Human Services 703-838-0750

Arlington County

Child Care Resource and Referral 703-358-5101
   referrals for day care

Fairfax County

Child Care Resource System 703-449-9555
   lists of child care resources; assessment and help for a family's child care
   needs

Falls Church

Department of Housing and Human Services 703-241-5005

Office of Community Education 703-241-7676

CHILD CARE AND
SCHOOL RESOURCES

Child Care Special Resources

BACKGROUND CHECKS AND SURVEILLANCE

Angel Watch 703-975-9770
      child protection through video tape monitoring of child care

Consolidated Consulting Services 703-823-9233
      background checks on day care providers

GLOBAL INVESTIGATIVE SERVICES, Inc. 301-589-0088
      background checks, serving suburban MD, DC, and Northern VA

Nanny Check 301-670-5988
      background investigations on child care personnel

DROP-IN CHILD CARE CENTERS

See also **CHILD CARE AND SCHOOL RESOURCES: Babysitting Services**

Our Kids, Inc. 202-267-6075
      2100 2nd Street, SW, L'Enfant Plaza   FAX: 202-267-4038
      Washington, DC 20593
            drop-in federal daycare center; initial fee, then fee for drop-in service

SCHOLARSHIPS AND SLIDING FEE CHILD CARE

District of Columbia

Washington's CHILD Project (WCP) 202-966-7543
3031 Oregon Knolls Drive
Washington, DC 20015
> directory of area services for economically disadvantaged, single parent
> families

Maryland

Arc, The, Family, Infant, and Child Care Center 301-279-2165
332 W. Edmonston Drive
Rockville, MD 20852
> childcare for children 6 weeks to 5 years, with and without medical con-
> ditions; sliding fee scale; nurse onsite; medicare and subsidies accepted

Families Foremost Center 301-585-3424
1109 Spring Street, Suite 300
Silver Spring, MD 20910
> Montgomery County program offering free child care and schooling for
> mothers age 26 and under, whose child is less than 4 years old; parenting
> classes, peer support, parent and child activities; toddler care offered free;
> home visits

Maryland Council of Parent Participation Nursery Schools (MCPPNS)
Mariana Hildesheim 301-527-1273
> scholarship funds to help families who cannot afford full tuition to a
> Maryland cooperative nursery school

Working Parents Assistance Program 301-217-1155
child care subsidies in Montgomery County
Working Parents Assistance
Child Care Provider Scholarship Program
Barbara McCreedy 301-946-1213
Nancy Richardson 301-948-3172
Mary Ellen Sevarese 301-279-1260
> scholarships for child care provider services

SICK CHILDREN CHILD CARE

General Care

METRO AREA

Doctor Care "Nanny Services" 703-799-7852
    serving the metropolitan area
        "Leave Your Child in Doctor Care"; 24 hour service

DISTRICT OF COLUMBIA

Peters Pediatric Nursing Team, Inc. 202-291-0062
    6856 Eastern Ave, NW
    Washington, DC
        licensed home health agency

MARYLAND

Peters Pediatric Nursing Team, Inc. 410-486-3800
    1700 Reistertown Road, Suite 210
    Baltimore, MD 20012
        licensed home health agency

VIRGINIA

Peters Pediatric Nursing Team, Inc. 703-941-8600
    5501 Backlick Road
    Springfield, VA 22003
        licensed home health agency

Sick Child Care 703-758-9419
    Reston and Herndon area
        day care for ill children; pick up from school or day care; individual bed-
        room with telephone, TV, books, toys

WeeSIT Sitting Services 703-764-1542
        serving Northern Virginia; sick child care available

Respite Care

See also **PARENT RESOURCES: Parent Info, Disabled and/or Chronically Ill Children**

NATIONAL

ARCH National Resource Center 914-490-5577
800 Eastown Drive, Suite 105   FAX: 919-490-4905
Chapel Hill, NC 27514
    help in finding respite care

DISTRICT OF COLUMBIA

Family Friends Department of Community Action
Ann King 202-387-4434
    part of Easter Seals; trains citizens to work with children for respite care

Pediatrics AIDS/HIV Care, Inc. 202-328-1421
Stephen Kosk, M.Div., Residential Program Director
1317 G Street, NW
Washington, DC 20005

United Cerebral Palsy of Washington, DC, and Northern Virginia 202-269-1500
Respite Care Program
3135 8th Street, NE
Washington, DC 20017
    temporary relief from caring for a family member with a disability

MARYLAND

Arc, The, Family, Infant, and Child Care Center 301-279-2165
332 W. Edmonston Drive,
Rockville, MD 20852
    childcare for children 6 weeks to 5 years, with and without medical
    conditions; sliding fee scale, nurse onsite; medicare and subsidies accepted

Family Friends Department of Community Action
Ann King 202-387-4434
    part of Easter Seals; trains citizens to work with children for respite care

VIRGINIA

Family Friends Department of Community Action
Betty Buchanan 703-324-5607
    part of Easter Seals; trains citizens to work with children for respite care

Respite Subsidy Program, Fairfax County 703-912-6206
The Hartwood Foundation

United Cerebral Palsy of Washington, DC, and Northern Virginia
Respite Care Program 202-269-1500
3135 8th Street, NE
Washington, DC 20017
    temporary relief from caring for a family member with a disability

Consultants about Child Care and Schools

EDUCATIONAL CONSULTANTS

See also **MENTAL HEALTH RESOURCES: Counseling Centers**

MENTAL HEALTH RESOURCES: Mental Health Practitioners

Referrals and Information

Independent Educational Consultants Association 703-591-4860
5085 Chain Bridge Road, Suite 401   FAX: 703-591-4860
Fairfax, VA 22030
advising families on educational options; free directory of educational
consultants

WISER, Directory of Educational Services in the Washington Area 301-816-0432
11140 Rockville Pike, #105
Rockville, MD 20852
referrals to local educational consultants

District of Columbia

Dranitzke, Susan, M.Ed., M.W.S., L.C.S.W. 202-544-5222
Resources for Children
124 12th Street, SE
Washington, DC 20003
educational consultant; family therapy, play therapy

Early Childhood Consultation Center, The 301-593-5992
Irene Shere, Director
11506 Michale Court
Silver Spring, MD 20904
consultations for families on finding appropriate schools; school adjustment;
school observations; kindergarten readiness; home visits

School Counseling Group, Inc., The 202-333-3530
Ethna Hopper, M.A., Director   FAX: 202-333-3212
4725 MacArthur Blvd., NW
Washington, DC 20007
educational consulting firm

Wake, Kendall, Springer, Isenman, & Associates 202-686-7699
5247 Wisconsin Avenue, NW
Washington, DC 20015
educational consultants

Maryland

Beardsley, Mary, M.Ed. 301-652-1947
5101 River Road, Suite 106
Bethesda, MD 20816
    evaluation; preschool admissions testing; developmental issues

Certified Learning Centers, Inc. 301-774-3700
Patricia Felton, M.Ed., Director
3403 Olanwood Court, Suite 102
Olney, MD 20832
    testing, evaluation, home visits, consultation, treatment

Early Childhood Consultation Center, The 301-593-5992
Irene Shere, Director
11506 Michale Court
Silver Spring, MD 20904
    consultations for families on finding appropriate schools; school adjustment;
    school observations; kindergarten readiness; home visits

Grobel, Anna, Ph.D. 301-229-0044
Brookmont Associates   FAX: 301-229-0151
6109 Broad Street
Bethesda, MD 20816
    educational consultant

Gross, Carol, M.A. 301-654-1833
3208 Pickwick Lane   FAX: 301-654-1437
Chevy Chase, MD 20815
    parent support, consultation, testing, diagnosis

Irvin, Georgia, and Associates 301-951-0131
4701 Willard Avenue, Suite 227   FAX: 301-951-1024
Chevy Chase, MD 20815   gki@eworld.com
    consultations for students from nursery to grad school; French and
    Spanish spoken

Learn for Life 301-949-4422
    consultation for learning for children grades K-6; learning styles and
    multi-sensory approach to tutoring; serving Montgomery County

Mogel, Judy, M.A. 301-320-6506
Bethesda, MD
    educational consultant, diagnostician, parent consultant

National Educational Consulting Services 301-983-4033
P.O. Box 1572
Rockville, MD 20849
    educational consulting

Reynolds, Rebecca B. 410-494-0209
School Search   FAX: 410-828-6178
P.O. Box 734
Brooklandville, MD 21022
    educational consultant

Slattery, Valerie G., Ph.D. 301-299-8085
10428 Masters Terrace
Potomac, MD 20854
psychoeducational assessment; school admissions; ADD, LD

Solomon, Laura, Ed.D. 301-495-0046
8720 Georgia Avenue, Suite 701   FAX: 301-565-2217
Silver Spring, MD 20910
educational consultant; special needs

Turner, Frances, M. Ed. 301-299-2012
35 Wisconsin Circle, Suite 560
Chevy Chase, MD 20815
educational consultant

Virginia

Educational Consulting Services of Northern VA .703-519-7181
100 West Howell Avenue
Alexandria, VA 22301
psychoeducational evaluation; special needs; deaf children

MULTI-CULTURAL EDUCATIONAL CONSULTANTS

Findlay, Judith M. 703-845-1131
Marchbanks & Ellis, Inc.   FAX: 703-931-4896
5119-A Leesburg Pke, Suite 280
Falls Church, VA 22041
international educational consultant with curriculum development,
cross-cultural awareness

SPECIAL NEEDS EDUCATIONAL CONSULTANTS

District of Columbia

Stultz, Sylvia, Ph.D. 202-686-4084
5153 34th Street, NW
Washington, DC 20008
special needs; counseling; preschool consultation

CHILD CARE AND
SCHOOL RESOURCES

Maryland

Certified Learning Centers, Inc.
11301 Classical Lane, Silver Spring 301-593-3700
4303 Olandwood Court, Suite 102, Olney 301-774-3700
7801 Norfolk Avenue, Suite 102, Bethesda 301-907-9427
special needs consultants

Creative Differences 301-320-4222
Susan J. Kline, M.A.E.E.
Bethesda, MD
specializing in individualized creative planning and enrichment;
multi-sensory, hands-on approach; free initial consultation

Neuberger, Sally, L.C.S.W. 301-424-5200
Rockville, MD
workshops or individual topics offered on coping and advocacy for
caretakers of children who have special needs

Solomon, Laura, Ed.D. 301-495-0046
8720 Georgia Avenue, Suite 701   FAX: 301-565-2217
Silver Spring, MD 20910
educational consultant; special needs

Spodak, Ruth B., Ph.D., & Associates 301-770-7507
6155 Executive Boulevard
Rockville, MD 20852
psychological and educational consultants concerning LD

Slattery, Valerie G., Ph.D. 301-299-8085
10428 Masters Terrace
Potomac, MD 20854
psychoeducational assessment; school admissions; ADD, LD

Stern, Judith 301-424-1941
205 Watts Branch Parkway
Rockville, MD 20850
ADD/ADHD; LD consultant; educational consultant

Virginia

Educational Consulting Services of Northern VA 703-519-7181
100 West Howell Avenue
Alexandria, VA 22301
psychoeducational evaluation; special needs; deaf children

Marks, Susan, L.C.S.W. 703-827-8815
7700 Leesburg Pike, Suite 221
Falls Church, VA 22043
ADD; Tourettes Syndrome; autism; obsessive compulsive disorder

Educational Information and Resources

See also **GENERAL RESOURCES: Advocacy Groups**
GENERAL RESOURCES: Books, Etc., Library Resources
GENERAL RESOURCES: Computer Online Services
CHILD CARE AND SCHOOL RESOURCES: Private School Info
CHILD CARE AND SCHOOL RESOURCES: Public School Info
EC PROFESSIONAL RESOURCES: Child Care, Licensing

ERIC-Educational Resources Information Center 1-800-LET-ERIC
**ERIC-Clearinghouse on Elementary and
    Early Childhood Education** . . . . .http://ericps.crc.uiuc.edu/ericeece.html
                                                                                ericeece@uiuc.edu
    University of Illinois at Urbana-Champaign 1-800-583-4135
    51 Gerty Drive   217-333-1386
    Champaign, IL 61820   FAX: 217-333-3767

National Association for the Education of Young Children 202-232-8777
    1509 16th Street, NW   1-800-424-2460
    Washington, DC 20036   FAX: 202-328-1846
        books, brochures, and videos about education for children

ReadyWeb . . . . .http://ericps.crc.uiuc.edu/readyweb/readyweb.html
        information and resources pertaining to school readiness

U.S. Department of Education Information Resource Center 1-800-872-5327

Nannies

AGENCIES

National

All-American Nanny, Ltd. 1-800-3-NANNYS
      health, DMV, and criminal checks; immediate, live-in

Au Pair in America 1-800-928-7247
                            http://www/aifs.org/aifsaup.htm
      largest U.S. government-designated program; au pair safety and training program

Au Pair Intercultural 1-800-654-2051
      P.O. Box 147
      Marlhurst, OR 97201

Au Pair USA Interexchange, Inc. . . . . .1-800-AU PAIRS
                            703-742-0377
      qualified, experienced live-in European au pairs; government designated program

EF Au Pair 1-800-333-6056
      1 Memorial Drive
      Cambridge, MA 02124

Metro Area

Abbye Ashton 301-469-0082
      serving the Washington area in nannies, housekeepers

A Choice Nanny
      Bethesda, MD 301-652-BABY
      Columbia, MD 410-730-BABY
      Gaithersburg, MD 301-963-BABY
      Rosslyn, VA 703-535-BABY
      Tysons, VA 703-827-BABY

Added Hands Agency 703-684-3149
      1800 Diagonal Road, Suite 600
      Alexandria, VA

Au Pair Care 703-549-7498
      P.O. Box 2065
      Arlington, VA

Au Pair Homestay 202-408-5380
      serving DC, MD, and northern VA

B & G Regal Domestics, Inc. 301-569-6817
      specializing in nannies, live in or out, full or part time

Carriage Trade Nannies, Ltd. 703-534-NANY
    2946 Sleepy Hollow Road, Suite 2B   FAX: 703-534-0069
    Falls Church, VA 22044
        live in or out, full or part time, temporary, on-call; CPR

Extra Assistance, Inc. 301-495-9587
    1109 Spring Street, Suite 401
    Silver Spring, MD 20910
        serving suburban MD, DC, and northern VA; live in or out

Extra Hands 301-567-0997
        live in or out, full or part time; on-call; criminal and DMV checks, CPR
        required; serving DC, MD, and VA

Mothers' Aides, Inc. 703-250-0700
        serving suburban DC, MD, and northern VA

Nannies, Inc.
    6701 Democracy Boulevard, Bethesda 301-718-0100
    3031 Borge Street, Oakton, VA 703-255-5312
        live in or out nannies with long-term references; available immediately

Nanny Dimensions 703-691-0334
    Gail Lyon, M.S.W.
    10560 Main Street, Suite 513
    Fairfax, VA 22030

Nanny Factor, The
    8001 Spring Road, Cabin John, MD 301-320-5245
    5975 New England Woods Drive, Burke, VA 703-764-9021

Nanny Match 703-273-7077
                                                         301-365-7078
        serving DC, MD, and VA; available immediately

Nanny Poppins 703-938-0444
    333 Maple Avenue East, #530
    Vienna, VA

Potomac Nannies 301-986-0048
    7315 Wisconsin Avenue, Suite 1300W
    Bethesda, MD 20814
        serving DC, MD, and northern VA since 1985

Quality Care Alternatives Placement Services 301-559-6755
        nannies, live in or out, full or part-time; discount placement fees

Shining Times, Inc. 1-888-889-8009
        placement service for nannies

Storybook Nannies 703-830-2094
        live in or out, full or part time; CPR; fluent English

White House Nannies, Inc. 301-654-1242
    4733 Bethesda Avenue, Suite 805A
    Bethesda, MD 20814

CHILD CARE AND SCHOOL RESOURCES

HEALTH INSURANCE FOR NANNIES

Eisenberg, Richard A., and Associates 1-800-777-5765
1340 Centre Street, Suite 203
Newton, MA 02159
official insurance representative of the International Nanny Association

Med Plans 301-881-5435
11300 Rockville Pike   FAX: 301-881-2341
Rockville, MD 20852
health insurance for nannies

HIRING

International Nanny Association, Member Services 402-691-9628
125 S. Fourth Street
Norfolk, Nebraska 68701
information available on hiring a nanny

NEWSLETTERS AND PUBLICATIONS

Keeping Kids, **by Barbara Cunningham** 703-527-8750
guide for employers of nannies; includes model contract

Nanny News 1-800-634-6266
bi-monthly newsletter for nannies and employers

SUPPORT AND TRAINING FOR NANNIES

See also **PARENT RESOURCES: Parent Education Classes**

Association of DC Area Nannies 202-561-2922
activities, lectures, newsletter

Fairfax County Office of Children 703-218-3700
Division of Community Education and Provider Services
3701 Pender Drive, Fourth Floor
Fairfax, VA 22030
training for nannies

International Nanny Association, Member Services 402-691-9628
125 S. Fourth Street
Norfolk, NE 68701
information and advocacy for nannies

TAX GUIDANCE FOR HOUSEHOLD EMPLOYERS

Canady, Edwin N., CPA 703-516-4584
tax guidance for federal and state payroll tax requirements for employing
a nanny

Nanitax 1-800-NANITAX
2 Pidgeon Hill Drive, Suite 210   FAX: 703-404-8155
Sterling, VA 20165   http://www.4nannytaxes.com
payroll tax service

Private Preschools and Kindergartens

See also   CHILD CARE AND SCHOOL RESOURCES: Child Care Referrals and Information

CHILD CARE AND SCHOOL RESOURCES: Consultants

PARENT RESOURCES: Parent Info: Home Schooling

GENERAL SCHOOL REFERRALS AND INFORMATION

See also EC PROFESSIONAL RESOURCES: CHILD CARE, Licensing

National

National Academy of Early Childhood Programs 202-328-2601
1509 16th Street, NW
Washington, DC 20036
list of NAEYC accredited childcare centers and preschools

National Association of Independent Schools (NAIS) 202-973-9700
1620 L Street, N.W.
Washington, DC 20036

Parent's Guide to Alternatives in Education, The
Ronald F. Koetzsch, author   . . . . .http://www.shambhala.com
Shambhala Publications, Inc.
300 Massachusetts Avenue
Boston, MA 02115
in-depth guide to full range of choices in alternative schooling

Metro Area

Association of Independent Schools of Greater Washington (AISGW) 202-538-1114
3609 Woodley Road, NW
Washington, DC 20016

Independent School Guide: Washington DC & Surrounding Area
Independent Schools Guides 301-986-5370
7315 Brookville Road   301-652-8635
Chevy Chase, MD 20815   301-986-0698
over 340 private schools from preschool up; includes summer programs, day
care LD, ED; area book stores or send $14.95 + $2.00 postage & handling

Metropolitan Washington Preschool and Day Care Guidebook
Merry Cavanaugh 202-338-7257
3833 Calvert Street, NW
Washington, DC 20007
1,000 listings in MD, DC, and VA; available by phone or at Crown Books and
The Cheshire Cat Book Store

District of Columbia

Department of Consumer and Regulatory 202-727-7225
    lists of approved private schools

Maryland

Association of Independent Maryland Schools (AIMS) 301-621-0787
    P.O. Box 813
    Millersville, MD 21108

Maryland State Department of Education
Nonpublic School Approval Branch 410-767-0408
    Virginia Cieslicki   FAX: 410-333-8963
    200 W. Baltimore Street   vcieslic@state.md.us
    Baltimore, MD 21201
        lists of approved schools, centers, and programs; approval agency for
        nursery schools, daycare centers, and special needs programs for children
        ages 2,3, and 4; preschoolers in Maryland may also attend nursery school
        programs operated by churches or temples that are not approved by the
        State Board of Education, but are registered with the State Department of
        Human Resources

Virginia

Licensing and Regulation
    Alexandria 703-838-0750
    Arlington County 703-358-5101
    Fairfax County 703-324-8100
        lists of approved preschools

COOPERATIVE PRESCHOOL INFORMATION

National

Parent Cooperative Preschools International (PCPI) 1-800-721-PCPI
P.O. Box 90410
Indianapolis, IN 46290
> information on starting and managing cooperative preschools; annual conference

Metro Area

Maryland Council of Parent Participation Nursery Schools (MCPPNS)
Lisa Blasey, President 301-649-6482
Kirsten Rhoades, Executive Vice President 301-933-9840
> organization of cooperative preschools in suburban Maryland; lists of
> cooperative preschools

Potomac Association of Cooperative Teachers (P.A.C.T.)
Irene Shere 301-593-5992
> lists of cooperative preschools in DC, MD, and VA; information on
> cooperative preschools

Virginia Cooperative Preschool Council (VCPC)
Kathryn Conklin 703-361-0146
> Virginia cooperative preschool organization; lists of cooperative preschools
> in Virginia

MONTESSORI SCHOOL INFORMATION

Washington Montessori Institute 202-387-8020
2119 S Street, NW   FAX: 202-332-6345
Washington, DC 20008
> listings of Montessori Schools in DC, MD, and VA

REGGIO EMILIA PRESCHOOL INFORMATION

ERIC/EECE 1-800-583-4135
Children's Research Center   http://ericps.ed.uiuc.edu/eece/reggio.html
University of Illinois
51 Gerty Drive
Champaign, IL 61820
> publications, information relating to Reggio Emilia approach

Model Early Learning Center 202-675-4148
Erica Hamlin
800 3rd Street, NE
Washington, DC 20002
> certified Reggio Emilia Preschool

St. John's Episcopal Church Preschool 202-338-2574
Kathy Price, Director
3240 O Street, NW
Washington, DC 20007
> Reggio Emilia inspired preschool

SPECIAL NEEDS SCHOOLS INFORMATION

See also CHILD CARE AND SCHOOL RESOURCES: Public Preschools and Kindergartens

Referrals and Information

American Association of Children's Residential Centers .703-838-7522
1021 Prince Street
Alexandria, VA 22314
    national directory of residential treatment facilities for severely emotionally
    disturbed children

National Association of Private Schools for Exceptional Children
1522 K Street, NW, Suite 1032 202-408-3338
Washington, DC 20005

Tomorrow's Child 609-354-9106
Daycare for Medically Dependent Children
Barklay Pavilion West, Suite 203B
Cherry Hill, NJ 08034
    information on national centers providing medical care and education

District of Columbia

Kennedy, Lt. Joseph P., Institute 202-529-7600
801 Buchanan Street, NE
Washington, DC 20007
    ungraded program for children with developmental disabilities

Lab School of Washington, The 202-965-6600
4759 Reservoir Road, NW
Washington, DC 20007
    K-12 special education program for children of average to superior intelli-
    gence with specific learning disabilities

Therapeutic Educational Day Care for Infants 202-832-4400
Hospital for Sick Children
1731 Bunker Hill Road, NE
Washington, DC 20017
    special program for children birth through age 5 with disabilities

Maryland

Centers for the Handicapped Child Care Center 301-593-8822
10611 Tenbrook Drive
Silver Spring, MD 20901
 inclusive preschool program for disabled and non-disabled children ages 2-5

Ivymount School, The 301-469-0223
11614 Seven Locks Road
Rockville, MD 20854
 ungraded program for children with LD, behavioral and/or emotional
 problems and/or multiple handicaps

Jewish Community Center of Greater Washington 301-881-0100
6125 Montrose Road
Rockville, MD 20852
 school with mainstreaming; special needs summer camp

Maryland School for the Blind 410-444-5000
3501 Taylor Avenue
Baltimore, MD 21236

Maryland School for the Deaf 301-662-5133
101 Clarke Place, P.O. Box 250
Frederick, MD 21701

McLean School of Maryland 301-299-8277
8224 Lochinver Lane
Potomac, MD 20854
 mainstream program with a special program for children with minimal LD;
 K-9th grade

St. Columba School 301-567-6212
7800 Livingston Road
Oxon Hill, MD 20745
 K-8th grade; ungraded school for children with LD

CHILD CARE AND SCHOOL RESOURCES

Virginia

Child Development Center of Northern Virginia 703-534-5353
educational and therapeutic center and program for developmentally
delayed or disabled children ages birth-5

Oakwood School 703-941-5788
7210 Braddock Road
Annandale, VA 22003
K-9th grade program for children whose potential is emerging

Special Love, Inc. 703-667-3774
117 Youth Development Court
Winchester, VA 22602
year-round programs for cancer patients from birth to 25

St. Coletta School 703-525-4433
3130 Lee Highway
Arlington, VA 22201
training for children ages 5-21 with mental retardation and other disabilities

WALDORF SCHOOL INFORMATION

Acorn Hill Children's Center 301-565-2282
9504 Brunett Avenue
Silver Spring, MD 20901
preschool based on Waldorf School /Rudolf Steiner philosophy

Washington Waldorf School 301-229-6107
4800 Sangamore Road
Bethesda, MD 20816
school based on the educational philosophy of Rudolf Steiner

CHILD CARE AND SCHOOL RESOURCES

Public Preschools and Kindergartens

NATIONAL INFORMATION

Head Start 1-800-27-START
federally funded preschool programs for 3 and 4 year olds; located in public schools

National Parent Teacher Association (P.T.A.) 312-787-0977
700 North Rush Street
Chicago, IL 60761

U.S. Department of Education Information Resource Center 1-800-872-5327

DISTRICT OF COLUMBIA PUBLIC SCHOOL INFORMATION

Board of Education 202-724-4283

Department of Education 202-401-2000

Head Start 202-645-3707
federally funded preschool programs for 3 and 4 year olds;
located in public schools

Public School Information 202-724-4044
Special Education 202-724-4800
HOTLINE 202-724-4016

P.T.A., D.C. Congress of Parents and Teachers 202-543-0333
Thriftone Jones, President
Hamilton Junior High School Bldg.
6th Street and Brentwood Parkway, NE
Washington, DC 20002

Superintendent of Public Schools 202-724-4222
District of Columbia Public Schools
415 12th Street, NW
Washington, DC 20004

CHILD CARE AND SCHOOL RESOURCES

"How Can I Help My Child?" Early Childhood Resource Directory

169

MARYLAND PUBLIC SCHOOL INFORMATION

Board of Education
Montgomery County 301-279-3617
Prince George's County 301-952-6000

Department of Education 410-767-0100
Special Education 410-767-0238
Disability Programs 410-767-0237
200 West Baltimore Street
Baltimore, MD 21201

Head Start, Maryland 301-464-5770
Montgomery County 301-230-0676
Prince George's County 301-985-1782
federally funded preschool programs for 3 and 4 year olds;
located in public schools

P.T.A., Maryland Congress of Parents and Teachers .410-235-7290
John R. Allen II, President
3121 St. Paul Street, Suite 25
Baltimore, MD 21218

Public School Information
Montgomery County 301-279-3000
Information Office 301-279-3391
Special Needs: PEATC 301-657-4969
Prince Georges County 301-952-6000
Special Needs: PEATC 301-731-4571

Superintendent of Schools 410-396-1783
State Department of Education
200 East North Avenue
Baltimore, MD 21202

VIRGINIA PUBLIC SCHOOL INFORMATION

Board of Education
Arlington County 703-358-6010
Alexandria 703-824-6610
Fairfax County 703-246-3646

Department of Education 804-225-2755
Special Education 804-225-2402
Disability Programs 804-371-8592
P.O. Box 2120
Richmond, VA 23218

Head Start, Virginia 703-836-5774
Alexandria 703-768-9644
Annandale 703-846-8720
Arlington County 703-979-2400
Bailey's Crossroads 703-820-2457
Fairfax County 703-324-8290
        federally funded preschool programs for 3 and 4 year olds;
        located in public schools

P.T.A., Virginia Congress of Parents and Teachers 804-355-2816
David Goodrich, President
3810 Augusta Avenue
Richmond, VA 23230

Public School Information
Alexandria 703-824-6600
    Special Education 703-824-6631
Arlington County 703-358-6000
    Arlington County, Extended Day 703-358-6069
    Special Education 703-358-6040
Fairfax County 703-246-2502
    Special Needs: PEATC 703-691-7826
Falls Church 703-241-7600
Loudoun County 703-771-6440
Prince William County 703-791-7200

Superintendent of Public Instruction 804-225-2023
State Department of Education
P.O. Box 6Q, James Monroe Building
Fourteenth and Franklin Streets
Richmond, VA 23216

"How Can I Help My Child?" Early Childhood Resource Directory

171

SPECIAL NEEDS PROGRAMS

District of Columbia

Public School Special Education Information 202-724-4800

Maryland

Department of Education, Special Education 410-767-0238
    Disability Programs 410-767-0237
    200 West Baltimore Street
    Baltimore, MD 21201
        program for children with disabilities, ages 3 through 5

Interact, Montgomery County Public Schools 301-649-8057
    Interdisciplinary Augmentative Communication and Technology Team
        speech and language programs for students with physical disabilities

LEAP (Language-Learning Early Advantage Program) 301-405-4228
    Daralee Baker, Director
    University of Maryland Department of Hearing and Speech Sciences
    College Park, MD 20742
        preschool for language-delayed children

Parent Education Program (PEP), Montgomery County .301-929-2155
        free program for children birth through age 5 with developmental delays;
        parent education classes

Public School Information
    Montgomery County, Special Needs: PEATC 301-657-4969
    Prince Georges County, Special Needs: PEATC 301-731-4571

Virginia

Department of Education, Special Education 804-225-2402
    Disability Programs 804-371-8592
    P.O. Box 2120
    Richmond, VA 23218
        programs for children with disabilities, ages 2 through 8

Fairfax County Department of Health Daytime Development Center 703-246-7850
    teaching, therapeutic, and stimulation program for children birth to 2
    who have disabilities or developmental delays

Public School Information
    Alexandria, Special Education 703-824-6631
    Arlington County, Special Education 703-358-6040
    Fairfax County, Special Needs: PEATC 703-691-7826

Parent Resources

Resources for Parents

PARENT RESOURCES includes:

- **Child Safety**

- **Child Transportation**

- **Computer Online Services**

- **Consultants for Parents**

- **Organizations for Parents**

- **Parent Education Classes:** includes multi-cultural, multi-lingual, and special needs parent education

- **Parent Information and Support:** includes extensive information on specific topics of interest to parents

- **Parent Resource Centers:** includes centers that provide a broad spectrum of information, education, support, and services, sometimes including child care, for young families

The Table of Contents on the next page provides a detailed listing of this section.

Note:

<u>**Be sure to look in "Metro Area" when available.**</u> <u>Metro Area</u> resources are available throughout the entire Washington metropolitan area. These resources are not repeated in the separate <u>District of Columbia</u>, <u>Maryland</u>, and <u>Virginia</u> listings.

"How Can I Help My Child?" Early Childhood Resource Directory

173

Parent Resources
Table of Contents

Child Safety 175
    Child Photo-ID Registration 175
    Child Safety Education 175
    Home and Product Safety 176
Child Transportation 177
Computer Online Services for Parents 178
Consultants for Parents 179
    Family Consultants 179
    Special Needs Family Consultants 180
Organizations for Parents 182
    Cooperative Preschool Parent Organizations 182
    Parent Teacher Associations (P.T.A.s) 182
Parent Education Classes 183
    Referrals and Information 183
    National 184
    Metro Area 184
    District of Columbia 185
    Maryland 185
    Virginia 190
    Multi-cultural, Multi-lingual Parent Education 192
    Special Needs Parent Education 193

Parent Information and Support 195
    Adoption 195
    African-American Families 198
    Allergy and Asthma 199
    Asian-American Families 200
    Attention Deficit Disorder (ADD) 201
    Attention Deficit Hyperactivity
       Disorder (ADHD) 201
    Autism 203
    Bedwetting 203
    Cancer 203
    Cerebral Palsy 204
    Challenging Children 204
    Child Abuse Prevention 205
    Death and Bereavement 207
    Diabetes .208
    Disabled and/or Chronically Ill Children . .209
    Divorce and Separation 212
    Down's Syndrome 216
    Emotionally Disturbed Children 217
    Epilepsy .217
    Fathers 218
    Foster Care 219
    Gay and Lesbian Parents 220
    Grandparents 221
    Hearing-Impaired Children 223
    Home Schooling 225
    Latino-American Families 227
    Learning Disabilities (LD) 228
    Low Income Resources 230
    Mothers .234
    Multicultural Resources 237
    Parents of Multiple Births 239
    Playgroups 240
    Sibling Relationships 240
    Single Parents 240
    Special Needs 242
    Stepfamilies 245
    Stuttering 245
    Support Groups 246
    Tourette's Syndrome 247
    Visually-Impaired Children 248
    Working Parents 248
Parent Resource Centers 249
    National 249
    Maryland 250
    Virginia 251

PARENT RESOURCES

Child Safety

See also CHILD CARE AND SCHOOL RESOURCES: Background Checks

CHILD PHOTO-ID REGISTRATION

BirthNet Family Registry 1-888-263-8548
http://www.birthnet.com
> color photo-ID cards and ID tags; photo-ID web page created for families

IDENT-A-KID Services of America 703-971-1709
5405 Dunsmore Road
Alexandria, VA 22315
> child identification program; will travel to private schools, day care centers

SAFETY-ID 301-460-7768
Brian Swartz   301-460-1105
14226 Clayton Street
Rockville, MD 20853
> child photo-ID registration on computer diskette for parents and schools;
> on-site for schools; kiosk at Cabin John Mall in Potomac, MD

CHILD SAFETY EDUCATION

National

Child Lures 1-802-985-8458
http://www.childlures.com
> abduction prevention materials; 20 page publication for $4

Child Shield 703-426-2693
> 24-hour information line to help parents safeguard their children

Kid Watch 1-916-893-1154
> Bob Stuber's book and program for empowering children against abduction

National Center for Missing and Exploited Children 703-235-3900
> child safety education information

Safe-T-Child, National 1-800-828-0098
> free copy: "Keeping your Child Safe from Abduction & Abuse"

Metro Area

Personal-Touch 202-537-7200
> "Keeping Kids Safe" class taught by pediatric R.N.

Safe-T-Child, DC and Prince George's County 301-350-1444
> free copy: "Keeping your Child Safe from Abduction & Abuse"

PARENT RESOURCES

HOME AND PRODUCT SAFETY

Information and Resources

Consumer Product Safety Commission 1-800-638-2772
current and past recall information for products .... http://www.cpsc.gov

Kids Gear Up Guide, The 202-662-0600
National Safe Kids Campaign
1301 Pennsylvania Avenue, NW, Suite 1000
Washington, DC 20004
$2 guide to car seat use and car safety

Maryland K.I.S.S. (Kids in Safety Seats) 1-800-370-7328
car seat rentals; car seat checks

Poison Control Center 202-625-3333
National Capital Poison Center
3201 New Mexico Avenue, Suite 310
Washington, DC 20016

Safety P.I.N., The 301-681-1584
P.O. Box 86031
Gaithersburg, MD 20886
child safety newsletter providing up-to-date safety information for children

Inspections and Products

BABYGUARD 703-821-1231
home safety inspection; installation of safety products; member of
International Association for Child Safety

Children's Safety Care 301-977-8334
in-home safety evaluation; installation of safety devices

Consolidated Consulting Services 703-823-9233
health and safety inspections for homes and day care providers; background
checks on day care providers

Guardian-Child Safety Consultants 703-960-6452
on-site safety evaluations and installations; "do-it-yourself" kits for products

Healthy Spaces 1-800-290-4436
environmental home inspection and consultation

Perfectly Safe 1-800-837-KIDS
7835 Freedom Avenue, NW, Suite 3
North Canton, Ohio 44720
catalog of safe products and safety products for children birth to 5

SAFE KIDS Childproofing 301-621-9770
708 South Overlook Drive
Alexandria, VA 22304
safety devices and installation; serving DC, MD, and VA

SafetyNest Childproofing, Inc. 703-379-7030
childproof advisors; in-home survey; video surveillance; member of
International Association for Child Safety

Child Transportation

DISTRICT OF COLUMBIA

Errands & Elephants, Ltd. 301-654-1841
550 Friendship Blvd.
Chevy Chase, MD 20815
child transportation; bonded and insured; household errands

MARYLAND

Door-to-Door Shuttle Service 410-465-8577
transportation for children ages 2-5 in Howard County

Errands & Elephants, Ltd. 301-654-1841
550 Friendship Blvd.
Chevy Chase, MD 20815
child transportation; bonded and insured; household errands

Mom's Shuttle 410-227-1958
transportation service for Howard County

VIRGINIA

Children's Chariot, Inc. 703-354-6493
prescheduled, private transportation for children; door-to-door service

Errands-4-U 703-938-4790
Claire T. West, R.N.
pick-up for children

"How Can I Help My Child?" Early Childhood Resource Directory

177

PARENT RESOURCES

Computer Online Services for Parents

See also GENERAL RESOURCES: Computer Resources

Cybermom Dot Com, The . . . . .http://www.thecybermom.com/index.html
mothers' web-site; reviews of videos, child safety, health; chat room

Family Education Network . . . . .www.familyeducation.com
20 Park Plaza, Suite 1215   info@familyeducation.com
Boston, MA 02116
free online service that gives parents information, advice, and discounts on
educational products

Family Web Corner . . . . .http://www.nauticom.net/www/cokids/
lists of resources and connections on www

Kathy's Parent Page . . . . .http://www.mcs.net/~kathyw/parent.html
essential information for parents

National Association for the Education of Young Children . . . . . .http://www.naeyc.org/naeyc
naeyc@naeyc.org

National Parent Information Network (NPIN) 1-800-583-4135
ericeece@ux1.cso/uiuc.edu
articles; question-answering service; discussions; access to other parents and
organizations serving parents, ERIC digests

Parenting . . . . .http://www.inetcom.net/test/index.html
preschool readiness skills manual

Parenting Education . . . . .nnfr3@mes.umn.edu

Parentsplace.com . . . . .http://www.parentsplace.com/
information for parents of children of all ages

Parenting Q & A . . . . .www.parenting-qa.com
online answers to parenting questions; searchable database of answers from
experts in child development and behavior

Parent Resource Page . . . . .http://www.thegrapevine.com/daycare/

Parents AskERIC 1-800-583-4135
askeric@ericir.syr.edu
parent part of AskERIC designed as a service for parents with questions about
development, education, and care of children from birth through high school years

Parentsoup . . . . .http://www.parentsoup.com

Parenttime . . . . .www.parenttime.com
online community of experts, resources, and parents available 24 hours a
day to answer questions or chat

Special Needs Families . . . . .http://www.pacifier.com/~estiles/

***Washington Parent* newspaper** . . . . .http://family.com

PARENT
RESOURCES

Consultants for Parents

FAMILY CONSULTANTS

See also **MENTAL HEALTH RESOURCES: Counseling Centers**
MENTAL HEALTH RESOURCES: Mental Health Practitioners
MENTAL HEALTH RESOURCES: Testing and Assessment
CHILD CARE AND SCHOOL RESOURCES: Consultants
PARENT RESOURCES: Parent Info, specific topics

Maryland

Early Childhood Consultation Center, The 301-593-5992
Irene Shere, Director
11506 Michale Court
Silver Spring, MD 20904
consultations for families concerning social and emotional issues of
preschoolers; anger management; sibling issues; separation and divorce;
challenging children; home visits

Maryland Council of Parent Participation Nursery Schools(MCPPNS)
Parent Education
P.O. Box 9383
Silver Spring, MD 20916
answers to child development issues through consultation with librarians,
Internet searches, and professionals

National Educational Consulting Services 301-983-4033
P.O. Box 1572
Rockville, MD 20849
parenting consultants

Parent Care, Inc. 1-800-224-3893
Scott Buehler, Director   301-770-CARE
6239 Executive Boulevard   drscott@parentcare.com
Rockville, MD 20852   www.parentcare.com
family consultation

Snyder, Lenni Gimple, M.A. 301-320-9282
4933 Auburn Avenue, Suite 202
Bethesda, MD 20814
child play therapy

Stein, Sharyn, M.S. 410-486-6001
Columbia, MD
social skills groups for young children

Virginia

Crosby, Terri 703-406-4471
    8 Worthington Court
    Sterling, VA 20165
        parent coaching; educational consultant; family consultant

Weiss, Sharon K., M.D. 703-356-5534
    1420 Beverly Road, Suite 300
    McLean, VA 22101
        behavioral consultation; child-parent counseling

SPECIAL NEEDS FAMILY CONSULTANTS

See also **MENTAL HEALTH RESOURCES: Mental Health Practitioners**
         MENTAL HEALTH RESOURCES: Testing and Assessment
         CHILD CARE, SCHOOL RESOURCES: Consultants, Special Needs
         PARENT RESOURCES: Parent Info, LD
         PARENT RESOURCES: Parent Info, Special Needs

Referrals

Learning Disabilities Association of DC 202-265-8869
Learning Disabilities Association of Maryland 410-484-0499
Learning Disabilities Association of Montgomery Co. .301-933-1076
Learning Disabilities Association of Virginia 703-569-3710
        referrals to special needs consultants

District of Columbia

Kingsbury Center 202-232-5878
    Carolyn Atkinson Thornell, Director   202-232-5989
    2138 Bancroft Place, NW   FAX: 202-667-2290
    Washington, DC 20008
        consultations and workshops on learning disabilities

Stultz, Sylvia, Ph.D. 202-686-4084
    5153 34th Street, NW
    Washington, DC 20008
        special needs; counseling; preschool consultation

PARENT RESOURCES

180   "How Can I Help My Child?" Early Childhood Resource Directory

Maryland

Ivymount School, The 301-469-0223
    Judi Greenberg   301-469-0228
    11614 Seven Locks Road
    Rockville, MD 20854
        child evaluations; consultations with families on helping children who may
        have developmental delays or special needs

Neuberger, Sally, L.C.S.W. 301-424-5200
    Rockville, MD
        workshops or individual topics offered on coping and advocacy for
        caretakers of children who have special needs

Solomon, Laura, Ed.D. 301-495-0046
    8720 Georgia Avenue, Suite 701   FAX: 301-565-2217
    Silver Spring, MD 20910
        educational consultant; special needs

Spodak, Ruth B., Ph.D., & Associates 301-770-7507
    6155 Executive Boulevard
    Rockville, MD 20852
        psychological and educational consultants concerning LD

Stern, Judith, M.A. 301-424-1941
    205 Watts Branch Parkway
    Rockville, MD 20850
        educational consultant specializing in ADD, LD

Virginia

Marks, Susan, L.C.S.W. 703-827-8815
    7700 Leesburg Pike, Suite 221
    Falls Church, VA 22043
        ADD; Tourette's Syndrome; autism; obsessive compulsive disorder

PARENT RESOURCES

Organizations for Parents

See also GENERAL RESOURCES: Advocacy Groups
PARENT RESOURCES: Parent Info, specific topics

COOPERATIVE PRESCHOOL PARENT ORGANIZATIONS

Maryland Council of Parent Participation Nursery Schools (MCPPNS)
Lisa Blasey, President 301-649-6482
Kirsten Rhoades, Executive Vice President 301-933-9840
annual conference, newsletter, and information about parent cooperatives

Parent Cooperative Preschools International 800-721-PCPI
P.O. Box 90410
Indianapolis, IN 46290
publications and information about cooperative preschools; information
about starting a cooperative preschool; newsletter

Virginia Cooperative Preschool Council (VCPC)
Kathryn Conklin 703-361-0146
newsletter and information about parent cooperatives in Virginia

PARENT TEACHER ASSOCIATIONS (P.T.A.s)

D.C. Congress of Parents and Teachers 202-543-0333
Thriftone Jones, President
Hamilton Jr. High School Bldg.
6th Street and Brentwood Parkway, NE
Washington, DC 20002

Maryland Congress of Parents and Teachers 410-235-7290
John R. Allen, II, President
3121 St. Paul Street, Suite 25
Baltimore, MD 21218

National P.T.A. 312-787-0977
700 North Rush Street
Chicago, IL 60761

Virginia Congress of Parents and Teachers 804-355-2816
David Goodrich, President
3810 Augusta Avenue
Richmond, VA 23230

Parent Education Classes

See also **GENERAL RESOURCES: Books, Etc., Resource Guides**
GENERAL RESOURCES: Conferences and Speaker Series
GENERAL RESOURCES: Videos for Adults
HEALTH RESOURCES: Courses in CPR, First Aid, and Health
MENTAL HEALTH RESOURCES: Counseling Centers
MENTAL HEALTH RESOURCES: Mental Health Practitioners
PARENT RESOURCES: Child Safety Education
PARENT RESOURCES: Consultants
PARENT RESOURCES: Parent Resource Centers

REFERRALS AND INFORMATION

Metro Area

Coalition for Marriage, Family and Couples Education
Diane Sollee, Director, CMFCE, L.L.C 202-966-5376
5310 Belt Road, NW   FAX: 202-362-0973
Washington, DC 20015   CMFCE @his.com
http://www.his.com/~CMFCE
information exchange to help families locate and select educational courses

District of Columbia

Washington's CHILD Project (WCP) 202-966-7543
3031 Oregon Knolls Drive
Washington, DC 20015
directory of area parenting education programs and services for
economically disadvantaged, single parent families

Virginia

Work and Family Institute 703-358-7215
Parenting Education Resource Center   703-358-7214
Clarendon Education Center   703-358-7216
2801 Clarendon Blvd, Suite 306
Arlington, VA 22201
information about parenting programs in Arlington County; free directory

PARENT RESOURCES

NATIONAL

Active Parenting Publishers 1-800-825-0060
810 Franklin Court, Suite B
Marietta, GA 30067
book and video kits on parenting skills

Faber/Mazlish Workshops, LLC 1-800-944-8584
Dept. 103A   FAX: 914-967-8130
P.O. Box 37   customer counselor 914-967-8130
Rye, NY 10580
workbooks, audio tapes, video tapes from the book *How to Talk
So Kids will Listen and Listen So Kids Will Talk*

S.T.E.P., Systematic Training for Effective Parenting
Early Childhood S.T.E.P 1-800-328-2560
ags@skypoint.com
www.agsnet.com

METRO AREA

Early Childhood Consultation Center, The 301-593-5992
Irene Shere, Director
11506 Michale Court
Silver Spring, MD 20904
workshops and support groups on child development topics such as anger
management, creative discipline, challenging children, and separation issues

Family Education Network, Inc. 301-888-1020
P.O. Box 318   1-800-888-1020
Brandywine, MD 20613   FAX: 301-888-1474
parenting classes in DC, MD, and VA

Ivymount School, The 301-469-0223
11614 Seven Locks Road
Rockville, MD 20854
workshops for parents concerning special needs children

Montgomery Child Care Association, Inc. 301-946-1213
Training Institute
2730 University Blvd. West, Suite 616
Wheaton, MD 20902
parenting classes on-site

National Educational Consulting Services 301-983-4033
P.O. Box 1572
Rockville, MD 20849
parenting classes

Parent Encouragement Program (P.E.P.) 301-929-8824
FAX: 301-929-8834
parenting and family relationship classes and workshops based on the
teachings of psychologist Alfred Adler; payment plan and scholarships

Stern, Judith, M.A. 301-424-1941
205 Watts Branch Parkway
Rockville, MD 20850
classes and workshops on ADD, LD

Television Project, The 301-588-4001
2311 Kimball Place   76507.1755@compuserve.com
Silver Spring, MD 20910   http://www.tvp.org
workshops for parents and educators on television and children;
newsletter, *Beyond TV*

DISTRICT OF COLUMBIA

Early Childhood Consultation Center, The 301-593-5992
Irene Shere, Director
11506 Michale Court
Silver Spring, MD 20904
workshops and support groups on child development topics such as anger
management, creative discipline, challenging children, and separation issues

Georgetown University Medical Center 202-342-2400
2233 Wisconsin Avenue, NW, Suite 317
Washington DC 20007
S.T.E.P. (Systematic Training for Effective Parenting) parenting classes;
parenting seminars

Jewish Social Service Agency 202-887-1644
parent classes and support groups for parents

Lab School of Washington, The 202-965-6600
workshops on LD, ADD/ADHD

MARYLAND

Affiliate Community Counselors, Inc. 301-251-8965
50 West Montgomery Avenue, Suite 110
Rockville, MD 20850

Bethesda Young Services 301-229-1347
workshops for parents of children of all ages

Awakening Spirit 301-656-6420
parenting classes

Child Care Management Resources 301-897-8272
5620 Greentree Road
Bethesda, MD 20817

Childcare Management Solutions 301-248-0358
9300 Livingston Road, Suite 205
Fort Washington, MD 20744
workshops for parents

Ciardi, Charmaine, Ph.D. 301-365-5929
Parent-Child Development Services
8203 Woodhaven Blvd.
Bethesda, MD 20817
workshops on child development issues

Commission for Women Counseling and Career Center 301-279-1800
255 North Washington Street, 4th Floor
Rockville, MD 20850
workshops for mothers based on Adele Faber book *How to Talk So Kids
Will Listen and Listen So Kids Will Talk*

Community Psychiatric Center 301-656-5220
8311 Wisconsin Avenue   301-933-2402
Bethesda, MD 20814
parenting groups, separation workshops, counseling; private, non-profit

Early Childhood Consultation Center, The 301-593-5992
Irene Shere, Director
11506 Michale Court
Silver Spring, MD 20904
workshops and support groups on child development topics such as anger
management, creative discipline, challenging children, and separation issues

Even Start Family Learning Center 301-808-8106
H. Winship Wheatley Special Center
8801 Ritchie Drive
Capital Heights, MD 20743
parent education for adults with low literacy skills with a child between
ages of birth and 7 years

Families Foremost Center 301-585-3424
1109 Spring Street, Suite 300
Silver Spring, MD 20910
community-based center that offers support to young families and their
children; parenting classes; peer support

Family Education Center of Southern Maryland 301-705-8527
P.O. Box 537
Waldorf, MD 20604
parent education classes

Family Education Network, Inc. 301-888-1020
P.O. Box 318   1-800-888-1020
Brandywine, MD 20613   FAX: 301-888-1474
parenting classes in DC, MD, and VA

Family Education of Southern Maryland 301-705-8527
parenting classes

Family Services Agency 301-840-2000
640 East Diamond Avenue
Gaithersburg, MD 20895
parenting classes

Family Works Home Visitor Program, The 301-424-5666
   Child Care Connection
   332 W. Edmonston Drive
   Rockville, MD 20852
      parent educators from Montgomery County visit homes to teach "Parents
      as Teachers" curriculum to economically or educationally-disadvantaged
      families who have at least one child age birth to 3; bi-lingual; professional
      referral or self-referral

Goldman, Linda 301-942-6440
   Center for Loss and Grief Therapy
   10400 Connecticut Avenue, Suite 514
   Kensington, MD 20895
      grief and loss workshops for children and parents

Head Start 301-230-0676
      federally funded preschool programs for 3 and 4 year olds;
      located in public schools; parent education

Health Quest, Inc. 410-869-0454
   9 Newburg Avenue   FAX: 410-869-0452
   Catonsville, MD 21228
      child development courses; coping with ADD courses

HUG (Helping Understanding Grow) 301-299-5513
   Sandra C. Burt, M.A.T., and Linda J. Perlis, M.A.
   8200 Gainsboro Court
   Potomac, MD 20854
      parenting lectures

Jewish Community Center of Greater Washington 301-881-0100
   6125 Montrose Road   301-230-3759
   Rockville, MD 20852
      parent and child classes

Jewish Social Service Agency
   22 Montgomery Village Avenue, Gaithersburg 301-990-6880
   6123 Montrose Road, Rockville 301-881-3700
      parent classes and support groups for parents

LifeWork Strategies, Inc. 301-309-1466
   710 East Gude Drive
   Rockville, MD 20850
      parent education classes

Maryland Committee for Children 410-752-7588
   608 Water Street
   Baltimore, MD 21202
      parent training and lectures

Montgomery County Parenting Education and Family Support Programs 301-929-2025

Montgomery Child Care Association, Inc. 301-946-1213
    Training Institute
    2730 University Blvd.,West, Suite 616
    Wheaton, MD 20902
        parenting classes on-site

Mother Voyage, The
    Lisa Makstein, L.C.S.W. 301-963-5696
    Marlin Zipin, Ph.D 301-899-4733
        workshops for mothers

Mustafa Counseling Services 1-800-876-1123
    Diana Z. Mustafa, M.A.   301-890-7416
    3009 Memory Lane
    Silver Spring, MD 20904
        parenting skills workshops

National Educational Consulting Services 301-983-4033
    P.O. Box 1572
    Rockville, MD 20849
        parenting classes

National Institute of Relationship Enhancement, The (NIRE) 301-986-1479
    William Nordling, Ph.D., Director   FAX: 301-986-1479
    4400 East-West Hwy, Suite 28
    Bethesda, MD 20814
        parent education; child play therapy

PACT (Parents and Children Together) 410-721-7719
    1657 Crofton Parkway
    Crofton, MD 21114
        parent education classes

Parent Care, Inc. 1-800-224-3893
    Scott Buehler, Director   301-770-CARE
    6239 Executive Boulevard   www.parentcare.com
    Rockville, MD 20852   drscott@parentcare.com
        Confident Parenting workshops and retreats

Parent Connection, Inc. 301-320-2321
    5606 Knollwood Road
    Bethesda, MD 20816

Parent Education Centers, Parent Line 301-942-8304
    classes offer education, information, and support for parents

Parent Education Network of Montgomery County .301-424-3747
    monthly parent education and network meetings

Parent Education Program (PEP), Montgomery County 301-929-2155
    parent education classes; free program for children birth through age 5
    with developmental delays

PARENT RESOURCES

Parent Encouragement Program (P.E.P.) 301-929-8824
    The Family Encouragement Center, 10100 Connecticut Avenue, Kensington   FAX: 301-929-8834
    Good Shepherd Lutheran Church, 16420 Westland Drive, Gaithersburg
    Marvin Memorial United Methodist Church, 33 E. University Blvd, Silver Spring
    Oneness School, 6701 Wisconsin Avenue, Chevy Chase
        non-profit educational organization sponsoring parenting and family
        relationship classes and workshops based on the teachings of psychologist
        Alfred Adler; payment plan and scholarships

Parenting Resource Centers 301-424-5566
    Children's Resource Center 301-279-8497
        332 W. Edmonston Drive, Room D-4, Rockville
    Connecticut Park Center 301-929-2037
        12518 Greenly Street, Room 10, Silver Spring
    New Hampshire Estates 301-431-7690
        8720 Carroll Avenue, Room 104, Silver Spring
    Sally K. Ride Elementary School 301-601-0360
        21301 Seneca Crossing Drive, Rm 2, Germantown
    Strawberry Knoll Elementary 301-840-4508
        18820 Strawberry Knoll Rd, Rm 13, Gaithersburg

        Parent-Child Drop-In Program where parents and young children and parents
        play and learn together with a parent educator on-site; parenting classes

Parent University
    Germantown Children's Center 301-353-1202
        19400 Crystal Rock Drive, Germantown
    Kentlands Children's Center 301-590-7355
        10 Kent Garden Circle, Gaithersburg
    Olney Children's Center 301-924-5919
        17717 Prince Phillip Drive, Olney

        free parenting workshops; free babysitting

Play Pals 301-596-2504
    Bonnie Bricker, M.S.
    7431 First League
    Columbia, MD 21046
        parenting classes; parent and child classes up to age four; classes in
        Columbia, Ellicott City, and Laurel

Project Family Outreach 301-656-5220
        parenting classes for parents of children with special needs

Shady Grove Adventist Hospital 301-279-6529
    parent education, grandparent classes

VIRGINIA

Active Parenting 703-237-3854
4829 N. 29th Street
Arlington, VA 22207
    seven-week classes to improve parenting skills

Center for Therapy and Education, The 703-442-7723
7700 Leesburg Pike, Suite 113
Falls Church, VA 22043
    parenting skills classes

Early Childhood Consultation Center, The 301-593-5992
Irene Shere, Director
11506 Michale Court
Silver Spring, MD 20904
    workshops and support groups on child development topics such as anger
    management, creative discipline, challenging children, and separation issues

Fairfax County Mental Health Centers
Mt. Vernon Center for Community Mental Health 703-360-6910
    8119 Holland Road, Alexandria
Northwest Center for Community Mental Health 703-481-4100
    1850 Cameron Glen Drive, Reston
Woodburn Center for Community Mental Health 703-573-0523
    3340 Woodburn Road, Annandale

    parenting classes on child development, tantrums, etc.

Fairfax County Parenting Education Center 703-506-2221
    parent education classes

How to Talk So Kids Will Listen and Listen So Kids Will Talk 703-536-4364
3560 N. Nottingham Street
Arlington, VA 22207
    seven-week course teaching parents positive communication skills

Jewish Social Service Agency
7345 McWhorter Place, Annandale 703-750-5400
12523 Lalwyers Road, Herndon 703-750-5400
    parent classes and support groups for parents

Northern Virginia Family Service 703-533-9727
100 N. Washington Street, #400
Falls Church, VA 22046
    parent education; parent support groups; speakers

Parent Education Network Support Group of Northern Virginia 703-548-8083
    support groups with speakers   703-841-5133

Parent Encouragement Program (P.E.P.) 301-929-8824
Montessori School of McLean
1711 Kirby Road
McLean, VA 22101
    non-profit educational organization sponsoring parenting and family relationship
    classes and workshops based on the teachings of psychologist Alfred Adler

Parenting Education Center, Fairfax County Public Schools 703-846-8670
    Parenting Education Center   703-846-8600
    3705 Crest Drive   703-846-8739
    Annandale, VA 22003
        parenting classes covering over 30 topics; free brochure
    SPEAKERS 703-846-8670
        bi-lingual speakers (Spanish, Korean, and Vietnamese) for schools
    PROJECT IMPACT Parenting Series 703-846-8600
        free community-sponsored parenting series
    WORK & FAMILY SEMINARS 703-846-8739
        workplace seminars for business, schools, and government agencies   ext. 64

Parenting Education Resource Center 703-358-7214
    Clarendon Education Center   703-358-7215
    2801 Clarendon Blvd, Suite 306   703-358-7216
    Arlington, VA 22201
        parenting seminars; free directory of parenting programs in
        Arlington County

Parenting 2000
    Terri Crosby 703-406-4471
    Bill Sanda 202-862-8514
        parenting classes

Parent University
    Fair Lakes Children's Center 703-818-9002
        4750 Rippling Pond Drive, Fairfax
    Franklin Barn Children's Center 703-264-9078
        3005 Dower House Drive, Herndon
    McNair Farms Children's Center 703-713-0093
        2487 McNair Farms Road, Herndon
        free workshops; free babysitting

PATHFINDERS, Inc. 703-239-2750
        parent education workshops

Project Impact 703-846-8600
    Falls Church, Fairfax, Reston, Mount Vernon   press 64
        free community-sponsored parenting classes offered by Fairfax County

SCAN (Stop Child Abuse Now of Northern Virginia)
    Parent Nurturing Program 703-836-1820
        parents and children attend together and learn parenting skills; training to
        groups interested in running their own programs

Weiss, Sharon K., M.D. 703-356-5534
    1420 Beverly Rd., Sutie 300
    McLean, VA 22101
        workshops for parents

Women's Center, The 703-281-2657
    133 Park Street, N.E.
    Vienna, VA 22180
        parenting classes

PARENT RESOURCES

MULTI-CULTURAL, MULTI-LINGUAL PARENT EDUCATION

See also **MENTAL HEALTH RESOURCES: Counseling Centers, Multi-cultural**
PARENT RESOURCES: Parent Info, Multi-cultural

National

California Department of Education 1-800-995-4099
parenting videos available in Spanish

Multicultural Education Training and Advocacy, Inc. (META) 617-628-2226
240A Elm Street, #22   FAX: 617-628-0322
Sommerville, MA 02145
advocacy for immigrant youth from low-income households; training for
parents and teachers

Virginia

ACAP (Arlington Community Action Program) 703-358-4732
Hispanic parent education classes

ESOL/HILT 703-358-6095
multi-lingual parent education classes offered by Arlington Public Schools;
bi-lingual resource assistants available as liaison between school and families

Foreign-born Parent Network 703-812-8716
2700 N. Wakefield Street
Arlington, VA 22207
workshops for parents and children dealing with intercultural skills

"Multicultural Parenting," Virginia Channel 25 Cable TV
Korean program descriptions . . . . .703-846-8763, press 2
Middle Eastern program descriptions . . . . .703-846-8760, press 2
Spanish program descriptions . . . . .703-846-8760, press 2
Vietnamese program descriptions . . . . .703-846-8761, press 2

Parenting Education Center, Fairfax County Public Schools 703-846-8670
3705 Crest Drive   703-846-8600
Annandale, VA 22003   703-846-8739
parenting classes covering over 30 topics; free brochure
SPEAKERS 703-846-8670
bi-lingual speakers (Spanish, Korean, and Vietnamese) for schools

Project Family 703-358-5694
parenting classes for Hispanics at different Arlington locations

Strengthening Families 703-358-4904
703-358-5130
10-session course to help Hispanic families deal with conflicts of
dual cultures

SPECIAL NEEDS PARENT EDUCATION

See also **PARENT RESOURCES: Consultants, Special Needs**
PARENT RESOURCES: Parent Info, Disabled Children

Parent Advocacy Training

See also **GENERAL RESOURCES: Advocacy Groups**

NATIONAL

PACER, Parent Advocacy Coalition for Educational Rights
PACER Center
4826 Chicago Avenue, South
Minneapolis, MN 55417
help for parents of children with disabilities; to order publications catalog,
send request to above address

METRO AREA

Creating Opportunities for Parent Empowerment (COPE) .202-543-6482
300 I Street, NE, Suite 112   FAX: 202-543-6682
Washington, DC 20002
parent training on the rights of children with special needs

MARYLAND

Parent Educational Advocacy Training Centers (PEATC)
Montgomery County Public Schools 301-657-4969
Prince Georges County Public Schools 301-731-4571

VIRGINIA

Parent Educational Advocacy Training Center (PEATC) 703-691-7826
Cherie Takemoto, Executive Director   1-800-869-6782
10340 Democracy Lane, Suite 206
Fairfax, VA 22030
parent advocacy training project for special needs; consultations; workshops

Parent Education Classes

DISTRICT OF COLUMBIA

ARC (Association for Retarded Citizens) Childcare Center 202-636-2956
        parenting classes

Lab School of Washington, The 202-965-6600
        4759 Reservoir Road, NW
        Washington, DC 20007
            workshops on LD, ADD/ADHD

MARYLAND

Health Quest, Inc. 410-869-0454
        9 Newburg Avenue   FAX: 410-869-0452
        Catonsville, MD 21228
            child development courses; coping with ADD courses

Ivymount School, The 301-469-0223
        11614 Seven Locks Road
        Rockville, MD 20854
            workshops for parents concerning special needs children

Parenting: The Family and the Child with Learning Disabilities 301-652-2820
        ten week course for parents

Project Team 301-984-5792
        Rockville, MD
            training for parents of children with mental, physical, and emotional
            disorders

Special Education Parent Information and Training Center
        Bethesda, MD 301-657-4969

VIRGINIA

Special Education Parent Resource Center 703-358-7238
        Clarendon Education Center   703-358-7239
        2801 Clarendon Blvd, Suite 304
        Arlington, VA 22201
            support and education for parents and staff of children with disabilities;
            newsletter; phone consultations; library

PARENT RESOURCES

Parent Information and Support

See also GENERAL RESOURCES: Computer Resources
GENERAL RESOURCES: Government Information and Resources
GENERAL RESOURCES: Resource Guides
HEALTH CARE RESOURCES: Health Information and Resources
MENTAL HEALTH RESOURCES: Mental Health Information
CHILD CARE AND SCHOOL RESOURCES: Educational Information
PARENT RESOURCES: Computer Online Services

ADOPTION

National

AASK (Adopt a Special Kid) 415-543-2275
2201 Broadway, Suite 702   FAX: 510-451-2023
Oakland, CA 94612

***Adoptive Families* Magazine** 1-800-372-3300
bi-monthly magazine published by Adoptive Families of America   612-645-9955

Adoptive Families of America (AFA), Inc. 1-800-372-3300
2309 Como Avenue
St. Paul, MN 55108
Guide to Adoption available

International Family Alliance (IFA) 713-454-5018
P.O. Box 16248
Houston, TX 77222
information for biracial families; newsletter

National Adoption Center 1-215-925-0200
Adoption Work Benefits policies 1-215-735-9988
Adopting a child with special needs 1-800-862-3678
1500 Walnut Street, Suite 701
Philadelphia, PA 19107

National Adoption Information Clearinghouse 703-352-3488
P.O. Box 1182   http://www.calib.com/naic
Washington, DC 20013
free publications; comprehensive library of adoption materials

National Resource Center for Special Needs Adoption .810-443-7080
16250 Northland Drive, Suite 120
Southfield, MI 48075
information and resources for adoption of special needs children

North American Council on Adoptable Children 612-644-3036
970 Raymond Avenue, Suite 106
St. Paul, MN 55114
conference for adoptive parents of special needs children

"How Can I Help My Child?" Early Childhood Resource Directory

195

Roots & Wings Adoption Magazine 908-637-8828
P.O. Box 577 FAX: 908-637-4259
Hackettstown, NJ 07840 adoption@interactive.net
quarterly publication focusing on all aspects of adoption

Metro Area

Adoption and Infertility Counseling 202-234-6483
3000 Connecticut Avenue, NW
Washington, DC 20008
family issues with adoption

Adoption Information, Montgomery County, MD 301-217-1641

Adoption Resource Center, Inc. 410-377-8975
international adoptions; personal service and attention

Adoption Service Information Agency, Inc.
7720 Alaska Avenue, NW, Washington, DC 202-726-7193
8555 16th Street, Suite 200, Silver Spring, MD 301-587-7068
adoption counseling and support; cultural events

Adoptive Family Network, Inc. 301-984-6133
P.O. Box 7 1-410-353-0889
Columbia, MD 21045
organization of adoptive families and professionals that provides support
and education to prospective adopters and to adoptive families; seminars,
newsletter

Adoption Resource Group 703-440-5771
support and education group for adoptive parents to explore the
relationships and challenges of adoption; meets fourth Sunday of the month

Adoptions Together 301-439-2900
Center for Adoptive Families
10230 New Hampshire Avenue, Suite 200
Silver Spring, MD 20903
counseling and educational workshops for adoptive families

American Adoption Agency 202-638-1638
1228 M Street, NW, 2nd Floor FAX: 202-638-1543
Washington, DC 20005
support through newsletter, referral, and hotline services

Arlington County Adoption 703-358-5085
Department of Human Services
Arlington, VA

ASIA Family and Friends 202-726-7193

Barker Foundation, The 301-229-8300
7945 MacArthur Blvd., Suite 206 202-363-7751
Cabin John, MD 20818
serving adoptive families since 1945; continuing education on adoption

Catholic Charities Maternity Counseling and Adoption Services 1-800-CARE-002
19 W. Franklin Street   410-659-4050
Baltimore, MD 21201

Center for Adoptive Families 301-439-2900
support and services for adoptive families

Children in Common 410-719-0939
support group for families with Eastern European children

Children's Adoption Support Services 202-362-3264
3824 Legation Street, NW
Washington, DC 20015
support services for adoptive families with special needs children

Children's Choice Inc. 1-800-LA-CHILD
adoptions of children from Latin America and Asia

Cradle of Hope Adoption Center 301-587-4400
8630 Fenton Street, Suite 310   FAX: 301-588-3091
Silver Spring, MD 20910

Datz Foundation, The
16220 Frederick Road, Gaithersburg, MD 301-258-0629
4545 42nd Street, NW, Suite 302, Washington, DC. 202-686-3400
404 Pine Street, #202, Vienna VA 703-242-8800

Families Adopting Children Everywhere (FACE) 410-488-2656
P.O. Box 28058, Northwood Station
Baltimore, MD 21239
adoption classes, magazine, support groups

Families Like Ours (FLO) 202-488-3967
700 Seventh Street, SW, #827
Washington, DC 20024
support and activities for families with Korean children

Families for Private Adoption 202-722-0338
P.O. Box 6375
Washington, DC 20015
support, workshops, newsletter

Families for Russian and Ukrainian Adoption 703-560-6184

Families with Open Adoptions Support Group 301-598-3690

Interracial Family Circle (IFC) 301-384-6826
support group for interracial families; monthly meetings, transracial
adoption workshops; newsletter: *Collage*

Jewish Adoptive Families 301-622-4757
social activities, support group

Jewish Social Service Agency 301-881-3700
 6123 Montrose Road, Rockville, MD 301-881-3700
 22 Montgomery Village Avenue, Gaithersburg, MD 301-990-6880
 7345 McWhorter Place, Annandale, VA 703-750-5400
  support for adoptive families

Latin America Parents Association (LAPA), Maryland Chapter 301-431-3407
 P.O. Box 4403
 Silver Spring, MD 20904
  information and activities for families with Latin American children, newsletter

Project Succeed 301-439-2900
  support groups for adoptive parents whose children have special needs;
  division of Adoptions Together

Single Adoptive Parents
 Margie Carpenter 202-208-4881
 3322 South 2nd Street
 Arlington, VA 22204
  support group and classes for single adoptive parents and for singles
  considering adoption

World Child, Inc. 301-588-3000
 9300 Columbia Blvd.
 Silver Spring, MD 20910
  adoptions from Eastern Europe, Asia, Latin America

AFRICAN-AMERICAN FAMILIES

Afro-American Counseling 301-589-5707
 8121 Georgia Avenue
 Silver Spring, MD 20910
  counseling, psychotherapy; children 2-5 and up and adults

This is My Child 301-588-4435
  "the newsletter for African-American parents who care"

Mocha Moms 301-322-8190
 Jolene Ivy, Editor
  quarterly newsletter for African-American stay-at-home mothers

National Black Child Development Institute 1-800-556-2234
 1023 15th Street, NW, Suite 600   202-387-1281
 Washington, DC 20005   FAX: 202-234-1738
  information for parents and providers; publications; advocacy; quarterly
  publication "Child Advocate"

PARENT RESOURCES

198   "How Can I Help My Child?" Early Childhood Resource Directory

ALLERGY AND ASTHMA

See also HEALTH CARE RESOURCES: Pediatricians, Allergists
HEALTH CARE RESOURCES: Nutritionists

National

Allergy & Asthma Network/Mothers of Asthmatics, Inc. 1-800-878-4403
non-profit organization that offers parents information on how to manage
and control asthma and allergies

Allergy Control Products 1-800-422-DUST
anti-allergy products

Allergy Information Referral Line 1-800-822-ASMA
American Academy of Allergy, Asthma & Immunology 1-800-822-ASMA
611 East Wells Street   414-272-6071
Milwaukee, WI 53202   http://www.aaai.org/

American College of Allergy, Asthma & Immunology 847-427-1200
85 West Algonquin Road, Suite 550   http://allergy.mcg.edu/
Arlington Heights, IL 60005

National Asthma Center
1400 Jackson Street, P.O. Box 61269
Denver, CO 80206

National Asthma Education and Prevention Program
National Heart, Lung and Blood Institute Information Center
P.O. Box 30105   http://www.nhlbi.nih.gov/nhlbi/nhlbi.htm
Bethesda, MD 20824

Metro Area

Allergy & Asthma Network/Mothers of Asthmatics,Inc. 703-385-4403
3554 Chain Bridge Road, Suite 200   http://www.podi.com/health/aanma/
Fairfax, VA 22030
non-profit organization that offers parents information on how to manage
and control asthma and allergies

Developmental Delay Registry 301-652-2263
Kelly Dorfman, nutritionist
Patricia Lemer, counselor
6701 Fairfax Road
Chevy Chase, MD 20815
counseling on nutrition and behavior

Feingold Association of the Washington Area 703-524-5566
P. O. Box 6550
Alexandria, VA 22306
controlling hyperactivity through diet management

Food Allergy Network 703-691-3179
10400 Eaton Place, Suite 107   fan@worldweb.net
Fairfax, VA 22030   http://www.foodallergy.org
> non-profit organization to provide education and support to families dealing
> with food allergies

Healthy Spaces 1-800-290-4436
> inspection and consultation for an allergy-free home

ASIAN-AMERICAN FAMILIES

See also   **GENERAL RESOURCES: Helplines, Multi-cultural Helplines**
            MENTAL HEALTH RESOURCES: Counseling Centers, Multi-cultural
            PARENT RESOURCES: Parent Education Classes, Multi-cultural
            PARENT RESOURCES: Parent Info, Multi-cultural

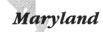

District of Columbia

Korean Community Service Center 202-882-8270
7720 Alaska Avenue, NW
Washington, DC 20012

Maryland

Korean Family Counseling and Research Center 301-949-5902
10914 Georgia Avenue
Wheaton, MD 20902
> counseling for young children and families; Koreans only

Montgomery County Public Schools
Counseling Center 301-230-0675
Parent Center 301-230-0674
ESOL/Bilingual Parent Services 301-231-5930
> counseling services in Spanish, Chinese, Vietnamese, Cambodian, Russian,
> French, Yiddish, Hindi, and Korean

Virginia

Center for Multicultural Human Services 703-533-3302
Fairfax County Services
701 W. Broad Street, Suite 305
Falls Church, VA 22046
> serving children and families in fifteen languages; counseling for young
> children; reduced fee or free services for eligible individuals

Korean Community Service Center 703-354-6345
7610 New Castle Drive
Annandale, VA 22003

ATTENTION DEFICIT DISORDER (ADD)
ATTENTION DEFICIT HYPERACTIVITY DISORDER (ADHD)

See also **PARENT RESOURCES: Parent Education Classes, Special Needs**
INDEX, Special Needs

National

ADD Warehouse 1-800-233-9273
300 NW 70th Avenue
Plantation, FL 33317

Attention Deficit Information Network (AD-IN) 617-455-9895
475 Hillside Avenue
Needham, MA 02194

Attention Deficit Disorders Association (ADDA)
4300 West Park Blvd.
Plano, TX 75093

Children and Adults with Attention Deficit Disorder (C.H.A.D.D.) 1-800-233-4050
499 N.W. 70th Ave   954-587-3700
Plantation, FL 33317
mail service for information requests

Feingold Association of the United States 703-768-FAUS
P.O. Box 6550
Alexandria, VA 22306
non-profit parent organization offering drug-free solutions for ADD;
information on controlling hyperactivity through diet management

Hyperactive Helpline 703-524-5566

National Attention Deficit Disorder Association (NADDA) 1-800-487-2282
P.O. Box 488
West Newbury, MA 01985
parent support group

National Information Center for Children and Youth with Disabilities 1-800-695-0285
P.O. Box 1492   202-884-8200
Washington, DC 20013   FAX: 202-884-8441
nichy@aed.org

PARENT RESOURCES

Metro Area

A.D.D. Concerned Parents Network 301-515-7739

ADHD/LD Counseling Services Helpline 703-849-9476
        sponsored by Virginia Pediatric Group

Feingold Association of the Washington Area 703-524-5566
        P.O. Box 6550
        Alexandria, VA 22306
            non-profit parent organization offering drug-free solutions for ADD;
            information on controlling hyperactivity through diet management

District of Columbia

Children and Adults with Attention Deficit Disorder (C.H.A.D.D.)
        District of Columbia 301-493-4159
            support groups for children and adults with attention deficit disorders

Maryland

Children and Adults with Attention Deficit Disorder (C.H.A.D.D.)
        Anne Arundel County 410-721-5376
        Baltimore 410-377-0249
        Catonsville, Ellicott City 410-655-4544
        Carroll County, Owings Mills 410-876-8615
        Frederick County 301-845-2801
        Harford County 410-838-8534
        Laurel 301-498-2162
        Montgomery County 301-869-3628
        Rockville 301-231-8602
        Southern Maryland 301-884-7061
            support groups for children and adults with attention deficit disorders

Virginia

Children and Adults with Attention Deficit Disorder (C.H.A.D.D.)
        Virginia C.H.A.D.D. 703-641-5451
        Arlington, Alexandria 703-525-1683
        Fredericksburg 703-720-5410
        Northern Virginia 703-641-5451
            support groups for children and adults with attention deficit disorders

Loudoun ADHD Parent Teacher Support Group 703-771-8010
                                                                                                              703-882-4133

PARENT RESOURCES

AUTISM

Autism Society of America 1-800-3-AUTISM
    7910 Woodmont Avenue, Suite 650   301-657-0881
    Bethesda, MD 20814
        list of local autism groups

Autism Society of America, Montgomery County 301-652-3912

Autism Research Institute 619-281-7165
    4182 Adams Avenue
    San Diego, CA 92116
        research into autism and nutrition

Carl Pfeiffer Treatment Center
    1804 Center Point Drive
    Naperville, IL 60540
        research into autism and nutrition

National Society for Children and Adults with Autism 202-783-0215
    1234 Massachusetts Avenue, NW, Suite 1017
    Washington, DC 20005

BEDWETTING

American Enuresis Foundation 918-627-8656
    P.O.Box 33061
    Tulsa, Oklahoma 74153
        send self-addressed, stamped business envelope for information about
        bed-wetting

CANCER

American Cancer Society 1-800-ACS-2345
    District of Columbia 202-483-2600
    Montgomery County, MD 301-933-9350
    Potomac, MD 301-261-6000
    Northern Virginia 703-938-5550

Cancer Information Hotline 1-800-4-CANCER

Candlelighters Childhood Cancer Foundation
    1312 19th Street, N.W., Suite 200, DC 1-800-366-2223
                                      FAX: 202-659-5136
    7910 Woodmont Avenue, Suite 460, Bethesda, MD 301-657-8401
        education and support for children with cancer and for their families

Special Love, Inc. 540-667-3774
    117 Youth Development Court
    Winchester, VA 22602
        year-round programs for cancer patients from birth to 25

PARENT RESOURCES

CEREBRAL PALSY

See also **PARENT RESOURCES: Parent Info/Support, Special Needs**

United Cerebral Palsy of Southern Maryland 410-263-9600
Mitzi Bernard, Executive Director
1616 Forest Drive, Suite 5
Annapolis, MD 21403

United Cerebral Palsy of Washington and Northern Virginia 202-269-1500
Family Support Services
Stanley Pryor, Executive Director
3135 8th Street, NE
Washington, DC 20017
short term loans of donated wheelchairs, walkers, etc.; respite care;
temporary relief from caring for a family member with a disability

CHALLENGING CHILDREN

Parenting the Difficult Child 703-569-1768
meets twice monthly

Parents Supporting Parents 301-424-0656
parents of children with emotional, behavior, and mental disorders

Support Groups for Parents of Challenging Children 301-593-5992
The Early Childhood Consultation Center
11506 Michale Court
Silver Spring, MD 20904
support groups, workshops for parents of challenging children

CHILD ABUSE PREVENTION

See also **GENERAL RESOURCES: Helplines, HOTLINES**
MENTAL HEALTH RESOURCES: Counseling Centers
MENTAL HEALTH RESOURCES: Information and Resources

National

American Professional Society on the Abuse of Children 312-554-0166
407 South Dearborn Street, Suite 1300   FAX: 312-554-0919
Chicago, IL 60605   APSACMems@aol.com
professional resource for those affected by child abuse and neglect; journal,
professional networking

National Committee to Prevent Child Abuse 1-800-244-5373
332 S. Michigan Avenue, Suite 1600   312-663-3520
Chicago, IL 60604   FAX: 312-939-8962
                                                                            HN2655@handsnet.org

National Coalition on Domestic Violence 202-638-6388

Parents Anonymous, Parents Stressline 909-621-6184
parent support, crisis intervention and referral service;   FAX: 909-625-6304
"breaking the cycle of abuse for generations"   HN3831@handsnet.org

District of Columbia

Child Abuse Reporting 202-727-0995

Parents Anonymous, Parents Stressline 909-621-6184
parent support, crisis intervention and referral service;   FAX: 909-625-6304
"breaking the cycles of abuse for generations"   HN3831@handsnet.org

PARENT RESOURCES

Maryland

Child Abuse Reporting
Montgomery County 301-217-4417
Prince George's County 301-699-8605

Intra-Familial Sexual Abuse Resource Directory 410-893-3857
Clinical Committee of the Central Maryland Sexual Abuse Task Force
sexual abuse resource directory for Anne Arundel, Baltimore, Cecil, Carroll,
Frederick, Harford, and Howard Counties

Parents Anonymous, Parents Stressline, in Maryland .1-800-243-7337
Baltimore metro area 410-243-7337
733 West 40th Street, Suite 20   FAX: 909-625-6304
Baltimore, MD 21211   HN3831@handsnet.org
Montgomery County, upcounty 301-963-4138
Montgomery County, downcounty 301-565-8272
Self-help and Supportive Listening Groups Hotline 301-738-2255
(24-hour anonymous listening service)
parent support, crisis intervention and referral service;"breaking the cycle
of abuse for generations"

Virginia

Child Abuse Reporting
Alexandria 703-838-0800
Arlington County 703-358-5100
Fairfax County 703-324-7400

Parents Anonymous, Parents Stressline 909-621-6184
parent support, crisis intervention and referral service;   FAX: 909-625-6304
"breaking the cycles of abuse for generations   HN3831@handsnet.org

SCAN (Stop Child Abuse Now of Northern Virginia), Parent Nurturing Program . . .703-836-1820
parents and children attend together and learn parenting skills;
training to groups interested in running their own programs

DEATH AND BEREAVEMENT

National

Children's Hospice International 1-800-24-CHILD
901 N. Washington Street, Suite 700
Alexandria, VA 22314

Compassionate Friends 312-323-5010
P.O. Box 3696   708-990-0010
Oak Brook, IL 50422
support groups for parents whose child has died; will locate local groups;
information available

Life and Loss, A Guide to Help Grieving Children 1-800-222-1166
Linda Goldman, M.S., author
counseling guide to help grieving children; national and local resources

National Hospice Organization 1-800-658-8898
1901 N. Moore Street, Suite 910
Arlington, VA 22209
education and support for dealing with dying

Metro Area

Bereaved Parents, Jewish Social Service Agency 301-881-3700

Center for Loss and Grief Therapy 301-942-6440
Goldman, Linda, M.S.
Zinner, Ellen, Psy.D.
10400 Connecticut Avenue, Suite 514
Kensington, MD 20895
grief and loss therapy with parents and children; Goldman is author of *Life
and Loss, A Guide to Help Grieving Children* (call 1-800-222-1166 to order)

Compassionate Friends Trinity Presbyterian Church 202-244-1026
support in grief resolution of death of a child

Grief Therapy Workshops 301-588-3225
Melinda Salzman, M.S.W.

Holy Cross Resource Institute 301-754-7742
9805 Dameron Drive
Silver Spring, MD 20910
bereavement support group for children coping with death of a family
member or friend; no fee

Montgomery Hospice 301-279-2566

Montgomery Hospice Society 301-951-9009

Shady Grove Adventist Hospital 301-469-6222
        support for infant death and stillborn

Steven Daniel Jeffreys Foundation Grief Counseling Service 410-997-4884
        5430-F Lynx Lane, Suite 256
        Columbia, MD 21044
        grief counseling with professionals

Washington Home, The 202-895-0124
        support for children and families who are grieving

DIABETES

American Diabetes Association 202-331-8303
                                                    703-549-1500

Juvenile Diabetes Foundation 202-371-0044
        parent-to-parent counseling

Juvenile Diabetes Foundation International 1-800-223-1138
        120 Wall Street, 19th Floor   http://www.jdfcure.com
        New York, NY 10005

DISABLED AND/OR CHRONICALLY ILL CHILDREN

See also **CHILD CARE AND SCHOOL RESOURCES: Child Care Special Resource,**
     Sick Children, Respite Care
     CHILD CARE AND SCHOOL RESOURCES: Schools, Special Needs
     PARENT RESOURCES: Parent Education Classes: Special Needs

National Information

ABLEDATA 1-800-588-9284
    8455 Colesville Road, Suite 935   301-588-9284
    Silver Spring, MD 20910
        database listing more than 15,000 commercial products for people with dis-
        abilities

Americans with Disabilities Act Information Center .1-800-949-4232
    2111 Wilson Blvd., Suite 400   703-525-3268
    Arlington, VA 22201

Association for the Care of Children's Health 301-654-6549
    7910 Woodmont Avenue, Suite 300
    Bethesda, MD 20814
        publications for helping children and families cope with hospitalization;
        some coloring books for ages 2 to 5

Clearinghouse on Disability Information 202-205-8241

Clearinghouse for Rehabilitation and Technology 1-800-638-8864
        information referral service for disabled persons, including young children

Council for Exceptional Children 703-629-3660
    1920 Association Drive
    Reston, VA 22091
        clearinghouse for information and resources about disabilities of all types

Disability Information 202-205-8241

Exceptional Parent, Parenting Your Child or Young Adult
    ***with a Disability* Magazine** 1-800-247-8080
    Exceptional Parent
    P.O. Box 3000, Dept. EP
    Denville, NJ 07834
        monthly magazine for families and professionals

Flaghouse 1-800-793-7900
    150 North MacQuestion Parkway, Suite 95083
    Mt. Vernon, NY 10550
        products, such as toys and games, adapted for children with disabilities

National Information Center for Children and Youth with Disabilities 1-800-695-0285
    P.O. Box 1492   FAX: 202-884-8441
    Washington, DC 20013   nichcy@aed.org
        free research and information   http://www.aed.org.nichcy

PARENT RESOURCES

National Parent Network on Disabilities 703-684-6763
1727 King Street, Suite 305   FAX: 703-836-1232
Alexandria, VA 22314
information for parents on disabilities

Pediatric Projects, Inc. 818-705-3660
P.O. Box 571555
Tarzana, CA 91357
medically-oriented therapeutic toys and books for children coping with
illness, hospitalization, and disability

Sick Kids Need Involved People (SKIP) 301-261-2602
216 Newport Drive
Severna Park, MD 21146
information and education for families coping with a child's special medical
care

Specialized Training of Military Parents (STOMP) 206-588-1741
12208 Pacific Highway, SW
Tacoma, WA 98499
information to military families on disabilities and available services

Special-Needs Collection Catalog, The 1-800-843-7323
Woodbine House
6510 Bells Mill Road
Bethesda, MD 20817
free catalog of books for parents, providers, and teachers of children with
disabilities, such as LD, visual and hearing impairments, ADD, Tourette's
Syndrome, epilepsy, etc.

Tomorrow's Child 609-354-9106
Daycare for Medically Dependent Children
Barklay Pavilion West, Suite 203B
Cherry Hill, NJ 08034
information on national centers providing medical care and education

Toy Guide for Differently-Abled Kids 703-684-6763
National Parent Network on Disabilities
1727 King Street, Suite 305
Alexandria, VA 22314
free guide to toys, games, etc., for children with special needs

Metro Area

Coordination Center for Home and Community Care, Inc. 301-621-7830
P.O. Box 613, Brightview Business Center
Millersville, MD 21108
home care monitoring for chronically ill children in Baltimore and
Washington areas

District of Columbia

Family Friends Department of Community Action
Ann King 202-387-4434
> part of Easter Seals; information and referral for parents with chronically ill
> and/or disabled children; trains citizens to work with children for
> companionship and brief respite care

Parent to Parent Programs of DC 202-232-2342
Easter Seal Society
2800 13th Street, NW
Washington, DC 20009
> matches families of newly diagnosed children with disabilities to similar
> families

Maryland

Family Friends Department of Community Action
Ann King 202-387-4434
> part of Easter Seals; information and referral for parents with chronically ill
> and/or disabled children; trains citizens to work with children for
> companionship and brief respite care

Family Friends Project 301-649-2158
Silver Spring, MD   301-635-5949
> non-professional support for chronically ill or disabled children through
> weekly visits to the home

Governor's Office for Individuals with Disabilities 410-333-3098
1 Market Center
300 W. Lexington Street, Box 10
Baltimore, MD 21201

Noyes Children's Library 301-929-5533
> Irene Briggs works with parents and adults involved with children for
> outreach to children who can't easily attend libraries

Project Team 301-984-5792
Rockville, MD
> training for parents of children with mental, physical, and emotional
> disorders

Virginia

Family Friends Department of Community Action
Betty Buchanan, VA 703-324-5607
> part of Easter Seals; information and referral for parents with chronically ill
> and/or disabled children; trains citizens to work with children for
> companionship and brief respite care

PARENT RESOURCES

DIVORCE AND SEPARATION

See also MENTAL HEALTH RESOURCES: Counseling Centers
MENTAL HEALTH RESOURCES: Mental Health Practitioners
PARENT RESOURCES: Parent Info, Single Parents
PARENT RESOURCES: Parent Info, Stepfamilies

National

Association for Children for the Enforcement of Support (ACES) 1-800-537-7072
parent education on ways to obtain child support

Child Support Collection Services, Inc. 703-266-1000
collection agency for past due child support payments

Family Matters . . . . .http://www.montana.edu/wwwpb/home/divorce.html
helping children adjust to divorce

Fathers United for Equal Rights 703-451-8580
P.O. Box 1323   301-927-7638
Arlington, VA 22210
support groups for fathers and second wives, girlfriends, sisters, and grandparents involved in separation and divorce

Mothers without Custody 1-800-457-MWOC
self-help group for women living apart from one or more of their children

Parents without Partners 1-800-637-7974
                                                                                        1-800-638-8078
international organization with six Washington area chapters

District of Columbia

Children of Separation and Divorce Support Group 202-589-3209
Dr. Dolores Cummings, DC Public Schools, Cluster 5
support groups restricted to DC residents

Parents without Partners 202-638-1320

Pro-Se-Plus Divorce Clinic 202-879-1010
DC Superior Court
500 Indiana Avenue, NW, Room 4230
Washington, DC 20001
classes that help unrepresented litigants better understand legal aspects of
divorce; by DC Bar Public Service

Separated and Divorced Catholics of the Archdiocese of Washington 301-961-2432
support groups for adults, regardless of religion

Maryland

Center for Divorcing Families 301-840-2004
    640 E. Diamond Avenue, Suite A, Gaithersburg   301-840-2006
    10335 Kensington Parkway, Kensington
        education and support for separating and divorcing families;
        works with Family Services Agency

Children of Separation and Divorce Center
    2000 Century Plaza, Suite 121, Columbia, MD 410-740-9553
    2400 Research Blvd, Suite 202, Rockville, MD 301-384-0079
        services for families dealing with separation and divorce

Child Support Recovery Services 301-770-5437
    1749 Rockville Pike, Suite 300
    Rockville, MD

Commission for Women Counseling and Career Center 301-279-8301
    255 North Washington Street, 4th Floor   301-279-1800
    Rockville, MD 20850   TDD: 301-279-1034
        workshops on separation and divorce; Displaced Homemaker Program
        (for women 30 yrs or older who have lost all or part of their income)
        provides counseling and training; divorce adjustment counseling.

Community Psychiatric Clinic 301-656-5220
    8311 Wisconsin Avenue, Bethesda 301-933-2402
    15944 Luanne Drive, Gaithersburg 301-840-9636
        "Make It Work: Workshop for Divorcing Families"

Family Center for Mediation and Counseling 301-946-3400
    3514 Plyers Mill Road
    Kensington, MD 20895

Fathers United for Equal Rights 301-927-7638
    P.O. Box 1323
    Arlington, VA 22210
        support groups for fathers and second wives, girlfriends, sisters, and grand-
        parents involved in separation and divorce

Lifebridge Family Mediation 301-215-7933
    7104 Exfair Road
    Bethesda, MD 20814
        divorce, custody, and family conflict resolution; male and female
        co-mediation team

Mothers without Custody, Montgomery County 301-890-6159
        self-help group for women living apart from one or more of their children

New Beginnings 301-384-0111
    Carol Randolph
    13129 Clifton Road
    Silver Spring, MD 20904
        provides support for separated and divorced adults

Rainbows 301-270-6777
    Sligo Seventh-Day Adventist Church   FAX: 301-270-3518
    7700 Carroll Avenue
    Takoma Park, MD 20912
        support groups for young children dealing with separation and divorce

Single Again Programs 410-721-2313
    Brad Mauzy
    Prince of Peace Presbyterian Church
    1657 Crofton Parkway
    Crofton, MD
        support and education for parents and children experiencing separation or
        divorce

Single Parents Raising Kids (SPARK) 301-340-8047
    Rockville 301-598-6395
    Rockville 301-774-4127
    P.O. Box 1631, Wheaton 301-598-6395
        weekly programs of family, social, and education events for single parents
        with at least one child under 18

Virginia

Alexandria Mediation 703-684-7677
        services to help families cope with conflict, separation, custody; blended
        families

Children Cope with Parental Separation, Northern Virginia Family Service 703-533-9727
    Alexandria, Baileys Crossroads, Dale City, Falls Church, Herndon,
    Leesburg, and Manassas
        four hour educational seminar for parents dealing with separation and
        divorce

Conflict ReSolutions 703-385-3383
    10617 Judicial Drive, Suite 101
    Fairfax, VA 22030
        mediation for family issues

Coping of Northern Virginia 703-533-3632
    Alan Meagher
    120 West Greenway Boulevard
    Falls Church, VA 22046
        six- and nine-week programs for parents coping with divorce

Divorce Anonymous
    Falls Church 703-573-3808
    Reston and Leesburg 1-800-777-8855
        12-step program for parents going through divorce

Divorce Mediation Services 703-318-0937
    12110 Sunset Hills Road
    Reston, VA 20190

Family Dynamics Institute 703-691-8547
9302 Swinburne Court
Fairfax, VA 22031
parent education seminars for separating and divorcing parents; mediation
services also available; variable fee

Fathers United for Equal Rights 703-451-8580
P.O. Box 1323
Arlington, VA 22210
support groups for fathers and second wives, girlfriends, sisters, and
grandparents involved in separation and divorce

Helping Children Cope with Divorce 703-476-4500
Kids Cope 703-968-4000
Northwest Center for Community Mental Health and Reston Community Center
2310 Colts Neck Road
Reston, VA 20190
support and educational groups for divorced parents concerning how to
raise their children; groups for children ages 4 to 7

Women's Center, The 703-281-2657
133 Park Street, NW
Vienna, VA 22180
workshops on coping with divorce

PARENT RESOURCES

DOWN'S SYNDROME

See also **PARENT RESOURCES: Parent Info/Support, Special Needs**

Down's Syndrome Society Hotline 1-800-221-4602

Parents of Children with Down's Syndrome 1-800-435-7309
11600 Nebel Street, Rockville, MD 301-984-5777
3358 Annandale Road, Falls Church, VA 703-451-6328

EMOTIONALLY DISTURBED CHILDREN

National

National Alliance for the Mentally Ill 1-800-950-6264
2102 Wilson Blvd, Suite 302   703-524-7600
Arlington, VA 22201

U.S. Dept. of Health and Human Services
Substance Abuse and Mental Health Services Administration 1-800-789-1763
    free information and materials on symptoms of mental illness in children;
    resources for families

Metro Area

Alliance for Mentally Ill Children and Adolescents (AMICA) 301-229-7811

Children and Youth with Serious Emotional Problems
A Guide for Families Seeking Help
    Maryland Mental Health Association 301-235-1178

Parents Supporting Parents 301-424-0656
    parents of children with emotional, behavior, and mental disorders

Prince George's County Family Home Intervention .301-817-3235
    in-home services to children and families with serious psychiatric problems

Project Team 301-984-5792
    Rockville, MD
        training for parents of children with mental, physical, and emotional
        disorders

PARENT RESOURCES

EPILEPSY

National

Epilepsy Foundation of America 1-800-332-1000
    4351 Garden City Drive   301-459-3700
    Landover, MD 20785

Metro Area

Epilepsy Association of Maryland 1-800-492-2523
    Lee Kingham, Executive Director   410-828-7700
    Hampton Plaza, Suite 1103
    300 East Joppa Road
    Towson, MD 21286

Epilepsy Foundation of the National Capital Area 202-638-5229

PARENT RESOURCES

FATHERS

 *National*

At-Home Dad 508-684-7931
    Peter Baylies, publisher   Athome-dad@aol.com
    61 Brightwood Avenue
    North Andover, MA 01845
        quarterly newsletter for stay-at-home dads; lists of names and phone
        numbers of at-home dads in 35 states

Marguerite Kelly's Family Almanac
    Marguerite Kelly, author
    Fireside
    Rockefeller Center
    1230 Avenue of the Americas
    New York, NY 10020
        helpful guide to navigating through everyday issues of fathering;
        extensive bibliography; area bookstores and libraries

Maryland

DADS (Dads Advising Dads) 301-217-4453

Father Focus 301-718-0402
    5480 Wisconsin Avenue, Suite 220   FAX: 301-589-1414
    Chevy Chase, MD 20815
        support group for fathers; newsletter

Virginia

At-Home Dad's Networking Group 703-430-9123
    at-home dads in northern Virginia

Fathers United for Equal Rights 703-451-8580
    P.O. Box 1323   301-927-7638
    Arlington, VA 22210
        support groups for fathers and second wives, girlfriends, sisters, and
        grandparents involved in separation and divorce

FOSTER CARE

National

National Foster Care Resource Center 313-487-0374
Eastern Michigan University   FAX: 313-487-0284
102 King Hall
Ypsilanti, MI 48197
   resource and information center for foster care parents

National Foster Parent Association 713-467-1850
Information and Services Office
226 Kilts Drive
Houston, TX 77024
   information and services relevant to foster care

Metro Area

For Love of Children 202-462-8686
   foster care services for children ages birth to 21

Helping Children Grow 202-546-4064
   foster care services for children ages birth to 21

Maryland

Boys and Girls Homes of MD 301-589-8444
   foster care service for children of all ages

Foster Care Homes, Montgomery County 301-217-1641

Virginia

Special Foster Care Program of Northern Virginia Family Service 703-533-2594
   foster parents for children with special needs; on-going training and support
   provided

GAY AND LESBIAN PARENTS

Gay/Lesbian Parents Coalition International 301-762-4828
five area chapters; national newsletter and annual conference; local chapters
meet once a month for families and also for parents with a parent education
facilitator

National Lesbian, Gay, and Bisexual Youth Organizations Directory 212-633-8920
Hetrick-Martin Institute
2 Astor Place
New York, NY 10003

National Federation of Parents and Friends of Gays 202-726-3223
8020 Eastern Avenue, NW
Washington, DC 20012

Parents and Friends of Lesbians and Gays (PFLAG) 202-638-4200
1012 14th Street, NW, Suite 700   301-439-3524
Washington, DC 20005

Project 10 213-651-5200
7850 Melrose Avenue
Los Angeles, CA 90046
information, support, resources pertaining to gay and lesbian parents; for
parents and teachers

PARENT RESOURCES

220   "How Can I Help My Child?" Early Childhood Resource Directory

GRANDPARENTS

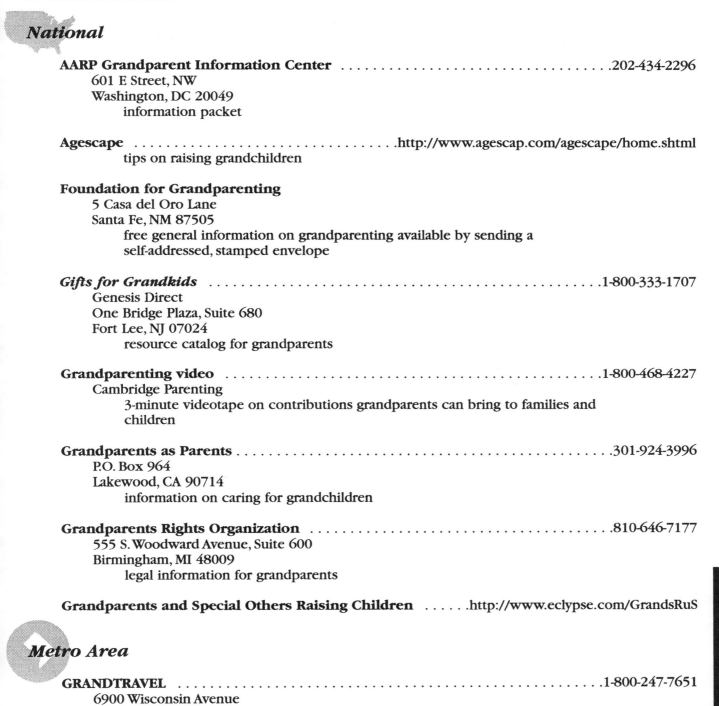

National

AARP Grandparent Information Center 202-434-2296
601 E Street, NW
Washington, DC 20049
information packet

Agescape . . . . .http://www.agescap.com/agescape/home.shtml
tips on raising grandchildren

Foundation for Grandparenting
5 Casa del Oro Lane
Santa Fe, NM 87505
free general information on grandparenting available by sending a
self-addressed, stamped envelope

Gifts for Grandkids 1-800-333-1707
Genesis Direct
One Bridge Plaza, Suite 680
Fort Lee, NJ 07024
resource catalog for grandparents

Grandparenting video 1-800-468-4227
Cambridge Parenting
3-minute videotape on contributions grandparents can bring to families and
children

Grandparents as Parents 301-924-3996
P.O. Box 964
Lakewood, CA 90714
information on caring for grandchildren

Grandparents Rights Organization 810-646-7177
555 S. Woodward Avenue, Suite 600
Birmingham, MI 48009
legal information for grandparents

Grandparents and Special Others Raising Children . . . . . .http://www.eclypse.com/GrandsRuS

Metro Area

GRANDTRAVEL 1-800-247-7651
6900 Wisconsin Avenue
Chevy Chase, MD 20815
vacations for grandparents and grandchildren; fully escorted itineraries

PARENT RESOURCES

District of Columbia

Family Friends Department of Community Action
Ann King 202-387-4434
> part of Easter Seals; trains senior citizens to work with disabled and/or
> chronically ill children for companionship and brief respite care

Maryland

Family Friends Department of Community Action
Ann King 202-387-4434
> part of Easter Seals; trains senior citizens to work with disabled and/or
> chronically ill children for companionship and brief respite care

Shady Grove Adventist Hospital 301-279-6529
> grandparent classes

Virginia

Family Friends Department of Community Action
Betty Buchanan 703-324-5607
> part of Easter Seals; trains senior citizens to work with disabled and/or
> chronically ill children for companionship and brief respite care

Fathers United for Equal Rights 703-451-8580
P.O. Box 1323   301-927-7638
Arlington, VA 22210
> support groups for fathers and second wives, girlfriends, sisters, and
> grandparents involved in separation and divorce

Grandparents Raising Grandchildren 703-533-9727
Northern Virginia Family Service   703-533-9727
100 N. Washington Street, #400
Falls Church, VA 22046
> program for grandparents raising their grandchildren; newsletter, support
> groups, family outings

Grandparent Support Group 703-533-2548

HEARING-IMPAIRED CHILDREN

See also **HEALTH RESOURCES: Speech and Hearing Specialists**
MENTAL HEALTH RESOURCES: Mental Health Practitioners, Specialists: Special Needs

National

American Society for Deaf Children 301-585-5400
National Association of the Deaf   TTY: 301-585-5400
814 Thayer Avenue   nadhq@juno.com
Silver Spring, MD 20910

International Association of Parents of Deaf 202-337-5200
International Organization for the Education of the Hearing Impaired   TTY:202-337-5220
Alexander Graham Bell Association for the Deaf   agbell2@aol.com
3174 Volta Place, NW
Washington, DC 20007

National Association for Hearing and Speech Action .1-800-638-8255
10801 Rockville Pike
Rockville, MD 20852

National Crisis Center for the Deaf 1-800-466-9876
University of Virginia Medical Center   TTY: 1-800-466-9876
Charlottesville, VA 22908

National Information Center on Deafness 202-651-5051
Gallaudet University   TTY: 202-651-5052
7th Street and Florida Avenue, NE   mcoogan@gallua.gallaudet.edu
Washington, DC 20002

National Institute on Deafness and Other Communication Disorders
National Institutes of Health 1-800-241-1044
1 Communication Avenue   TTY: 1-800-241-2055
Bethesda, MD 20892
      produces an annual Directory of Information Resources
      (NIH Publication #96-3987)

TRIPOD Grapevine 1-800-352-8888
2901 N. Keystone Street
Burbank, CA 91504
      information and resources about raising a hearing-impaired child

PARENT RESOURCES

District of Columbia

Washington Hearing and Speech Center 202-244-4420
5255 Loughboro Road, NW
Washington, DC

Maryland

Maryland School for the Deaf 301-620-8500
101 Clarke Place, P.O. Box 250   TTY: 301-620-8555
Frederick, MD 21705   frederick@msd.edu

Virginia

Northern Virginia Resource Center for Deaf and Hard-of-Hearing Persons 703-352-9055
10359 Democracy Lane   TTY: 703-352-9057
Fairfax, VA 22030
information on audiologists, support groups, educational programs, videos,
etc., in northern Virginia for families with hearing-impaired children;
resource guide for services; monthly newsletter, *The Update*

***Resources for Parents of Deaf and Hard of Hearing Infants and Toddlers
in the Northern Virginia Area*** 703-352-9055
10359 Democracy Lane   TTY: 703-352-9056
Fairfax, VA 22030
handbook on support groups, educational programs, audiologists, videos,
etc.; free to parents of hearing- impaired children, $25 to others

PARENT RESOURCES

HOME SCHOOLING

National

Christian Home Educators Association
P.O. Box 2009
Norwalk, CA 90651

Christian Home Educators Network 410-744-8919
304 N. Beechwood Avenue
Catonsville, MD

Distance Education and Training Counsel 202-234-5100
1601 18th Street, NW
Washington, DC 20009
    an accrediting information service for home school

Home Education Magazine 509-486-2477
Home Education Press   FAX: 509-486-2628
P.O. Box 1083   http://www.home-ed-press.com
Tonasket, WA 98855   HomeEdMag@aol.com
    bimonthly magazine with articles and information on home schooling

Homeschooling Today 954-962-1930
ProServices
P.O. Box 5863
Hollywood, FL 33083
    magazine on home schooling

Home School Legal Defense Association 703-338-5600
Box 159
Paeonian Springs, VA 22129

Independent School Guide: Washington DC & Surrounding Area
Independent Schools Guides 301-986-5370
7315 Brookville Road   301-652-8635
Chevy Chase, MD 20815   301-986-0698
    home schooling information and listings for courses; area book stores or
    send $14.95 + $2.00 postage & handling

John Holt's Bookstore 617-864-3100
2269 Massachusetts Avenue   FAX: 617-864-9235
Cambridge, MA 02140
    bookstore established by the founder of home schooling; variety of books,
    videos, and home schooling materials

Parents as Teachers National Center, Inc. 314-432-4330
9374 Olive Blvd.   FAX: 314-432-8963
St. Louis, MO 63132
    home-school-community partnership for advocacy of parent education for
    parents with children birth through age 5

District of Columbia

Boiling Area Home Schoolers of DC
1516 Carswell Circle
Washington, DC 20336

Maryland

Maryland Association of Christian Home Education 301-663-3999
Box 1041
Emmitsburg, MD 21727

Montgomery Home Education Network 301-871-6431
      secular home schooling information and support, newsletter   301-831-8832

Virginia

Community of Independent Learners, The 703-780-2691
      secular group of home schooling families

Home Education Support Group 703-573-7121
      support group for families that home educate

Home Educators Association of Virginia 703-635-9322
P.O. Box 1810
Front Royal, VA 22630

Welcome 703-573-7121
      support group of home education families

PARENT RESOURCES

LATINO-AMERICAN FAMILIES

See also GENERAL RESOURCES: Helplines, HOTLINES, Multi-cultural
MENTAL HEALTH RESOURCES: Counseling Centers, Multi-cultural
PARENT RESOURCES: Parent Education Classes, Multi-cultural
PARENT RESOURCES: Parent Info, Multi-cultural

General Information

Andromeda, Spanish Hotline 202-722-1245

El Montgomery 301-309-0129
biweekly newspaper in Spanish

California Department of Education 1-800-995-4099
parenting videos available in Spanish

Maryland

English as a Second Language, Montgomery County Public Schools
Counseling Center 301-230-0675
Parent Cemter 301-230-0674

Virginia

Hispanics Against Child Abuse and Neglect
P.O. Box 1802
Falls Church, VA 22041

Hispanic Parents Association 703-524-2529
P.O. Box 1536   703-358-6239
Arlington, VA 22210

Parent to Parent 703-524-8222
4729 N. 20th Street
Arlington, VA 22204
support groups for Spanish-speaking parents; matches families for support

Project Family 703-358-5694
800 S. Walter Reed Drive, Fenwick Center
Arlington, VA 22204

Strengthening Families 703-358-4909
ten week parent education course for Hispanic parents   703-358-5130

PARENT RESOURCES

LEARNING DISABILITIES (LD)

See also MENTAL HEALTH RESOURCES: Mental Health Practitioners, Specialists: Special Needs
CHILD CARE AND SCHOOL RESOURCES: Mental Health Practitioners, Special Needs
PARENT RESOURCES: Parent Education Classes, Special Needs
PARENT RESOURCES: Parent Info, Special Needs

National

"Last One Picked, First One Picked On"; "Learning Disabilities and Discipline"; "How Difficult Can This Be?" Understanding Learning Disabilities
PBS Videos 1-800-328-7271
video for parents and professionals; $49.95 each

Learning Disabilities 301-443-4513
National Institute for Mental Health
5600 Fishers Lane, Room 7C02
Rockville, MD 20857
free information packet from NIMH

Learning Disabilities Association of America 412-341-1515
Jean Petersen
4156 Library Road
Pittsburgh, PA 15234
free information packet

National Children's Center 202-722-2300
information on programs and care for learning disabled children

National Center for Law and Learning Disabilities 301-986-1422

National Center for Learning Disabilities 212-545-7510
381 Park Avenue South, Suite 1420   FAX: 212-545-9665
New York, NY 10016
information packets; referrals to local and national resources; magazine

District of Columbia

Lab School of Washington, The 202-965-6600
4759 Reservoir Road, NW
Washington, D.C. 20007
speaker series on children with learning disabilities; workshops on
LD, ADD/ADHD

Learning Disabilities Association of DC 202-265-8869
Karen Brock
1848 Columbia Road, NW, #45
Washington, DC 20009
support and referrals to LD consultants

Maryland

Learning Disabilities Association of Maryland 410-484-0499
76 Cranbrook Road, Suite 300
Cockeysville, MD 21030

Learning Disabilities Association of Montgomery County 301-933-1076
P.O. Box 623
Rockville, MD 20848
support and referrals to LD consultants

Orton Dyslexia Society 1-800-222-3123
Chester Bldg, 8600 LaSalle Road, Suite 382   410-296-0232
Baltimore, MD 21204

Parenting: The Family and the Child with Learning Disabilities 301-652-2820
ten-week course for parents

Parents of Gifted/Learning Disabled Children 301-986-1422
support groups; monthly meetings; newsletter

Virginia

ADHD/LD Counseling Services Helpline 703-849-9476
Virginia Pediatric Group

Learning Disabilities Association of Virginia 703-569-3710
Kristen Otte   703-451-5007
8007 Daffodil Court
Springfield, VA 22152
support and referrals to LD consultants

LOW INCOME RESOURCES

See also HEALTH CARE RESOURCES: Information and Resources

MENTAL HEALTH RESOURCES: Information and Resources

CHILD CARE AND SCHOOL RESOURCES, Child Care Special Resources,
Scholarships, Sliding Fee

CHILD CARE AND SCHOOL RESOURCES, Schools: Private, Cooperative Schools,
Scholarships

National

Head Start 1-800-27-START
federally funded preschool programs for 3 and 4 year olds;
located in public schools

Multicultural Education Training and Advocacy, Inc. (META) 617-628-2226
240A Elm Street, #22   FAX: 617-628-0322
Sommerville, MA 02145
advocacy for immigrant youth from low-income households;
training for parents and teachers

VISION USA 1-800-766-4466
243 North Lindbergh Boulevard
St. Louis, MO 63141
referrals to local free eye care offered for low-income children; screenings in
January; sponsored by the American Optometric Association

District of Columbia

Catholic Charities Social Services 202-526-4100
1438 Rhode Island Avenue, NE
Washington, DC 20018
counseling families and children in need, regardless of race, creed, or origin

Head Start 202-645-3707
federally funded preschool programs for 3 and 4 year olds;
located in public schools

Jewish Social Service Agency 202-887-1644
1640 Rhode Island Avenue, NW
B'nai B'rith Building, Suite 534
Washington, DC 20036
sliding fee scale services for children and parents; non-sectarian; parent
counseling; ADD

Washington's CHILD Project (WCP) 202-966-7543
3031 Oregon Knolls Drive
Washington, DC 20015
directory of area parenting education programs and services for
economically disadvantaged, single parent families

Maryland

Arc, The, Family, Infant, and Child Care Center .301-279-2165
332 W. Edmonston Drive
Rockville, MD 20852
    childcare for children 6 weeks to 5 years, with and without medical
    conditions; sliding fee scale, nurse onsite; medicare and subsidies accepted

Catholic Charities Social Services 301-434-2550
1504 St. Camillus Drive
Silver Spring, MD 20903
    counseling for families and children in need, regardless of race, creed, or origin

Dental Health Clinic, Montgomery County 301-217-1875
    dental services for low-income families

Family Counseling Center, The 301-840-2000
Family Services Agency, Inc.
640 E. Diamond Avenue
Gaithersburg, MD 20895
    family counseling, parenting classes; fees based on a sliding scale

Families Foremost Center 301-585-3424
1109 Spring Street, Suite 300
Silver Spring, MD 20910
    Montgomery County program offering free child care and schooling for
    mothers age 26 and under, whose child is less than 4 years old; parenting
    classes; peer support; parent and child activities; toddler care offered free;
    home visits

Family Works Home Visitor Program, The 301-424-5666
Child Care Connection
332 W. Edmonston Drive
Rockville, MD 20852
    parent educators from Montgomery County visit homes to teach "Parents
    as Teachers" curriculum to economically or educationally-disadvantaged
    families who have at least one child aged birth to 3; bi-lingual; professional
    referral or self-referral

Head Start 301-464-5770
Montgomery County 301-320-0676
Prince George's County 301-985-1782
    federally funded preschool programs for 3 and 4 year olds;
    located in public schools

Health Care, Montgomery County
Colesville Health Center 301-989-1900
Care for Kids, Health and Human Services 301-217-1856
Silver Spring Community Clinic 301-585-1250
    pediatric care and income eligibility

PARENT RESOURCES

Jewish Social Service Agency

6123 Montrose Road, Rockville 301-881-3700
TDD 301-984-5662

22 Montgomery Village Avenue, Gaithersburg 301-990-6880
TDD 301-990-7215

sliding fee scale services for children and parents; non-sectarian; parent
counseling; ADD

Maryland K.I.S.S. (Kids in Safety Seats) 1-800-370-7328
discounted car seat rentals for low income families

Prince George's County Family Home Intervention 301-817-3235
in-home services to children and families with serious psychiatric problems

Therapistline 301-738-7176
Montgomery County referral helpline for individuals who have limited
or no financial resources for therapy; links people with mental health
professionals who accept a sliding scale fee; Wednesdays and Fridays only

Working Parents Assistance Program 301-217-1155
child care subsidies in Montgomery County

Virginia

Alexandria Child Health Clinic 703-838-4414
517 N. St. Asaph Street
Alexandria, VA 22314
physical exams for children ages 3 to 11; children with medicaid

Annandale Counseling Center 703-750-0692
7008-B Little River Turnpike
Annandale, VA 22003
scaled fees; parent workshops; developmental issues; family conflict; ADHD, LD

Catholic Charities Social Services
Arlington 703-841-2531
Fairfax County 703-841-2531
counseling families and children in need, regardless of race, creed, or origin

Center for Multicultural Human Services 703-533-3302
701 W. Broad Street, Suite 305
Falls Church, VA 22046
serving children and families in 15 languages; counseling for young children;
reduced fee or free services for eligible individuals

Head Start, Virginia 703-836-5774
Alexandria 703-768-9644
Annandale 703-846-8720
Bailey's Crossroads 703-820-2457
Fairfax County 703-324-8290
federally funded preschool programs for 3 and 4 year olds;
located in public schools

Jewish Social Service Agency
7345 McWhorter Place, Annandale 703-750-5400
12523 Lawyers Road, Herndon 703-750-5400
sliding fee scale services for children and parents; non-sectarian; parent
counseling; ADD

Northern Virginia Family Service
Alexandria 703-370-3223
Dale City 703-680-9358
Fairfax County 703-533-9727
Falls Church 703-533-9727
Herndon 703-689-0208
counseling and psychotherapy; sliding fee scale   TDD: 1-800-828-1120

Training for Single Parents and Displaced Homemakers .703-506-6415
free career counseling; vocational training and support groups

"How Can I Help My Child?" Early Childhood Resource Directory

233

PARENT
RESOURCES

MOTHERS

National

Marguerite Kelly's Family Almanac
Marguerite Kelly, author
Fireside
Rockefeller Center
1230 Avenue of the Americas
New York, NY 10020
helpful guide to navigating through everyday issues of mothering; extensive
bibliography; area bookstores and libraries

Mother's Almanac, Revised, The
Marguerite Kelly, author
Bantam Doubleday Publishing Group, Inc.
666 Fifth Avenue
New York, NY 10103
child rearing guide with extensive bibliography; area bookstores and
libraries

Mothers at Home 1-800-783-4666
largest national non-profit organization providing support and
encouragment for at-home mothers; publications; publishes monthly journal,
Welcome Home, complimentary copy; provides networking

National Association of Mothers' Centers 1-800-645-3828
336 Fulton Avenue
Hempstead, NY 11550
information on how to start a mothers' center; provides resources for
discussion groups and will connect to a local existing group

Metro Area

MOMS (Moms Offering Moms Support)
Beth Mendelson 301-754-2529
groups for moms; activities, babysitting coops, meetings; Mendelson is
regional coordinator for DC, MD, and VA

Maryland

Commission for Women Counseling and Career Center 301-279-1800
255 North Washington Street, 4th Floor
Rockville, MD 20850
workshops for mothers based on Adele Faber book *How to Talk So Kids
Will Listen and Listen So Kids Will Talk*

Frederick County Family Counseling Center 301-694-9002
groups for mothers of children birth through 5

Gatherings 301-365-8860
Gatherings helps keep moms connected to the world of adult ideas and
opinions

Middle-Aged Moms Support Group 301-279-1800
Commission for Women Counseling and Career Center
255 North Washington Street, 4th Floor
Rockville, MD 20850
monthly meetings of mothers over 40 with infants and toddlers

MOMS (Moms Offering Moms Support)
Pat Waters, Maryland coordinator 301-540-6309
Mary Siegler, North Potomac, Gaithersburg 301-762-4731
Bethesda Region 301-754-2529
mothers of children five and under; meetings, field trips, playgroups;
groups for moms, babysitting coops; guest speakers and panels

Mothers' Access to Careers at Home (MATCH) 703-205-9664
support group for mothers with a home-based business

Mother Support Group 301-588-3225
Melinda Salzman, M.S.W.
Silver Spring, MD
"Now That I'm a Mother...Who Am I Really?" support group for mothers of
children six months through elementary school

Mother Voyage, The
Lisa Makstein, L.C.S.W 301-963-5696
Marlin Zipin, Ph.D 301-899-4733
eight session workshop for women to explore the mothering process

PARENT RESOURCES

Virginia

MOMS (Moms Offering Moms Support)
Allison Roberts 540-786-7777
> groups for moms; activities, babysitting coops, meetings; Roberts is Virginia
> coordinator

Moms Club and Playgroup, Lake Ridge 703-491-2154
> parents of children five and under; meetings, field trips, playgroups   ext. 113

Mothers' Access to Careers at Home (MATCH) 703-205-9664
> support group for mothers with a home-based business

Mothers at Home 1-800-783-4666
> support group for stay-at-home mothers; publisher of two books;   703-827-5903
> monthly journal

Mothers First 703-827-5922
P.O. Box 1526   301-946-0592
Vienna, VA 22183
> support group for women interrupting careers to raise their children at
> home; also, groups for moms over 40

Mothers of Preschoolers (MOPS) 703-644-5859
Kathy Rossell 703-644-7608
> non-profit international support group for mothers with children ages infant
> through 6 yrs

Women's Center of Northern Virginia 703-281-2657
133 Park Street, NE
Vienna, VA 22180
> mother support groups

MULTICULTURAL RESOURCES

See also **MENTAL HEALTH RESOURCES: Counseling Centers, Multi-cultural**
PARENT RESOURCES: Parent Education Classes, Multi-cultural
PARENT RESOURCES: Parent Info, Asian-American Families, Latino-American Families
PARENT RESOURCES: Parent Resource Centers, Multi-cultural

National

Center for Research on Education, Diversity, and Excellence (CREDE) 408-459-3500
University of California at Santa Cruz
1156 High Street
Santa Cruz, CA 95064
publications of relevant research findings on diversity

Clearinghouse for Immigrant Education (CHIME) 617-357-8507
100 Boylston Street, Suite 737   FAX: 617-357-9549
Boston, MA 02116
educational materials for parents and schools

Multicultural Education Training and Advocacy, Inc. (META) 617-628-2226
240A Elm Street, #22   FAX: 617-628-0322
Sommerville, MA 02145
advocacy for immigrant youth from low-income households;training to
parents and teachers; conferences; policy

National Association for Bilingual Education 202-898-1829
1220 L Street, N.W.   FAX: 202-789-2866
Washington, DC 20005
addresses educational needs of language-minority students; conference;
newsletter, journal

National Association for Multicultural Education (NAME) 703-243-4525
2101A N. Rolfe Street   FAX: 202-296-6620
Arlington, VA 22209
programs that foster multicultural education; conferences, magazine

Sparkes, Louise Derman 818-397-1306
Leadership in Diversity Project
Pacific Oaks College
Pasadena, CA 91103
publications and videos on multi-cultural education

PARENT RESOURCES

Metro Area

Center for Multicultural Human Services 703-533-3302
701 W. Broad Street, Suite 305
Falls Church, VA 22046
serving families in fifteen languages; counseling for young children; sliding
fee; free for children

ESOL/Bilingual Parent Services, Montgomery County 301-231-5930

Interracial Family Circle (IFC) 301-384-6826
P.O. Box 53290   301-229-7326
Washington, DC 20009
support group for interracial families; monthly meetings, transracial
adoption workshops; newsletter: *Collage*

Korean Books at Libraries:
Fairland Library, Burtonsville, MD 301-421-5400
Gaithersburg Regional Library, Gaithersburg MD 301-840-2515
Rockville Regional Library, Rockville, MD 301-217-3800
Wheaton Library, Wheaton, MD 301-929-5520
White Oak Library, Silver Spring, MD 301-622-2492

"Multicultural Parenting," Virginia Channel 25 Cable TV
Korean program descriptions . . . . .703-846-8763, press 2
Middle Eastern program descriptions . . . . .703-846-8760, press 2
Spanish program descriptions . . . . .703-846-8760, press 2
Vietnamese program descriptions . . . . .703-846-8761, press 2

Naim Foundation 202-462-5715
3000 Connecticut Avenue, NW, Suite 136
Washington, DC 20008
multi-cultural counseling for Arabic speakers; psychological testing; family
therapy; child therapy

Strengthening Families 703-358-4904
10-session course to help Hispanic families deal with conflicts of dual   703-358-5130
cultures

PARENT
RESOURCES

PARENTS OF MULTIPLE BIRTHS

 National

Double Talk 513-231-8946
Karen Kerkof Gromada
Box 412, Dept. ND
Amelia, OH 45102
quarterly newsletter for parents and professionals who work with twins and
children of multiple births

Mothers of Twins Clubs 1-800-243-2276
12404 Princess Jeanne, NE
Albuquerque, NM 87112
referrals to local parents and clubs

Triplet Connection 209-474-0885
quarterly newsletter; referrals to local support groups   FAX: 209-474-2233

Twins 1-800-821-5533
Box 12045   1-800-328-3211
Overland Park, KS 66212   FAX: 303-290-9025
newsletter about twins

Maryland

KWYS Parent Group, Wheaton 301-933-2818
Thursday evening meetings on parenting

Mothers of Multiples Club, Annapolis 410-757-4456
P.O. Box 372
Arnold, MD 21012

Mothers of Multiples of Prince George's County 301-474-0469
Bonnie Randolph 301-317-4867

Mothers of Twins Club, Columbia 410-750-1322
P.O. Box 1915
Ellicott City, MD 21041

Parents of Multiples 301-649-7868
Parents of Multiples, Montgomery County 301-294-0014

Virginia

Mothers of Multiples, Fairfax County 703-715-MOMS
Mothers of Multiples, Loudoun/Fairfax 703-631-4058

Parents of Multiples, Northern Virginia 703-528-7667

PLAYGROUPS

Playgroup Connections 301-838-0098
> organizes playgroups for parents and childen ages infant to 5 years;
> free brochure

SIBLING RELATIONSHIPS

See also **MENTAL HEALTH RESCURCES: Counseling Centers**
MENTAL HEALTH RESOURCES: Mental Health Practitioners

Early Childhood Consultation Center, The 301-593-5992
Irene Shere, Director
11506 Michale Court
Silver Spring, MD 20904
> workshops and consultations on sibling relationships

SINGLE PARENTS

National

National Organization of Single Mothers 704-888-KIDS
P.O. Box 68   http://www.parentsplace.com/readroom/nosm
Midland, NC 28107
> network of single mothers; newsletter, *SingleMOTHER*

Parents without Partners 1-800-637-7974
> international organization with local chapters   1-800-638-8078

Single Mothers By Choice (SMC) 212-988-0993
P.O. Box 1642 Gracie Square Station
New York, NY 10023
> quarterly newsletter; local chapters

Metro Area

Single Adoptive Parents
Margie Carpenter 202-208-4881
3322 South 2nd Street
Arlington, VA 22204
> support group and classes for single adoptive parents and for singles
> considering adoption

District of Columbia

Parents without Partners 202-638-1320

Single Mothers By Choice (SMC), DC Chapter 703-237-1924
      support group and education program

Washington's CHILD Project (WCP) 202-966-7543
    3031 Oregon Knolls Drive
    Washington, DC 20015
        resources for at-risk, economically disadvantaged single parents; newsletter,
        directory of area parenting education programs and services

Maryland

New Beginnings 301-384-0111

Parents without Partners 301-588-9354

Project PRIDE 301-983-4200

Single Parents Raising Kids (SPARK) 301-340-8047
    Rockville 301-598-6395
    Rockville 301-774-4127
    P.O. Box 1631, Wheaton 301-598-6395
        weekly programs of family, social, and education events for single parents
        with at least one child under 18

Single Parents 301-598-4792
        support group for separated, divorced, widowed, abandoned, adoptive or
        never-married parents who have a child under the age of 18

Virginia

Fathers United for Equal Rights 703-451-8580
    P.O. Box 1323   301-927-7638
    Arlington, VA 22210
        support groups for fathers and other relatives involved in separation and
        divorce

Training for Single Parents and Displaced Homemakers 703-506-6415
        free career counseling, vocational training and support groups

SPECIAL NEEDS

See also HEALTH CARE RESOURCES: Pediatricians, Special Needs
MENTAL HEALTH RESOURCES: Mental Health Practitioners, Special Needs
CHILD CARE AND SCHOOL RESOURCES: Schools, Special Needs
PARENT RESOURCES: Consultants, Special Needs
PARENT RESOURCES: Parent Education Classes, Special Needs

National

ARC (Association for Retarded Citizens) 817-261-6003
P.O. Box 1047
Arlington, TX 76004

Council for Exceptional Children 1-800-845-6232
1920 Association Drive
Reston, VA 22091
clearinghouse for information and resources about disabilities of all types

Directory for Exceptional Children 617-523-1670
Porter Sargent Publishers, Inc. FAX: 617-523-1021
11 Beacon Street, Suite 1400
Boston, MA 02108
directory of more than 3,000 schools and summer programs nationwide
serving children with disabilities

Easter Seal Society 410-298-0991
Jesse Hall, President
3104 Timanus Lane, Suite 200
Baltimore, MD 21244
services for people with all disabilities

ERIC-Educational Resources Information Center 1-800-LET-ERIC
special needs resource http://www.cec.sped.org./ericec.htm

Federation for Children with Special Needs 617-482-2915
95 Berkeley Street, Suite 104
Boston, MA 02116
information about mental and physical disabilities

Muscular Dystrophy Association 1-800-572-1717

National Information Center for Children and Youth with Disabilities 1-800-695-0285
Box 1492
Washington, DC 20013

National Parent Network on Disability 703-684-6763
1600 Prince Street, Suite 15 FAX: 703-836-1232
Alexandria, VA 22314
information for parents on disabilities

PACER, Parent Advocacy Coalition for Educational Rights
PACER Center
4826 Chicago Avenue South
Minneapolis, MN 55417
help for parents of children with disabilities; to order publications catalog,
send to above address

Parents and Children Coping Together 1-800-788-0097
Joyce Kube, Executive director   804-225-0002
201 West Broad Street, Suite 503
Richmond, VA 23220

Special-Needs Collection Catalog, The 1-800-843-7323
Woodbine House
6510 Bells Mill Road
Bethesda, MD 20817
free catalog of books for parents, providers, and teachers of children with
disabilities, such as LD, visual and hearing impairments, ADD, Tourette's
Syndrome, epilepsy, etc.

Toy Guide for Differently-Abled Kids 703-684-6763
National Parent Network on Disabilities
1600 Prince Street, Suite 115
Alexandria, VA
free guide to toys, games, etc. for children with special needs

Maryland

Parent Education Program (PEP), Montgomery County .301-929-2155
free program for children birth through age 5 with developmental delays;
parent education classes

Parents Supporting Parents 301-424-0656
Mental Health Association of Montgomery County
support group for parents of children with special needs

Project Family Outreach 301-656-5220
parent education discussion groups for families with special needs

Project TEAM 301-984-5792
training courses for parents of children with special needs

Special Education Parent Information and Training Center 301-657-4969
Bethesda, MD

Special Needs Library 301-897-2212
6400 Democracy Blvd.   TDD: 301-897-2217
Bethesda, MD 20817

PARENT RESOURCES

Virginia

ARC (Association for Retarded Citizens) of Virginia, The .804-649-8481
Steve K. Waldron, Executive Director
6 North 6th Street, 4th Floor
Richmond, VA 23219

Fairfax County Mental Retardation Services 703-324-4400

Parent Educational Advocacy Training Center (PEATC) 703-691-7826
Cherie Takemoto, Executive Director   1-800-869-6782
10340 Democracy Lane, Suite 206
Fairfax, VA 22030
parent training information project; publications, workshops, consultations

Parent-Infant Education/PIE (Special Needs) 703-358-4564
1810 N. Edison Street
Arlington, VA 22207

Parent Resource Center, Fairfax County 703-204-3941
Dunn Loring Center   TDD: 703-204-3956
2334 Gallows Road, Room 224
Dunn Loring, VA 22027
resources for parents of children with disabilities

Parent to Parent 703-524-8222
816 S. Walter Reed Road
Arlington, VA
matches special needs family with an experienced support family to provide
info and emotional support for families with special needs children birth to
age 5; available in Spanish; free service

Special Education Parent Resource Center 703-358-7238
Clarendon Education Center   703-358-7239
2801 Clarendon Blvd, Suite 304
Arlington, VA 22201
support and education for parents and staff of children with disabilities;
newsletter; phone consultations; library

Special Foster Care Program of Northern Virginia Family Service 703-533-2594
foster parents for children with special needs; on-going training and support
provided

STEPFAMILIES

See also **PARENT RESOURCES: Parent Info, Divorce**

Stepfamily Association of America 1-800-735-0329
    215 Centennial Mall South, Suite 212
    Lincoln, NE 68508
        free information packet on building stepfamilies and referrals to stepparent-
        ing resources in your area

STUTTERING

See also **HEALTH CARE RESOURCES: Speech and Hearing Specialists**

American Speech-Language-Hearing Association 1-800-638-8255
    10801 Rockville Pike
    Rockville, MD 20852
        information on stuttering

National Center for Stuttering 1-800-221-2483

Stuttering Foundation of America 1-800-992-9392
    P.O. Box 11749
    Memphis, TN 38111
        support and information about stuttering; nationwide list of speech
        pathologists who specialize in stuttering

**PARENT
RESOURCES**

SUPPORT GROUPS

National

See also **MENTAL HEALTH RESOURCES: Counseling Centers**
MENTAL HEALTH RESOURCES: Mental Health Practitioners
PARENT RESOURCES: Parent Info, specific topics

Parents Anonymous 1-909-621-6184
lists of free local support groups for parents

Self-Help Resource Book, The 201-625-7101
American Self-Help Clearinghouse   http://www.cmhc.com/selfhelp
Northwest Covenant Medical Center
Denville, NJ 07834
$9 resource book; contacts for any national self-help group; will help
start a group

Metro Area

Directory of Self-Help Support Groups 703-838-7535
National Mental Health Association Information Center
1021 Prince Street
Alexandria, VA 22314
over 1200 listings of support groups in the Washington metro area; $30 plus
$5 shipping and handling

Maryland

Child Study Association of Maryland 410-526-4000
educational support to parents of children of all ages

Parents Anonymous, in Maryland 1-800-243-7337
help in locating a free local parent support group

Parent Education Network of Montgomery County 301-424-3747
Julie Liss
1003 Willowleaf Way
Potomac, MD 20854
organizes mothers in Montgomery County area into chapters for monthly
parent education/ network meetings in evenings

Project Family Outreach, Community Psychiatric Center, Inc. 301-656-5220
support groups

Parenting Resource Centers 301-929-2025
drop-in centers for families under guidance of a parent educator

Parent Support Groups 301-593-5992
The Early Childhood Consultation Center
Silver Spring, MD 20904
parent support groups

Virginia

Parent Education Network Support Group of Northern Virginia 703-548-8083
    support groups with speakers   703-841-5133

Parent Power 703-358-6400
    Lubber Run Recreation Center
    300 N. Park Drive
    Arlington, VA 22203
        parent and child activity groups

TOURETTE'S SYNDROME

See also **HEALTH CARE RESOURCES: Pediatricians, Neurologists**
            MENTAL HEALTH RESOURCES: Mental Health Practitioners

Tourette's Syndrome Association 1-800-237-0717
    42-40 Bell Blvd.
    Bayside, NY 11361

Tourette's Syndrome Support Group 301-474-1969
        for parents of children with Tourette's Syndrome and related disorders

PARENT RESOURCES

VISUALLY-IMPAIRED CHILDREN

See also HEALTH CARE RESOURCES: Optometrists and Visual Training

National

National Association for Parents of the Visually Impaired 1-800-562-6265
P.O. Box 317   617-972-7441
Watertown, MA 02272   FAX: 617-972-7444
      newsletter, conferences, networking for parents

Metro Area

Children's Hospital 202-884-3015
Ophthalmology Department
111 Michigan Avenue, NW
Washington, DC 20010

Maryland School for the Blind 410-444-5000
3501 Taylor Avenue
Baltimore, MD 21236

Prevention of Blindness Society of Metropolitan Washington 202-234-1010
1775 Church Street, NW
Washington, DC 20036

Virginia State Department for the Visually Handicapped 804-371-3140
337 Azalea Avenue
Richmond, VA 23227

WORKING PARENTS

MATCH, Inc., Mothers' Access to Careers at Home 703-764-2320
      networking, support and advocacy to entrepreneurial mothers   703-205-9664

PARENT RESOURCES

248   "How Can I Help My Child?" Early Childhood Resource Directory

Parent Resource Centers

See also **MENTAL HEALTH RESOURCES: Counseling Centers**
MENTAL HEALTH RESOURCES: Mental Health Information
PARENT RESOURCES: Parent Education Classes
PARENT RESOURCES: Parent Info, specific topics
PARENT RESOURCES: Parent Info, Multi-cultural

National

Children's Foundation 202-347-3300
725 15th Street, NW, Suite 505
Washington, DC 20005
parent resources

National Childcare Information Center 1-800-616-2242
301 Maple Avenue, West, Suite 602   703-938-6555
Vienna, VA 22180
information packets provided for child concerns

ZERO TO THREE 202-638-1144
National Center for Infants, Toddlers, and Families   FAX: 202-638-0851
734 15th Street, NW, Suite 1000   0-3@zerotothree.org
Washington, DC 20005
resource center for the first three years of life; info and support to parents
and professionals; training; books, posters

PARENT
RESOURCES

Maryland

Arc, The, Family, Infant, and Child Care Center 301-279-2165
332 W. Edmonston Drive
Rockville, MD 20852
> childcare for children 6 weeks-5 years, with and without medical
> conditions; sliding fee scale; nurse onsite; medicare and subsidies accepted

ESOL/Bilingual Parent Services, Montgomery County 301-231-5930
Families Foremost Center 301-585-3424
1109 Spring Street, Suite 300
Silver Spring, MD 20910
> community-based center that offers support to young families with their
> children birth through 3; parenting classes, peer support, parent/child
> activities and toddler care offered free; home visits

Family Works Home Visitor Program, The .301-424-5666
Child Care Connection
332 W. Edmonston Drive
Rockville, MD 20852
> parenting information and support for economically disadvantaged
> Montgomery County families with children from birth to three years of age

Montgomery County Public Schools
Counseling Center 301-230-0675
Parent Center 301-230-0674
> counseling services in Spanish, Chinese, Vietnamese, Cambodian, Russian,
> French, Yiddish, Hindi, and Korean

Parenting Education and Family Support Programs 301-929-2025

Parenting Resource Centers 301-424-5566
Children's Resource Center 301-279-8497
> 332 W. Edmonston Drive, Room D-4, Rockville
Connecticut Park Center 301-929-2037
> 12518 Greenly Street, Room 10, Silver Spring
New Hampshire Estates 301-431-7689
> 8720 Carroll Avenue, Room 104, Silver Spring
Sally K. Ride Elementary School 301-601-0360
> 21301 Seneca Crossing Drive, Rm 2, Germantown
Strawberry Knoll Elementary 301-840-4508
> 18820 Strawberry Knoll Rd, Rm 13, Gaithersburg

> Parent-Child Drop-In Program where parents and young children can play
> and learn together with a parent educator on-site; parenting classes

Parent Resource Centers
Montgomery County 301-840-4508
Prince George's County 301-805-2710

Virginia

Parent Educational Advocacy Training Center (PEATC) 703-691-7826
Special Education Parent Resource Center   1-800-869-6782
Fairfax County Public Schools
10340 Democracy Lane, Suite 206
Fairfax, VA 22030
          parent training information project;consultations; workshops

Parenting Education Center 703-846-8670
Family and Early Childhood Education Program   703-846-8720
Fairfax County Public Schools   703-846-8678
          parenting classes, resource library, workshops, at various locations

Parenting Education Resource Center 703-358-7214
Clarendon Education Center
2801 Clarendon Blvd., Suite 306
Arlington, VA 22201

Parent Resource Center, Fairfax County 703-204-3941
Dunn Loring Center   TDD: 703-204-3956
2334 Gallows Road, Room 224
Dunn Loring, VA 22027
          resource center for parents of children with disabilities

Special Education Parent Resource Center 703-358-7238
Clarendon Education Center   703-358-7239
2801 Clarendon Blvd, Suite 304
Arlington, VA 22201
          support and education for parents and staff of children with disabilities;
          newsletter; phone consultations, library

Work and Family Institute 703-358-7215
Clarendon Education Center
2801 Clarendon Blvd, Suite 306
Arlington, VA 22201
          info about parenting programs in Arlington County; free directory; parenting
          seminars available

PARENT
RESOURCES

Early Childhood Professional Resources

Resources for Child Care and Schools; Resources for Early Childhood Professionals

The Early Childhood Professional Resource section provides information and resources for child care centers and schools, as well as for EC professionals such as directors, teachers, aides, home-care providers, and specialists. Professionals from many fields who work with young children and their families will also find this section helpful.

"Child care" refers to homecare providers and daycare centers. "Schools" refers to preschools and Kindergartens.

EC PROFESSIONAL RESOURCES includes:

Child Care and School Resources

- **Child Care and Schools: Business Management Resources**
- **Child Care and Schools: Educational Resources**
- **Child Care and Schools: Licensing and Accreditation**

EC Professional Resources

- **Computer Resources for EC Professionals**
- **Conferences and Speakers Series**
- **Consultants for EC Professionals:** includes multi-cultural and special needs consultants
- **Courses: College Programs:** includes graduate and undergraduate programs
- **Courses: General Training:** includes general training, MD certification courses, and specialized training
- **Courses: Mentoring Programs and Training for Trainers**
- **Courses: Scholarships for EC Professionals**
- **Helplines for EC Professionals**
- **Organizations for EC Professionals**
- **Videos for EC Professionals**

The Table of Contents on the next page provides a detailed listing of this section.

Note:

Be sure to look in "Metro Area" when available. Metro Area resources are available throughout the entire Washington metropolitan area. These resources are not repeated in the separate District of Columbia, Maryland, and Virginia listings.

"How Can I Help My Child?" Early Childhood Resource Directory   253

PROFESSIONAL RESOURCES

Early Childhood Professional Resources
Table of Contents

Child Care and Schools: Business Management Resources .... .255
    Grant Resources .... .255
    Insurance .... .255
    Management and Operation .... .255
    Start-up Resources .... .257
    Tax Services .... .258
Child Care and Schools: Educational Resources .... .259
    Assessments for Children .... .259
    Computer On-site Services .... .260
    Curriculum .... .260
    Organizations .... .262
    Scholarship .... .263
Child Care and Schools: Licensing and Accreditation .... .264
    General Licensing .... .264
    Montessori School Accreditation .... .266
    NAEYC Accreditation .... .266
Computer Resources for EC Professionals .... .267
    Online Services .... .267
    Information and Resources .... .269
Conferences and Speaker Series .... .270
Consultants for EC Professionals .... .272
    General Child Care and School Consultants .... .272
    Cooperative Preschool Consultants .... .274
    Multi-cultural Consultants .... .274
    Reggio Emilia Preschool Consultants .... .274
    Special Needs Consultants .... .275
Courses: College Programs .... .277
    Graduate Programs .... .277
    Undergraduate Programs .... .279
Courses: General Training .... .282
    General EC Professional Courses .... .282
    Maryland Certification Courses .... .286
    Montessori School Training .... .287
    Reggio Emilia Preschool Training .... .287
Courses: Mentoring Programs and Training for Trainers .... .288
Courses: Scholarships For EC Professionals .... .289
Helplines for EC Professionals .... .290
Job Clearinghouses for EC Professionals .... .291
Organizations for EC Professionals .... .292
    General Organizations .... .292
    Cooperative Preschool Organizations .... .294
    Directors' Organizations .... .295
    Family Child Care Organizations .... .295
Publications for EC Professionals .... .296
    Books for EC Professionals .... .296
    Journals and Magazines for EC Professionals .... .297
    Library Resources for EC Professionals .... .299
    Newsletters for EC Professionals .... .300
Videos for EC Professionals .... .301

PROFESSIONAL RESOURCES

254   "How Can I Help My Child?" Early Childhood Resource Directory

Child Care and Schools:
Business Management Resources

See also EC PROFESSIONAL RESOURCES: Computer Resources
EC PROFESSIONAL RESOURCES: Child Care, Educational, Start-up Resources

GRANT RESOURCES

Department of Education Grant Information 1-800-USA-LEARN
Teacher's Guide   http://www.ed.gov/pubs/TeachersGuide/

Education Funding Research Council 703-528-1000
4301 North Fairfax Drive, Suite 875
Arlington, VA 22203

Foundation Center, The 202-331-1400
1001 Connecticut Avenue, NW
Washington, DC 20035

Kidsnet Media Guide & News 202-291-1400
Kidsnet   FAX: 202-882-7315
6856 Eastern Avenue, NW, Suite 208
Washington, DC 20012
Media Guide includes a section on grants and awards for educators

INSURANCE

Markel Insurance Company 1-800-431-1270
4600 Cox Road   804-527-2700
Glen Allen, VA 23060   FAX: 804-527-7966
insurance for child care providers and teachers

MediVault 1-800-317-5977
liability insurance for child care centers and schools

"How Can I Help My Child?" Early Childhood Resource Directory   255

PROFESSIONAL RESOURCES

MANAGEMENT AND OPERATION

National

Child Care 2000 1-800-875-5002
6543 "C" Commerce Parkway   614-793-2000
P.O. Box 1530
Dublin, OH 43017
computer software child care administration system

Day Care Providers Home Page . . . . .http://www.io.org/~dlukas
software for business aspects of running a day care

EZ-CARE 1-800-220-4111
Child Care Management System Demonstration Disk   215-628-0400
SofterWare
540 Pennsylvania Avenue, Suite 200
Fort Washington, PA 29034
management software

Maryland

Child Care Connection Computer Database 301-294-4858
listing of all legally-operating child care in Montgomery County; call to add
information or update free listing

TECHNIC: Child Care 1-800-766-4900
608 Water Street, Baltimore 410-752-7588
Prince Georges' County 301-772-8420
information and help regarding start-up and operation of either a family
daycare or a daycare center in Maryland

PROFESSIONAL RESOURCES

256   "How Can I Help My Child?" Early Childhood Resource Directory

START-UP RESOURCES

See also **CHILD CARE AND SCHOOL RESOURCES: Child Care Referrals**
EC PROFESSIONAL RESOURCES: Child Care and Schools, Licensing
EC PROFESSIONAL RESOURCES: Child Care, Educational, Organizations for Schools
EC PROFESSIONAL RESOURCES: Organizations for EC Professionals

Metro Area

Childcare Management Solutions 301-248-0358
9300 Livingston Road, Suite 205
Fort Washington, MD 20744
consultations for starting daycare business

Child Care Startup . . . . .http://www.accesone.com/~hitflu/daycare/
steps for starting a daycare

Children's Foundation 202-347-3300
725 15th Street, NW, Suite 505
Washington, DC 20005
help with daycare center start-up

National Cooperative Business Association 202-638-6222
Leta Mach   FAX: 202-628-6726
1401 New York Avenue, N.W., Suite 1100
Washington, DC 20005
video on starting a cooperative preschool

Maryland

Child Care Connection, Montgomery County 301-279-1773
Child Care Connection: Providers 301-294-4958
C.O.N.T.A.C.T. Child Care, Montgomery County 301-279-1260
Children's Resource Center   TDD: 301-217-1246
332 W. Edmonston Drive
Rockville, MD 20852
child care start-up information

Early Childhood Advisory Council (ECAC) 301-279-1260
332 West Edmonston Drive   FAX: 301-279-1296
Rockville, MD 20852
licensing help for daycare providers in Montgomery County

Prince George's County Child Care Resource Center .301-772-8420
9475 Lottsford Road, Suite 202   FAX: 301-772-8410
Landover, MD 20774   TDD: 301-772-8408
child care center start-up information; helps providers get licensed

TECHNIC: Child Care 1-800-766-4900
608 Water Street, Baltimore 410-752-7588
Prince Georges' County 301-772-8420
information and help regarding start-up and operation of either a family day-
care or a daycare center in Maryland

Cooperative Preschools

National Cooperative Business Association 202-638-6222
Leta Mach   FAX: 202-628-6726
1401 New York Avenue, N.W., Suite 1100
Washington, DC 20005
   video on starting and operating a cooperative preschool

Potomac Association of Cooperative Teachers (P.A.C.T.)
Irene Shere 301-593-5992
Jeanne Porter 703-941-9791
   organization of teachers and directors in DC, MD, and VA cooperative
   preschools; consultations on starting a cooperative reschool

Parent Cooperative Preschool International (PCPI) 1-800-721-PCPI
P.O. Box 90410
Indianapolis, IN 46290
Kirsten Rhoades 301-933-9840
   international organization of cooperative preschools; literature on starting
   and operating a cooperative preschool

TAX SERVICES

Bennett, Duane, CPA 410-347-8544
Severna Park, MD   410-647-6741
   accountant specializing in family child care businesses   FAX: 410-347-8469

Tax Break, Inc. 301-854-0972
Bob Carroll, CPA
8568 Dark Hawk Circle
Columbia, MD 21045
   accountant specializing in tax service for family day care providers

PROFESSIONAL RESOURCES

258   "How Can I Help My Child?" Early Childhood Resource Directory

Child Care and Schools: Educational Resources

ASSESSMENTS FOR CHILDREN

See also MENTAL HEALTH RESOURCES: Testing and Assessment

Behavioral Assessments

anser system, the
Editors Publishing Service, Inc.
75 Moulton Street
Cambridge, MA 02138
parent and teacher questionnaires for children ages 3-5 for assessing behavior

Balzer-Martin Preschool Screening Program (BAPS)
Lynn Balzer-Martin, Ph.D., OTR 301-654-1828
screening method for identifying possible developmental problems in
children ages 3, 4, and 5 years old; based upon a sensory integration model;
on-site screening available; $60 manual available from St. Columba's Nursery
School, 4201 Albemarle Street, NW, Washington, DC 20016

Psychological Assessment Resources
P.O. Box 998
Odessa, FL 33556
catalog for assessment tools for professionals

Work Sampling System 1-800-435-3085
P.O. Box 4479
Ann Arbor, MI 48106
assessment tools for in-class use; developmental screening instruments for
children ages 3-6

ZERO TO THREE:
National Center for Infants, Toddlers, and Families Publications Catalog 1-800-899-4301
Suite 1000   202-638-0840
734 15th Street, NW
Washington, DC 20005
publications on assessment

Vision and Hearing Tests

Maryland Vision and Hearing Testing, Inc.
Wendy Chansky 301-474-4198
Patty Reeley 301-439-2536
8009 Brett Place
Greenbelt, MD 20770
private testing service on-site for children ages 3 and up

COMPUTER ON-SITE SERVICES

Computer Kids 301-983-9600
    10324 Windsor View Drive   301-983-4965
    Potomac, MD 20854
        on-site computer courses for children ages 4 through 12

Computer Tutors 301-384-ABCD

Computertots 1-800-531-5053
        on-site computer instruction for schools and centers

Computertots 301-365-8687
        serving Montgomery and Frederick Counties

CURRICULUM

See also **EC PROFESSIONAL RESOURCES: Computer Resources**

Curriculum Resources

NATIONAL

Committee for Children 1-800-634-4449
        curriculum on early childhood issues, classroom issues, free catalog of
        materials, videos, etc.

Project Construct National Center 1-800-335-PCNC
    27 S. 10th Street, Ste 202   http://www.missouri.edu/~pcncwww
    Columbia, MO 65211
        resources for professional development; consultation to support
        developmentally appropriate practice

METRO AREA

Learning Foundations for Children 301-428-0542
    Ruby Neville, Director
    P.O. Box 5
    Germantown, MD 20875
        consultations with EC providers on curriculum

Curriculum Units

Colgate Bright Smiles, Bright Futures 1-800-334-7734
    JMH Communications
    1133 Broadway, Suite 1123
    New York, NY 10010
        multi-cultural oral health education program kit

Committee for Children 1-800-634-4449
        free info packet on *Second Step* and *Talking About Touching,*
        social skills curricula for pre-K to grade 9

Insect Lore . . . . .1-800-LIVE BUG
    P.O. Box 1535
    Shafter, CA 93263
        live nature kits featuring butterflies, earthworms, ladybugs, silkworms, ants,
        and frogs

Junior Chef's Program, "Kids Know Best" 1-800-SCHOLAS
        free Scholastic classroom kit with teaching materials and recipe contest

Polaroid's Child Care Activity Kit 1-800-678-8014
        instant photography as an effective teaching tool   ext. 300

Project Learning Tree (PLT) Curriculum 202-463-2462
    1111 19th Street, NW, Suite 780
    Washington, DC 20036
        environmental curriculum for pre-K through grade 8

Scholastic Early Childhood Workshop, The 1-800-724-6527
        complete integrated curriculum for Pre-K and K classrooms in both English
        and bilingual versions

Social Skills Curriculum Activities Library, Pre-K 1-800-288-4745
    West Nyack, NY 10995
        social skills curriculum units

Team Nutrition 1-800-SCHOLAS
        classroom kits that provide an integrated approach to teaching nutrition;
        offered by Scholastic, Inc.

ORGANIZATIONS

See also EC PROFESSIONAL RESOURCES: Organizations for EC Professionals

Cooperative Preschool Organizations

Maryland Council of Parent Participation Nursery Schools, (MCPPNS)
Lisa Blasey, President 301-649-6482
Kirsten Rhoades, Executive Vice President 301-933-9840
> Maryland organization for parents and teachers and cooperative preschools;
> yearly conference; reduced fee school supplies; networking meetings with
> school representatives

Parent Cooperative Preschools International (PCPI) 1-800-721-PCPI
P.O. Box 90410
Indianapolis, IN 46290
Kirsten Rhoades 301-933-9840
> international organization of cooperative preschools; literature on starting
> and operating a cooperative

Potomac Association of Cooperative Teachers (P.A.C.T.)
Irene Shere 301-593-5992
Jeanne Porter 703-941-9791
> organization of teachers and directors in DC, MD, and VA cooperative
> preschools; two conferences per year

Virginia Cooperative Preschool Council (VCPC)
Kathryn Conklin 703-361-0146
> Virginia organization for parents and teachers and cooperative preschools;
> yearly conference; networking meetings with school representatives

Montessori School Organizations

INTERNATIONAL, NATIONAL

American Montessori Society, The (A.M.S.) 212-924-3209
150 Fifth Avenue
New York, NY 10011
A.M.S. accreditation; clearinghouse for teacher training and information

Association Montessori Internationale, The (A.M.I.) 31-20-679-8932
161 Koninginneweg
1075 CN
Amsterdam, Holland
A.M.I. accreditation; clearinghouse for teacher training and information

Montessori Institute of America (M.I.A.)
3550 Galt Ocean Drive
Fort Lauderdale, FL 33308
clearinghouse for information and training

National Center for Montessori Education (N.C.M.E.)
4544 Pocahontas Avenue
San Diego, CA 92117
publications, teacher training, and workshops information

METRO AREA

International Montessori Society (I.M.S.) 1-800-301-3131
912 Thayer Avenue, Suite 207   301-589-1127
Silver Spring, MD 20910
publications; clearinghouse for information and teacher training

Institute for Advanced Montessori Studies, The 301-871-6200
13500 Layhill Road   ext. 267
Silver Spring, MD 20906
teacher training

SCHOLARSHIPS

Maryland Council of Parent Participation Nursery Schools (MCPPNS)
Mariana Hildesheim 301-527-1273
scholarship funds to help families who cannot afford full tuition to a
Maryland cooperative nursery School

Child Care and Schools: Licensing and Accreditation

GENERAL CHILD CARE AND SCHOOL LICENSING

National

**National Association for Family Child Care Accreditation
Assessment Checklist** 817-831-5095
P.O. Box 16149
Fort Worth, TX 76161

National Resource Center for Health and Safety 1-800-598-KIDS
licensing regulations for every state   http://nrc.uchsc.edu/

Metro Area

Metropolitan Washington Preschool and Day Care Guidebook
Merry Cavanaugh 202-338-7257
3833 Calvert Street, NW
Washington, DC 20007
review of all required licensing and accreditation for child care and
preschools in MD, DC, and VA; available by phone or at Crown Books and
The Cheshire Cat bookstore

District of Columbia

Department of Consumer and Regulatory 202-727-7225

Department of Human Services 202-727-8500
1905 E Street, S.E., 5th Floor
Washington, DC 20003
child care licensing

Maryland

Licensing and Regulation

Montgomery County 301-294-0344
Prince George's County 301-808-1685
301-499-3600

Maryland State Department of Education

Nonpublic School Approval Branch 410-767-0408
    Virginia Cieslicki   FAX: 410-333-8963
    200 W. Baltimore Street   vcieslic@state.md.us
    Baltimore, MD 21201
        approval agency for nursery schools, daycare centers, and special needs
        programs for children ages 2,3, and 4; preschoolers in Maryland may also
        attend nursery school programs operated by churches or temples that are
        not approved by the State Board of Education, but are registered with the
        State Department of Human Resources

Virginia

Licensing and Regulation

Alexandria 703-838-0750
Arlington County 703-358-5101
Fairfax County 703-324-8100
        approval agencies for licenses for childcare centers, half-day preschools,
        family daycare home providers

Virginia State Licensing 703-934-1505
        child care licensing for 5 children or more; less than 5 children refer to
        county licensing agencies

MONTESSORI SCHOOL ACCREDITATION

American Montessori Society, The (A.M.S.) 212-924-3209
150 Fifth Avenue, Suite #203
New York, NY 10011
A.M.S. accreditation for Montessori Schools; "American-adapted" Montessori
accreditation

Association Montessori Internationale, The (A.M.I.) 31-20-679-8932
161 Koninginneweg
1075 CN
Amsterdam, Holland
A.M.I. accreditation for Montessori Schools; international Montessori
accreditation

NAEYC ACCREDITATION

LifeWork Strategies, Inc. 1-800-777-1720
710 East Gude Drive, Suite A
Rockville, MD 20850
courses in NAEYC accreditation process

National Academy of Early Childhood Programs 1-800-424-2460
National Association for the Education of Young Children (NAEYC)
1509 16th Street, N.W.   202-232-8777
Washington, D.C. 20036   FAX:202-328-1846
NAEYC accreditation agency for preschools and daycare centers; videos
available on NAEYC accreditation process

National Educational Consulting Services 301-983-4033
P.O. Box 1572
Rockville, MD 20849
courses in NAEYC accreditation process

Computer Resources for EC Professionals

See also GENERAL RESOURCES: Computer Online Services
PARENT RESOURCES: Computer Online Services
EC PROFESSIONAL RESOURCES: Child Care: Educational, Computer On-site Services

ONLINE SERVICES

America Tomorrow On-Line Center 1-800-PRODIGY
early childhood network   301-229-1067
professional chats through bulletin boards; news and policy information;
reduced rates for NAEYC members

AskERIC 1-800-583-4135
askeric@ericir.syr.edu
question and answering service designed for teachers, administrators, and
other education specialists

AT& T WorldNet Service . . . . .http://www.worldnet.att.net/atschool/lounge/index.html#top
curriculum and lesson plans; "Learning Network"; professional development;
grants and funding

California Child Care Health Project . . . . .http://ericps.crc.uiuc.edu/cchp/cchphome.html
information on health and safety in child care settings, particularly family
child care

Center for Career Development in Early Care and Education-CCDECE
http://ericps.ed.uiuc.edu/ccdece/ccdece.html
career development system for EC practitioners; promotes ECE as a
professional field

Child Care and the Americans with Disabilities Act . . . . .http://thearc.org/faqs/ccqal.html

Child Care Parent/Provider Information Network's Website . . . . . . .http://childcare-ppin.com

Child Care Resources . . . . .http://www.primenet.com/~starbrit/child.html#netlists
sponsored by the Star Brite Learning Program

Child Care Startup . . . . .http://www.accesone.com/~hitflu/daycare/
steps for starting a day care

Conference Calendar . . . . .http://ericps.ed.uiuc.edu/ncic/confcal.html

Day Care Providers Home Page . . . . .http://www.io.org/~dlukas
lists of www resources, class planning ideas; includes software
for business aspects

Day Care Provider Resources . . .http://www.thegrapevine.com/daycare/ProvLinks/LindIndex.html

Delphi's Child Care Network . . . . .http://people.delphi.com/punkyhaake/daycare.htm

Early Childhood Education . . . . .http://www.ume.maine.edu/~cofed/ecel/welcome.html

Early Childhood Education at North Seattle Community College
http://nsccux.sccd.ctc.edu/~eceprog/index.html
philosophy, class plans, etc.   http://nsccux.sccd.ctc.edu/~eceprog/pretzel.html

Early Childhood Education On Line (ECEOL) . . . . .bonniebine.maine.edu
Bonnie Blagojevic
32 Myrtle Street
Orono, ME 04473
connection for early childhood educators nationally and internationally
to support educational efforts through information exchange

Early Childhood Educators .http://www.nauticom.net/www/cokids/
list of resources and connections on www

***Early Childhood Today* Scholastic Magazine** . . . . .ect@scholastic.com

Early Childhood Website . . . . .http://www.pcix.com/~bharris/
professionals working with children birth through 5

ERIC-Clearinghouse on Elementary and Early Childhood Education 1-800-583-4135
University of Illinois at Urbana-Champaign   http://ericps.crc.uiuc.edu/ericeece.html
51 Gerty Drive   ericeece@uiuc.edu
Champaign, IL 61820   217-333-1386
ECENET-L: listserv for discussion of development, education and   FAX: 217-333-3767
care of children birth through age 8
ECPOLICY: listserv for discussing policy issues related to young children
REGGIO-L: listserv for discussing Reggio Emilia preschools
discussion group for early childhood educators; answers to educators'
questions

National Association for the Education of Young Children . . . . . .http://www.naeyc.org/naeyc
naeyc@naeyc.org
NAEYC Academy . . . . .academy@naeyc.org
NAEYC Affiliate . . . . .affiliate@naeyc.org
NAEYC Conference . . . . .conference@naeyc.org
NAEYC Editorial . . . . .editorial@naeyc.org
NAEYC Executive Director . . . . .exdir@naeyc.org
NAEYC Institute . . . . .institute@naeyc.org
NAEYC Membership . . . . .membership@naeyc.org
NAEYC Public Affairs . . . . .pubaff@naeyc.org
NAEYC Resource Sales . . . . .resource_sales@naeyc.org
NAEYC Young Children International . . . . .yci@naeyc.org

National Parent Information Network (NPIN) 1-800-583-4135
ericeece@uiuc.edu
articles, question-answering service, discussions; access to other parents and
organizations serving parents; ERIC digests

National Resource Center for Health & Safety 1-800-598-KIDS
licensing regulations for every state   http://nrc.uchsc.edu/

WebEd K-12 Curriculum Links . . . . . . .http://badger.state.wi.us/agencies/dpi/www/WebEd.html
        extensive resource for family issues, legal issues, curriculum, teacher
        resources of all kinds

Wee-Pak . . . . .http://www.datasys.net/edpak/weehome.html
        ideas for directors of schools, preschools and daycare centers

INFORMATION AND RESOURCES

A to Z: The Early Childhood Educator's Guide to the Internet 1-800-583-4135
    ERIC Clearinghouse reference book   ericeece@uiuc.edu
        ECE reference book for the Internet; $10 + $1.50 for shipping and handling

"How Can I Help My Child?" Early Childhood Resource Directory   269

PROFESSIONAL RESOURCES

Conferences and Speaker Series

See also GENERAL RESOURCES: Conferences and Speaker Series
PARENT RESOURCES: Parent Education Classes

NATIONAL

National Association for the Education of Young Children (NAEYC) 202-232-8777
1509 16th Street, NW   1-800-424-2460
Washington, DC 20036   FAX: 202-328-1846
    annual national conference in Fall

Parent Cooperative Preschool International (PCPI) 1-800-721-PCPI
P.O. Box 90410
Indianapolis, IN 46290
    annual conference; international organization of cooperative preschools

DISTRICT OF COLUMBIA

Lab School of Washington, The 202-965-6600
4759 Reservoir Road, NW
Washington, D.C. 20007
    speaker series on children with learning disabilities; workshops on LD,
    ADD/ADHD

MARYLAND

Charles County Community College Early Childhood Conference
Mary Hunt 301-934-7512
Charles County Community College   301-870-3008
Mitchell Road, P.O. Box 911   301-884-8131, ext. 7512
La Plata, Md 20646
    annual conference for early childhood educators

Child Care Conference 301-946-1213
    Fall conference every other year in Bethesda for child care professionals;
    collaborative effort of over 15 private and government child care agencies
    and associations

Ivymount Speakers Series 301-649-0223
The Ivymount School
11614 Seven Locks Road
Rockville, MD 20854
    speaker series on special needs children; babysitting

Maryland Association for Play Therapy Conference
Peg Bagwell, Conference Coordinator 410-461-2307
Nancy M. Schultz
7311 Wildwood Drive
Takoma Park, MD 20912
    annual Fall conference on child play therapy

**Maryland Community for the Association for the Education of
Young Children (MDAEYC)** 301-863-2322
301-373-8360
> annual Fall conference in Towson for educators and parents

Maryland Council of Parent Participation Nursery Schools (MCPPNS)
> Kirsten Rhoades 301-933-9840
>> annual spring conference for professionals and parents in cooperative
>> nursery schools

Maryland State Family Child Care Association Conference
> Children's Resource Center 301-279-1260
>> Fall Conference every other year; location varies

Potomac Association of Cooperative Teachers (P.A.C.T.)
> Jeanne Porter 703-354-2339
> Irene Shere 301-593-5992
>> two conferences per year for directors and teachers in cooperative
>> nursery schools; parents welcome; Fall Conference in Alexandria;
>> Spring Conference in Bethesda

VIRGINIA

Virginia Association for the Education of Young Children (VAEYC)
> Shirlie Anson, Conference Coordinator 804-595-8351
> 117 Sarazen Court
> Newport News, VA 23602
>> annual conference

Virginia Cooperative Preschool Council (VCPC)
> Kathryn Conklin 703-361-0146
>> conferences for parents and professionals in cooperative preschools

Wolf Trap Institute for Performing Arts For Educators 703-255-1900
> conference with music and storytelling workshops for educators

ZERO TO THREE:
National Center for Infants, Toddlers and Families 202-638-1144
> 734 15th Street, NW, Suite 1000   FAX: 202-638-0851
> Washington, DC 20005
>> annual Fall conference; resource center for the first three years of life; books

"How Can I Help My Child?" Early Childhood Resource Directory   271

PROFESSIONAL RESOURCES

Consultants for EC Professionals

See also **MENTAL HEALTH RESOURCES: Counseling Centers**
MENTAL HEALTH RESOURCES: Mental Health Practitioners
CHILD CARE AND SCHOOL RESOURCES: Consultants
PARENT RESOURCES: Consultants
EC PROFESSIONAL RESOURCES: Business Management Resources

GENERAL CHILD CARE AND SCHOOL CONSULTANTS

See also **CHILD CARE AND SCHOOL RESOURCES: Private Schools**

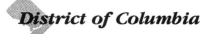

District of Columbia

Children's Foundation 202-347-3300
725 15th Street, NW, Suite 505
Washington, DC 20005
information and training for professionals; help with daycare center start-up

Early Childhood Consultation Center, The 301-593-5992
Irene Shere, Director
11506 Michale Court
Silver Spring, MD 20904
staff training; school, daycare, home care consultation; child consultations;
teacher evaluations; school, staff mediation

Maryland

Child Care Connection Computer Database 301-294-4858
listing of all legally-operating child care in Montgomery County; call to add
information or update free listing

Childcare Management Solutions 301-248-0358
9300 Livingston Road, Suite 205
Fort Washington, MD 20744
consultations for starting daycare business; workshops for daycare providers

Ciardi, Charmaine, Ph.D. 301-365-5929
Parent-Child Development Services
8203 Woodhaven Blvd.
Bethesda, MD 20817
workshops on child development issues

Early Childhood Consultation Center, The 301-593-5992
Irene Shere, Director
11506 Michale Court
Silver Spring, MD 20904
staff training; school, daycare, home care consultation; child consultations;
teacher evaluations, school, staff mediation

Family Services Agency, Connect for Success Program 301-840-2000
provides consultation to child care centers to train staff in dealing with
children's developmental and emotional needs, including special needs
children

Family Works 301-294-4956
free workshops and on-site consultations to child care programs

Learning Foundations for Children 301-428-0542
Ruby Neville, Director
P.O. Box 5
Germantown, MD 20875
workshops for professionals and parents; consultations with EC providers
on curriculum

Mustafa Counseling Services 1-800-876-1123
Diana Z. Mustafa, M.A.   301-890-7416
3009 Memory Lane
Silver Spring, MD 20904
management and staff training

National Educational Consulting Services 301-983-4033
P.O. Box 1572   FAX: 301-983-1901
Rockville, MD 20849
staff training; school consultations; teacher evaluations; NAEYC accreditation
consultation

Parent-Child Development Services . . . . .301-365-5929\
Charmaine Ciardi
8203 Woodhaven Blvd.
Bethesda, MD 20817
school consultations

Play Pals 301-596-2504
Bonnie Bricker, M.S.
7431 First League
Columbia, MD 21046
consultations to child care centers

Virginia

Education Unlimited, Inc. 703-848-1878
Judith Knotts, M.Ed.
1055 Swinks Mill Road
McLean, VA 22102
advisory services to school heads and boards of directors

Parent-Child Development Services . . . . .301-365-5929\
Charmaine Ciardi
8203 Woodhaven Blvd.
Bethesda, MD 20817
school consultations

COOPERATIVE PRESCHOOL CONSULTANTS

Early Childhood Consultation Center, The 301-593-5992
Irene Shere, Director
11506 Michale Court
Silver Spring, MD 20904
> cooperative preschool consultations; staff training; school child
> consultations; teacher evaluations; school, staff, parent mediation

Parent Cooperative Preschools International (PCPI) 1-800-721-PCPI
P.O. Box 90410
Indianapolis, IN 46290
> information on starting and managing cooperative preschools; annual
> conference

MULTI-CULTURAL CONSULTANTS

See also **MENTAL HEALTH RESOURCES: Counseling Centers, Multi-cultural**
MENTAL HEALTH RESOURCES: Mental Health Practitioners
PARENT RESOURCES: Parent Info, Multi-cultural

Findlay, Judith M.
Marchbanks & Ellis, Inc. 703-845-1131
5119-A Leesburg Pke, Suite 280   FAX: 703-931-4896
Falls Church, VA 22041
> international educational consultant with curriculum development,
> cross-cultural awareness

Marks, Susan, L.C.S.W. 703-827-8815
7700 Leesburg Pike, Suite 221
Falls Church, VA 22043
> multi-cultural concerns; special needs

REGGIO EMILIA PRESCHOOL CONSULTANTS

Price, Kathy 202-338-2574
3240 O Street, NW
Washington, DC 20007
> school consultant on Reggio Emilia-inspired preschools

SPECIAL NEEDS CONSULTANTS

See also HEALTH CARE RESOURCES: Physical and Occupational Therapists
MENTAL HEALTH RESOURCES: Mental Health Practitioners
CHILD CARE AND SCHOOL RESOURCES: Consultants, Special Needs
CHILD CARE AND SCHOOL RESOURCES: Schools, Special Needs
PARENT RESOURCES: Parent Info, Special Needs

District of Columbia

Kingsbury Center 202-232-5878
Carolyn Atkinson Thornell, Director   202-232-5989
2138 Bancroft Place, NW   FAX: 202-667-2290
Washington, DC 20008
consultations and workshops on learning disabilities

Stultz, Sylvia, Ph.D. 202-686-4084
5153 34th Street, NW
Washington, DC 20008
preschool consultation; special needs; counseling

Maryland

Ivymount School, The 301-469-0223
Judi Greenberg 301-469-0228
11614 Seven Locks Road
Rockville, MD 20854
on-site child evaluations; consultations on working with children with
special needs in a preschool setting

Family Services Agency, Connect for Success Program .301-840-2000
provides consultation to child care centers to train staff in dealing with
children's developmental and emotional needs, including special needs children

Solomon, Laura, Ed.D. 301-495-0046
8720 Georgia Avenue, Suite 701   FAX: 301-565-2217
Silver Spring, MD 20910
educational consultant; special needs

Spodak, Ruth B., Ph.D., & Associates 301-770-7507
6155 Executive Boulevard
Rockville, MD 20852
psychological and educational consultants concerning LD

Stern, Judith, M.A. 301-424-1941
205 Watts Branch Parkway
Rockville, MD 20850
educational consultant specializing in ADD, LD

Treatment and Learning Centers 301-424-5200
    9975 Medical Center Drive   TDD: 301-424-5203
    Rockville, MD 20850
        ADD, LD consultations

Virginia

Marks, Susan, L.C.S.W. 703-827-8815
    7700 Leesburg Pike, Suite 221
    Falls Church, VA 22043
        preschool consultations; ADD; Tourettes Syndrome; autism; obsessive
        compulsive disorder

PROFESSIONAL RESOURCES

276   "How Can I Help My Child?" Early Childhood Resource Directory

Courses: College Programs

GRADUATE PROGRAMS

Computer Online Programs

Pacific Oaks College/Distance Learning 1-800-613-0300
5 Westmoreland Place
Pasadena, CA 91103
    M.A. in Human Development, with specialization in ECE or Leadership in
    Education; Postgraduate Certificate in Human Development or ECE

District of Columbia

Catholic University 202-319-5800
620 Michigan Avenue, NE
Washington, DC 20064
    M.A. in education, specialization in EC

Gallaudet University 202-651-5330
Department of Education   TTY: 202-651-5330
800 Florida Avenue, NE   FAX: 202-651-5860
Washington, DC 20002   masasslehrer@gallua.gallaudet.edu
    M.A. in deaf education with specialization in family-centered EC; advanced
    master's degree program for family-centered EC specialists

George Washington University, The 202-994-6170
Graduate School of Education and Human Development   FAX: 202-994-7207
Teacher Preparation Department
2134 G Street, NW, Suite 416
Washington, DC 20052
    M.A. in EC special education

Howard University 202-806-7340
2441 Sixth Street, NW
Washington, DC 20059
    M.Ed. in EC; M.A. in EC; M.A. in teacher EC

Mount Vernon College 202-625-4542
2100 Foxhall Road, NW   1-800-MVC-INFO
Washington, DC 20007
    M.A. in EC Program Administration

Trinity College 202-884-9400
125 Michigan Avenue, NE
Washington, DC 20017
    M.A. in teaching with special EC graduate program in Education and
    Administration; many courses offered on Saturdays; summer courses

University of the District of Columbia 202-274-6465
4200 Connecticut Avenue, NW
Washington, DC 20008
    M.A. in EC

Maryland

Hood College 301-696-3471
401 Rosemont Avenue
Frederick, MD 21701
M.S. in Curriculum and Instruction; concentration in EC for certified teachers

Johns Hopkins University 301-294-7040
1601 Medical Center Drive
Rockville, MD 20850
M.Ed. in special education with an opportunity for specialization in EC;
M.A. in teaching, offers specialization and certification in EC

Johns Hopkins University 410-516-8273
101 Whitehead Hall
3400 N. Charles Street
Baltimore, MD 21218
M.A. in teaching (M.A.T.) with EC specialization; S.I.M.A.T. (School
Immersion Master of Teaching); M.S. in special ed, with specialization in
EC special education; Ed.D. in special education with specialization in
EC special education

Loyola College 410-617-2546
4501 N. Charles Street
Baltimore, MD 21218
M.A. in EC special education

University of Maryland
1210 Benjamin Building, College Park 301-405-1000
1000 Hilltop Circle, Baltimore 410-455-2465
M.A. in ECE; M.Ed. in ECE

Virginia

George Mason University
Office of Teacher Education 703-993-2080
Licensure Specialist 703-993-2079
Graduate School of Education, Robinson Hall A307
4400 University Drive
Fairfax, VA 22030
ECE post-licensure program; EC M.Ed.; teacher licensure with M.Ed. option
in: ECE, EC special education; EC ESOL

PROFESSIONAL RESOURCES

UNDERGRADUATE PROGRAMS

District of Columbia

Catholic University 202-319-5800
620 Michigan Avenue, NE
Washington, DC 20064
B.A. in ECE

Howard University 202-806-2750
2400 Sixth Street, NW   outside of DC 1-800-822-6363
Washington, DC 20059
B.A. in ECE

Mount Vernon College 202-625-4542
2100 Foxhall Road, NW   1-800-MVC-INFO
Washington, DC 20007
B.A. in ECE

Trinity College 202-884-9400
125 Michigan Avenue, NE
Washington, DC 20017
B.A. in Education with specialization in EC

University of the District of Columbia 202-274-6465
4200 Connecticut Avenue, NW
Washington, DC 20008
B.A. in ECE

Maryland

Anne Arundel Community College 301-541-2430
    101 College Parkway
    Arnold, MD 21012
        A.A. in EC, 2 year degree

Bowie State University 301-464-7562
    14000 Jericho Park Road
    Bowie, MD 20715
        B.A. in ECE

Catonsville Community College 410-455-4318
    800 South Rolling Road
    Catonsville, MD 21228
        A.A. in EC, 2 year degree

Charles County Community College 301-934-2251
    Mitchell Road, P.O. Box 910, La Plata 301-870-3008
    Smallwood Village Center, Waldorf 301-645-4446
        certificate in applied science in EC; A.A.S. in EC, 2 year degree; letter of
        recognition for child care providers who meet MD state requirements

College of Notre Dame of Maryland 1-800-435-0200
    Baltimore, MD 21210   outside of MD 1-800-435-0200
        B.A. in ECE   410-532-5330

Columbia Union College 1-800-835-4212
    7600 Flower Avenue   301-891-4064
    Takoma Park, MD 20912   FAX: 301-270-1618
        A.A.S. in ECE; 2 year degree; B.A. in ECE   http://www.cuc.edu/

Community College at Calvert County 410-586-3054
    3205 Broomes Island Road   301-855-1211
    Port Republic, MD
        certificate in applied science in EC; A.A.S. in EC, 2 year degree; letter of
        recognition for child care providers who meet MD state requirements

Community College at St. Mary's County 301-863-6681
    Great Mills Road, P.O. Box 98
    Great Mills, MD 20634
        certificate in applied science in EC; A.A.S. in EC, 2 year degree; letter of
        recognition for child care providers who meet MD state requirements

Coppin State College 1-800-635-3674
    2500 West North Street   410-383-5990
    Baltimore, MD 21216
        B.A. in ECE

Goucher College 410-337-6000
    1021 Dulaney Valley Road
    Baltimore, MD 21204
        B.A. in ECE

Hood College 1-800-922-1599
401 Rosemont Avenue
Frederick, MD 21701
B.A. in ECE

Montgomery College
20200 Observation Drive, Germantown 301-353-7700
51 Mannakee Street, Rockville 301-251-7471
7600 Takoma Avenue, Takoma Park 301-650-1300
A.A.S. in ECE, 2 year degree; A.A.S. in Early Childhood Education Technology
w/ ECE Certificate option

Prince George's County Community College 301-322-0059
301 Largo Road
Largo, MD 20774
A.A.S. in ECE, 2 year degree; A.A.S. in EC Management, 2 year degree;
cerficate degree in ECE

Sojourner-Douglass College 410-276-0306
500 North Caroline Street   ext. 249
Baltimore, MD 21205
B.A. in ECE

Towson State University . . . . .1-800-CALL TSU
Admissions Office
800 York Road
Towson, MD 21204
B.A. in ECE

University of Maryland 301-405-1000
1210 Benjamin Building
College Park, MD 20742
B.A. in ECE

Villa Julie College 410-486-7000
Green Spring Valley Road
Stevenson, MD 21153
B.A. in ECE

Washington Bible College 1-800-787-0256
6511 Princess Garden Parkway   301-552-1400
Lanham, MD 20706   ext. 212
B.A. in ECE

Virginia

Northern Virginia Community College 703-845-6333
20001 N. Beauregard Street
Alexandria, VA 22311
A.A. in EC, 2 year degree, Alexandria Campus only

Courses: General Training

See also **GENERAL RESOURCES: Conferences and Speaker Series**
HEALTH CARE RESOURCES: CPR, First Aid, and Health Courses
PARENT RESOURCES: Parent Education Classes
EC PROFESSIONAL RESOURCES: Courses: College Programs
EC PROFESSIONAL RESOURCES: Conferences and Speakers

GENERAL EC PROFESSIONAL COURSES

District of Columbia

Lab School of Washington International Training Center, The
4759 Reservoir Road, NW 202-944-2232
Washington, DC 20007   202-944-3082
    courses for teachers concerning identifying pre-schoolers with learning
    disabilities

Levine School of Music 202-337-2227
1690 36th Street, NW
Washington, DC 20007
    music classes for EC professionals

Children's Foundation 202-347-3300
725 15th Street, NW, Suite 505
Washington, DC 20005
    training for professionals

Trinity College Professional Workshops 202-884-9400
125 Michigan Avenue, NE
Washington, DC 20017
    professional graduate workshops on Saturdays and summers

Maryland

Academy Child Development Center 301-984-5612
6119 Executive Blvd.
Rockville, MD 20852
    childcare provider workshops

Carroll, Debbie 301-854-0972
8568 Dark Hawk Circle
Columbia, MD 21045
    training for daycare professionals

C.H.I.L.D. (Children's Health & Instructional Learning Development)
Pamela L. Walker, M.E.
Nida N. Saavedra, Ph.D.
Gaithersburg 301-977-8334
Silver Spring 301-776-0861
    health, safety, and early educational development courses for child care
    providers and child care center staff; training on weekends and evenings;
    will train one person on-site

PROFESSIONAL RESOURCES

282   "How Can I Help My Child?" Early Childhood Resource Directory

Child Care Bureau 301-330-8401
  9055-D Gaither Road
  Gaithersburg, MD 20877
    training and education for careers in child care

Child Care Connection Training Bulletin 301-294-4954
  332 West Edmonston Drive
  Rockville, MD 20852
    calendar of approved training for child care providers

Child Care Group II, Inc. 301-933-2291
  Celia Boykin, Director
    child care provider workshops

Childcare Management Solutions 301-248-0358
  9300 Livingston Road, Suite 205
  Fort Washington, MD 20744
    workshops for daycare providers

Child Care Training Institute *Healthy Beginnings* Training Manual 410-768-4351
  Anne Arundel Community College, Child Care Training Institute   410-760-7043
  101 Crain Highway, N.W., 5th Floor
  Glen Burnie, MD 21061
    3-part program manual to support child care providers and enable them to
    care for children with special needs; 268 pages; $45

Ciardi, Charmaine, Ph.D. 301-365-5929
  Parent-Child Development Services
  8203 Woodhaven Blvd.
  Bethesda, MD 20817
    workshops on child development issues

C.O.N.T.A.C.T. Child Care, Montgomery County 301-279-1260
  Children's Resource Center   TDD: 301-217-1246
  332 W. Edmonston Road
  Rockville, MD 20852
    continuing education for child care programs

Early Childhood Consultation Center, The 301-593-5992
  Irene Shere, Director
  11506 Michale Court
  Silver Spring, MD 20904
    courses on emotional and social needs of young children; staff training
    on-site; workshops in Silver Spring; Maryland CE credits for professionals

Family Education Network, Inc. 301-888-1020
  P.O. Box 318
  Brandywine, MD 20613
    workshops for educators

Family Services Agency Connect for Success Program 301-840-2000
    provides consultation to child care centers to train staff in dealing with
    children's developmental and emotional needs, including special needs children

PROFESSIONAL
RESOURCES

Family Works, The 301-294-4956
>free workshops and on-site consultation to child care programs to help staff
and providers develop positive partnerships with parents in caring for their
children

Given, Judy 410-367-6447
>speeches and workshops on movement therapy techniques; Baltimore,
Mt. Washington area

Goldman, Linda 301-942-6440
>Center for Loss and Grief Therapy
10400 Connecticut Avenue, Suite 514
Kensington, MD 20895
>>workshops for educators on grief and loss therapy for children

Health Quest, Inc. 410-869-0454
>9 Newburg Avenue   FAX: 410-869-0452
Catonsville, MD 21228
>>course on starting and maintaining a successful daycare; child development
courses; coping with ADD courses

Ivymount School, The 301-469-0223
>11614 Seven Locks Road
Rockville, MD 20854
>>workshops for professionals on working with children with special needs in
a preschool setting

Learning Foundations for Children 301-428-0542
>Ruby Neville, Director
P.O. Box 5
Germantown, MD 20875
>>workshops for professionals; consultations with EC providers on curriculum

Montgomery Child Care Association, Inc., Training Institute 301-946-1213
>2730 University Blvd. , West, Suite 616   301-949-3561
Wheaton, MD 20902
>>workshops for EC professionals

Mustafa Counseling Services 1-800-876-1123
>Diana Z. Mustafa, M.A.   301-890-7416
3009 Memory Lane
Silver Spring, MD 20904
>>management and staff training

National Educational Consulting Services 301-983-4033
>P.O. Box 1572
Rockville, MD 20849
>>workshops for educators

National Institute of Relationship Enhancement, The (NIRE) 301-986-1479
>William Nordling, Ph.D. Director   FAX: 301-986-1479
4400 East-West Hwy, Suite 28
Bethesda, MD 20814
>>workshops on child play therapy techniques

Parent Encouragement Program (P.E.P.) 301-929-8824
    10100 Connecticut Avenue   FAX: 301-929-8834
    Kensington, MD 20895
        classes for daycare providers

Play Pals 301-596-2504
    Bonnie Bricker, M.S.
    7431 First League
    Columbia, MD 21046
        caregiver workshops in Columbia, Ellicott City, and Laurel

Quality Time Early Learning Center Institute 301-588-3350
    8101 Georgia Avenue
    Silver Spring, MD 20910

Rubinoff, Laura, and Associates 301-493-4695
    6505 Democracy Blvd.
    Bethesda, MD 20817
        workshops on improving social language interactions

Shere, Irene 301-593-5992
    The Early Childhood Consultation Center
    11506 Michale Court
    Silver Spring, MD 20904
        courses on emotional and social needs of young children; staff training
        on-site; workshops in Silver Spring; Maryland CE credits for professionals

TECHNIC/TRAINING 410-752-7599
    Statewide Child Care Resource Center (SCCRC)
    Maryland Child Care Resource Network (MCCRN)
    Maryland Committee for Children, Inc. 410-752-7588
        608 Water Street
        Baltimore, MD 21202
    Prince George's Child Care Resource Center 301-772-8420
        9475 Lottsford Road, Suite 202   FAX: 301-772-8410
        Landover, MD 20785
                                              TDD: 301-772-8408
        workshops for child care providers, directors, and teachers; workshop
        locations: Baltimore County, Baltimore City, Western Maryland

Treatment and Learning Centers 301-424-5200
    9975 Medical Center Drive   TDD 301-424-5203
    Rockville, MD 20850
        workshops for professionals working with young children

Virginia

Weiss, Sharon K., M.D. 703-356-5534
    1420 Beverly Road, Suite 300
    McLean, VA 22101
        workshops for parents and staff

PROFESSIONAL RESOURCES

MARYLAND CERTIFICATION COURSES:
90 HOURS/45 HOURS/26 HOURS

Charles County Community College 301-934-2251
    Mitchell Road, P.O. Box 910, La Plata 301-870-3008
    Smallwood Village Center, Waldorf 301-645-4446
        letter of recognition for child care providers who meet MD state
        requirements

Child Care Group II, Inc. 301-933-2291
    Celia Boykin, Director
        certification courses

Community College at Calvert County 410-586-3054
    3205 Broomes Island Road   301-855-1211
    Port Republic, MD
        letter of recognition for child care providers who meet MD state
        requirements

Community College at St. Mary's County 301-863-6681
    Great Mills Road, P.O. Box 98
    Great Mills, MD 20634
        letter of recognition for child care providers who meet MD state
        requirements

Green Acres School 301-881-4100
    11701 Danville Drive
    Rockville, MD 20852
        certification courses

Montgomery Child Care Association, Inc., Training Institute 301-946-1213
    2730 University Blvd. West, Suite 616
    Wheaton, MD 20902
        certification courses

National Education Consulting Service 301-983-4033
    P.O. Box 1572   FAX: 301-983-1901
    Rockville, Md 20849
        certification courses

Quality Time Early Learning Center Institute 301-588-3350
    8101 Georgia Avenue
    Silver Spring, MD 20910
        certification courses

PROFESSIONAL RESOURCES

286   "How Can I Help My Child?" Early Childhood Resource Directory

MONTESSORI SCHOOL TRAINING

Institute for Advanced Montessori Studies 301-871-6200
13500 Layhill Road ext.267
Silver Spring, MD 20906
Montessori teacher training for early childhood

Montgomery Montessori Institute 301-762-4544
10500 Darnestown Road
Rockville, Maryland 20850
Montessori teacher training for early childhood

Virginia Commonwealth University 804-828-0100
Montessori Teacher School of Education Training Program
Richmond, Virginia 23284
Montessori teacher training

Washington Montessori Institute 202-387-8020
2119 S Street, NW FAX: 202-332-6345
Washington, DC 20008
Montessori teacher training

REGGIO EMILIA PRESCHOOL TRAINING

Model Early Learning Center 202-675-4148
Erica Hamlin
800 3rd Street, NE
Washington, DC 20002
teacher training for Reggio Emilia preschool teachers

Courses: Mentoring Programs and Training for Trainers

NATIONAL

National Center for the Early Childhood Work Force 202-737-7700
  733 15th Street, NW, Suite 1037   FAX: 202-737-0370
  Washington, DC 20005
      organization supporting mentoring programs at local, state, and national
      levels; annual conference; leadership development for mentors; publishes
      Early Childhood Mentoring Curriculum

ZERO TO THREE Publications Catalog 1-800-899-4301
  National Center for Infants, Toddlers, and Families   202-638-0840
  734 15th Street, NW, Suite 1000
  Washington, DC 20005
      publications on professional mentoring

MARYLAND

Montgomery Child Care Association, Inc., Training Institute 301-946-1213
  2730 University Blvd. West, Suite 616
  Wheaton, MD 20902
      mentoring program

Maryland Child Care Resource Network 410-752-7588
  608 Water Street   FAX: 410-752-6286
  Baltimore, Md 21202
      block grants for trainers

Maryland Department of Human Resources 410-767-7805
  Child Care Administration   FAX: 410-333-8699
  311 W. Saratoga Street
  Baltimore, MD 21201
      approval agency for Maryland individuals and organizations as trainers for
      EC professionals

Responsive Training Symposiums 410-752-7588
  Nancy Kohlhepp
  Maryland Child Care Resource Network
  608 Water Street
  Baltimore, MD 21202
      training for EC professional trainers

PROFESSIONAL RESOURCES

288   "How Can I Help My Child?" Early Childhood Resource Directory

Courses: Scholarships
For EC Professionals

Maryland Community Association for the Education of Young Children (MCAEYC)
Ann Byrne 301-929-2505
       two $500 scholarships awarded to MCAEYC members enrolled full- or   ext. 14
       part-time in a course related to early childhood education

Helplines for EC Professionals

See also **GENERAL RESOURCES: Computer Resources**
GENERAL RESOURCES: Helplines
CHILD CARE AND SCHOOL RESOURCES, Educational Information
PARENT RESOURCES: Computer Resources
PARENT RESOURCES: Helplines
EC PROFESSIONAL RESOURCES: Computer Resources

NATIONAL

ERIC-Clearinghouse on Elementary and Early Childhood Education 1-800-583-4135
University of Illinois at Urbana-Champaign   217-333-1386
51 Gerty Drive   FAX: 217-333-3767
Champaign, IL 61820

National Child Care Information Center 1-800-616-2242
Anne Goldstein, Director   agoldstein@acf.dhhs.gov
encourages communication within the child care community; analyzes
child care data; publishes *Child Care Bulletin*

METRO AREA

Child Care Administration 301-294-0344
51 Monroe Street
Rockville, MD 20852

Children's Resource Center 301-279-1260
332 West Edmonston Drive
Rockville, MD 20852

Community LINC of Montgomery County 301-217-0500
TTY 301-424-1087
computer bulletin board 301-424-5123
information and referral service for Montgomery County, MD; lists non-profit
organizations and resources of all types

Hyperactivity Helpline 703-524-5566

Montgomery County, MD, Department of Health and Human Services 301-217-8980
Public Health Service, Kathy Wood
help for child care providers about health care concerns

Job Clearinghouses for EC Professionals

COOPERATIVE PRESCHOOL PROFESSIONALS

Maryland Council of Parent Participation Nursery Schools(MCPPNS)
Marsy Desnoyers 301-564-1967
Cathy Leffler 301-890-6199
job clearinghouse for directors, teachers, aides in cooperative nursery
schools

Potomac Association of Cooperative Teachers
Cindy Walsh 202-363-2209
job clearinghouse for directors, teachers, aides in cooperative nursery
schools

MONTESSORI PROFESSIONALS

Washington Montessori Institute 202-387-8020
2119 S Street, NW   FAX: 202-332-6345
Washington, DC 20008
job clearinghouse for Montessori teachers

"How Can I Help My Child?" Early Childhood Resource Directory

291

Organizations for EC Professionals

See also **GENERAL RESOURCES: Advocacy Groups**
EC PROFESSIONAL RESOURCES: Center and School Resources:
Educational, Organizations

GENERAL ORGANIZATIONS

National

Advocates for Child Care Professionals, Inc.
Marian Green, President 301-251-7471
P.O. Box 10104
Rockville, MD 20849
advocates for child care professionals; annual Celebration of the Child Care
Profession

Association for Childhood Education International 1-800-423-3563
17904 Georgia Avenue, Suite 215   301-570-2111
Olney, MD 20832   FAX: 301-570-2212
organization of those concerned with children from infancy through early
adolescence; networking; public advoicacy; publishes *Journal of Research
in Childhood Education*

Council for Early Childhood Professional Recognition
CDA National Credentialing Program 1-800-424-4310
1341 G Street, NW, Suite 400   202-265-9090
Washington, DC 20005
credentialing program for preschool teachers, daycare providers, homecare
providers

Mid-Atlantic Association for the Education of Young Children (MAEYC)
Vickie Kaneko 410-333-7206
410-521-5204

National Association for the Education of Young Children (NAEYC) 202-232-8777
1509 16th Street, NW   1-800-424-2460
Washington, DC 20036   FAX: 202-328-1846
services and advocacy for young children ages birth to 8; books, brochures,
conferences for parents and professionals

National Association for Multicultural Education (NAME) 703-243-4525
2101A N. Rolfe Street   FAX: 202-296-6620
Arlington, VA 22209
organization for professionals interested in multicultural education;
conferences; magazine

PROFESSIONAL RESOURCES

292   "How Can I Help My Child?" Early Childhood Resource Directory

National Education Association (NEA) 202-833-4000
    1201 16th Street, NW
    Washington, DC 20006
        national teachers' union; preschool and kindergarten teachers included in
        membership

North American Montessori Teachers Association 216-421-1905
    11424 Bellflower Road, NE
    Cleveland, OH 44106

District of Columbia

DC Association for the Education of Young Children (DCAEYC) 202-332-3680
    Mattie Edwards, President

Maryland

Maryland Committee for Children, Inc. 410-752-7588
    608 Water Street
    Baltimore, MD 21202
        speaker series; conference; newsletter; public policy report; discounts at
        reSTORE craft store

Maryland Association for the Education of Young Children (MAEYC)
    Rivalee Gitomer 410-455-4236
    Vickie Kaneko 410-521-5204
        3928 Rolling Road, 7-C, Baltimore, MD 21208
    Arundel-Bowie AEYC 301-206-2082
        Ester Parker, 2307 Westport Lane, Crofton, MD 21114
    Central MD AEYC 410-296-2955
        Cathy Owings, 1015 Winsford Road, Towson, MD 21204
    Maryland Community AEYC (MCAEYC) 301-229-4146
        Ann Byrne, 5905 Namakagan Road, Bethesda, MD 20816
    Southern MD AEYC 301-855-4714
        Brenda Tyrrell, 8816 Donald's Way, Owings, MD 20736
    Western MD AEYC 301-689-2808
        Denise Payne, University Children's Center, 104 Pullen Hall, Frostburg, MD 21532

Virginia

Virginia Association for the Education of Young Children (VAEYC)
    Mary Landis, membership 757-272-9266
    Sharon Stottlemyer, information 540-786-2065
    President 804-560-2700
        services and advocacy for people concerned with the well-being of young
        children, ages birth to 8

COOPERATIVE PRESCHOOL ORGANIZATIONS

International, National

Parent Cooperative Preschools International (PCPI) 1-800-721-PCPI
P.O. Box 90410
Indianapolis, IN 46290
Kirsten Rhoades 301-933-9840
international organization of cooperative preschools; literature on starting
and operating a cooperative

Metro Area

Potomac Association of Cooperative Teachers
Jeanne Porter, Secretary of Publicity 703-941-9791
Irene Shere, President 301-593-5992
11506 Michale Court
Silver Spring, MD 20904
directors and teachers in cooperative preschools in DC, MD, and VA; two
conferences per year, two newsletters, lending library of educational videos,
coop school directory

Teacher Support Groups for Teachers of 2 Year-olds, 3-Year-olds, and 4-Year-olds
Potomac Association of Cooperative Teachers 301-593-5992
support groups for cooperative teachers of 2's, 3's, and 4's

Maryland

Maryland Council of Parent Participation Nursery Schools (MCPPNS)
Kirsten Rhoades 301-933-9840
organization of cooperative preschools parents and professionals operating
in four Maryland counties: Montgomery, Prince George's, Howard, and
Anne Arundel

Virginia

Virginia Cooperative Preschool Council (VCPC)
Kathryn Conklin, President 703-361-0146
Leslie Sirriani, Vice President 703-533-3181
VA organization for parents and teachers and cooperative preschools; yearly
conference; reduced school supplies; networking meetings with school
representatives

PROFESSIONAL RESOURCES

294

"How Can I Help My Child?" Early Childhood Resource Directory

DIRECTORS' ORGANIZATIONS

Directors Group, The 301-593-5992
Irene Shere, Administrator
11506 Michale Court
Silver Spring, MD 20904
seminars for preschool directors in DC, MD, and VA; four seminars per year;
Maryland CE credits

Organization of Child Care Directors (OCCD) 301-975-2152
332 W. Edmonston Drive
Rockville, MD 20852
training and support to administrators of children's programs

FAMILY CHILD CARE ORGANIZATIONS

National

National Association for Family Child Care
Membership 602-838-3446
Accreditation Assessment Checklist 817-831-5095
P.O. Box 16149
Fort Worth, TX 76161

National Association for Family Day Care 801-268-9148
P.O. Box 71268
Murray, UT 84107

Maryland

Family Child Care Association of Montgomery County 301-949-0728
P.O. Box 2396
Kensington, MD 20891
support organization for registered family child care providers; publishes
Naptime News

Maryland State Family Day Care Association 410-647-2334
Debbie Moore, President   FAX: 410-431-5416
457 Lynwood Court
Severna Park, MD 21146
information and support to family daycare providers

"How Can I Help My Child?" Early Childhood Resource Directory

295

Publications for EC Professionals

See also **GENERAL RESOURCES: Books, etc.**

BOOKS FOR EC PROFESSIONALS

Early Childhood Directors Association Resources for Child Caring 612-641-0305
Toys'n'Things Press
450 North Syndicate, Suite 5
St. Paul, MN 55104
      "survival book" kit for Directors, Forms Kit for Directors

Educational Services 703-476-5338
Charles Dunn
P.O. Box 393
Vienna, VA 22180
      books for EC professionals

Gryphon House, Inc. 1-800-638-0928
Early Childhood Book Collection   FAX: 301-595-0051
P.O. Box 207   http://www.ghbooks.com
Beltsville, MD 20704
      free teacher resource catalog

Kidsrights 1-800-892-KIDS
10100 Park Cedar Drive   FAX: 704-541-0113
Charlotte, NC 23210
      catalog for books, videos, and brochures dealing with difficult emotional
      issues for children

Redleaf Press 1-800-423-8309
Resources for Early Childhood Professionals
450 N. Syndicate, Suite 5
St. Paul, MN 55104
      resources for early childhood professionals

Scholastic *Family Bookshelf,* The Link Between Home and School 1-800-724-2424
2931 East McCarty Street
P.O. Box 7502
Jefferson City, MO 65102
      parenting books, tapes, software, and videos for parents to order through
      schools for school bonus points toward school purchases; free introductory
      copy

PROFESSIONAL RESOURCES

296   "How Can I Help My Child?" Early Childhood Resource Directory

JOURNALS AND MAGAZINES FOR EC PROFESSIONALS

Child Care Information Exchange Magazine 1-800-221-2864
P.O. Box 2890   206-883-9394
Redmond, WA 98073   FAX: 2106-867-5217
          magazine for directors and owners of daycare facilities and preschools;
          six issues per year; books for directors and teachers

Children's Literature Newsletter 301-469-2070
7513 Shadywood Road
Bethesda, MD 20817
          monthly review of children's literature

Children's Teacher 1-800-672-1789
Cokesbury Publishing
201 8th Avenue, South
Nashville, TN 37203
          quarterly publication

Early Childhood Education Journal 212-620-8473
Human Sciences Press, Inc.
233 Spring Street
New York, NY 10013
          journal for professionals about the social, physical, emotional, and
          intellectual development of children birth to age 8; descriptions of early
          childhood programs worldwide; case studies of young children; book
          reviews; for teachers, child care providers, and mental health practitioners

Early Childhood News 1-800-543-4383
The Journal of Professional Development   ext. 121
330 Progress Road   FAX: 937-847-5910
Dayton, OH 45449   webster@loopback.com
                                     http://www.earlychildhoodnews.com

Early Childhood Research Quarterly, The .FAX: 201-767-8450
Ablex Publishing Corporation
355 Chestnut Street
Norwood, NJ 07648
          NAEYC's research journal focusing on relevant social and educational
          topics; published quarterly

Early Childhood Teacher's Club 609-786-9778
A Newbridge Book Club
P.O. Box 6009
Delran, NJ 08370
          1-2-3 Early Learning Activities; books and materials for teachers

Early Childhood Today 1-800-544-2917
Scholastic, Inc.
P.O. Box 54813
Boulder, CO 80323
          magazine for EC professionals dealing with staff development, curriculum,
          program resources, etc.

PROFESSIONAL RESOURCES

ERIC-Educational Resources Information Center 1-800-583-4135
ERIC-Clearinghouse on Early and Elementary Childhood Education   ericeece@uiuc.edu
    University of Illinois at Urbana-Champaign   http://ericps.crc.uiuc.edu/ericeece.html
    51 Gerty Drive   217-333-1386
    Champaign, IL 61820   FAX: 217-333-3767
        free newsletter published twice a year; teaching articles, publications,
        computer reprints, child care program articles

Family Child Caring 1-800-423-8309
    Redleaf Press, a division of Resources for Child Caring
    450 N. Syndicate, Suite 5
    St. Paul, MN 55104
        newsletter for family child care providers; activities, resources, training
        opportunities; health, safety, tax info; photocopying permitted

Journal of Child Care Administration
    275 Metty Drive, Suite 1
    P.O. Box 8623
    Ann Arbor, MI 48107
        each issue contains 16 pages of information on business, staff issues;-
        interviews with leading child-care professionals

Journal of Research in Childhood Education 1-800-423-3563
    Association for Childhood Education International   301-570-2111
    17904 Georgia Avenue, Suite 215   FAX: 301-570-2212
    Olney, MD 20832
        reviews of research and professional publications; articles on classroom
        skills, fostering communication between staff and parents, and creating
        learning environments

Mailbox, The, **The Idea Magazine for Teachers** 910-273-9409
    The Education Center
    P.O. Box 29485
    Greensboro, NC 27499
        bimonthly magazine for cross-curricular, thematic, and timesaving teaching
        units, plus advice and teaching ideas; preschool level and kindergarten level
        available

Parent and Preschooler Newsletter 1-800-726-1708
    Preschool Publications, Inc.   516-626-1971
    P.O. Box 1167   FAX: 1-516-765-4927
    Cutchogue, NY 11935
        monthly exploration of early childhood topics for parents and educators; an
        international resource for parents and professionals; articles reproducible for
        school and center use; available in English and English/Spanish

School Administrator, The 703-875-0753
    American Association for School Administrators
    1801 North Moore Street
    Arlington, VA 22209
        11 issues per year

PROFESSIONAL RESOURCES

298   "How Can I Help My Child?" Early Childhood Resource Directory

Teacher Institute, The 703-323-9170
P.O. Box 397
Fairfax Station, VA 22039
    publishing company for newsletters and booklets for EC professionals;
    free catalog

Teaching Strategies, Inc. 1-800-637-3652
P.O. Box 42243   202-362-7543
Washington, DC 20015   TSI7543@aol.com
    books for centers and family child care providers and parents relating to
    early childhood issues

Young Children 202-232-8777
National Association for the Education of Young Children (NAEYC) 1-800-424-2460
1509 16th Street, N.W   .FAX: 202-328-1846
Washington, DC 20036
    magazine published six times per year; professional development resource
    tool

ZERO TO THREE Publications Catalog 1-800-899-4301
National Center for Infants, Toddlers, and Families
734 15th Street, NW, Suite 1000   202-638-0840
Washington, DC 20005
    bi-monthly bulletin; publications for professionals

LIBRARY RESOURCES FOR EC PROFESSIONALS

See also **GENERAL RESOURCES: Books, Etc., Library Resources**

Maryland

Children's Resource Center 301-217-3800
Rockville Regional Library
99 Maryland Avenue
Rockville, MD 20850
    extensive educational book, journal, and video collection for EC
    professionals; borrower need not be a Montgomery County resident

Virginia

Fairfax County Libraries 703-222-3155
On-line Library catalog; modem phone # 703-802-7447
Library Administration   http://www.co.fairfax.va.us/library
13135 Lee Jackson Highway, Suite 301
Fairfax, VA 22033
    professional library with over 400 audio and video tapes; parent handouts in
    eight languages; resource notebooks of parent handouts

NEWSLETTERS FOR EC PROFESSIONALS

Child Care Issues 410-752-7588
  TECHNIC: Child Care
  Maryland Committee for Children
  608 Water Street
  Baltimore, MD 21202
    newsletter for child care providers

Child Care Connection Training Bulletin 301-294-4954
  332 West Edmonston Drive
  Rockville, MD 20852
    bulletin of Montgomery County organizations providing training and workshops

Child Care Parent/Provider Information Network 301-262-0274
  P.O. Box 574   FAX: 301-262-1145
  Bowie, MD 20718   CCPPIN@AOL.com
    quarterly newsletter for family day care providers

Maryland Community Association for the Education of Young Children,
MCAEYC Courier
  Ann Byrne 301-229-4146
  5905 Namakagan Road
  Bethesda, MD 20816
    information newsletter for MCAEYC

Maryland Council of Parent Participation Nursery Schools MCPPNS Newsletter
  Cooperatively Speaking
  Kirsten Rhoades, Executive VP 301-933-9840
    newsletter for cooperative preschool parents and schools; published three times
    per school year; winter issue contains information about Spring Conference

Maryland Child Care Resource Network Training Calendar
  Susan Thorpe, Editor 410-752-7588
  Maryland Childcare Resource Network
  608 Water Street
  Baltimore, MD 21202
    quarterly publication of the Maryland Committee for Children and MD
    Child Care Administration; lists workshops throughout Maryland that are
    presented by organizations with MD Child Care Administration approval

Nap Time News, The 301-871-6810
  Family Day Care Association of Montgomery County
  P.O. Box 2396
  Kensington, MD 20891
    newsletter for family day care providers

Parenting Program Guide 703-846-8670
  Parenting Education Center, PPG
  Lacey Instructional Center
  3705 Crest Drive
  Annandale, VA 22203
    free reference document for professionals, listing parenting programs,
    classes and activities in Fairfax County; printed two times a year

PROFESSIONAL RESOURCES

300   "How Can I Help My Child?" Early Childhood Resource Directory

Videos for EC Professionals

See also GENERAL RESOURCES: Videos

NATIONAL

Association for Supervision and Curriculum Development (ASCD) 703-549-9110
        classroom management-curriculum videos for grades K-1; purchase-$345;
        rent-$75; preview-$20

Bev Bos Videos 1-800-959-5549
    Turn-the-Page Press
    203 Baldwin Avenue
    Roseville, CA
        Starting at Square One, Come On and Sing, $24.95; developmentally
        appropriate early childhood curriculum; developmentally appropriate early
        childhood music

California Department of Education 1-800-995-4099
        educational videos available in English, Spanish, Cantonese; $65

Child Development Videos 1-800-523-5503
        free catalog

Child Development Media 1-800-405-8942
    4632 Van Nuys Blvd, Suite 286
    Van Nuys, CA 91401
        child development videos from numerous sources

Childswork/ChildsPlay 1-800-962-1141
    Center for Applied Psychology
    P.O. Box 61586
    King of Prussia, PA 19406
        videos addressing the mental health needs of children and their families
        through play

Committee for Children 1-800-634-4449
    2203 Airport Way South, Suite 500
    Seattle, WA 98134
        educational videos for parents and professionals on early childhood issues;
        child safety; talking about touching; classroom issues; curriculum; free
        catalog

Educational Productions 503-292-9234
        educational videos with parent and teacher guides

Faber/Mazlish Workshops, LLC 1-800-944-8584
    Dept. 103A   FAX: 914-967-8130
    P.O. Box 37   customer counselor: 914-967-8130
    Rye, NY 10580
        video series from the Faber/Mazlish book *How to Talk So Kids Will Listen
        and Listen So Kids Will Talk*

National Association for the Education of Young Children (NAEYC) 202-232-8777
    1509 16th Street, NW
    1-800-424-2460
    Washington, DC 20036
    FAX: 202-328-1846
        videos for professionals about curriculum, child development, staff
        communication, etc.

METRO AREA

Children's Resource Center 301-217-3800
    Rockville Regional Library
    99 Maryland Avenue
    Rockville, MD 20850
        educational videos for parents and professionals; borrowers need not be
        Montgomery County residents

Fairfax County Libraries 703-222-3155
    www.co.fairfax.va.us/library
    On-line Library catalog; modem phone # 703-802-7447
    Library Administration
    13135 Lee Jackson Highway, Suite 301
    Fairfax, VA 22033
        professional library with over 400 audio and video tapes

Maryland Association for the Education of Young Children (MAEYC)
    Vickie Kaneko 410-767-6890
        educational videos for training/staff development

Potomac Association of Cooperative Teachers (P.A.C.T.)
    Cindy Walsh, DC and MD 202-363-2209
    Jeanne Porter, VA 703-941-9791
        free loans of educational videos to P.A.C.T. members

PROFESSIONAL RESOURCES

302   "How Can I Help My Child?" Early Childhood Resource Directory

Glossary

A.A.: Associate of Arts, two-year college degree

A.A.S.: Associate of Applied Science, two-year college degree

ADD: see Attention Deficit Disorder in glossary

ADHD: see Attention Deficit Hyperactivity Disorder in glossary

ADTR: Registered American Dance Therapist

aide: a person who assists professional teachers or childcare providers

AMI: Association Montessori Internationale

AMS: American Montessori Society

art therapy: therapy in which art is used for evaluation and treatment

A.T.R.: Registered Art Therapist

A.T.R.-B.C.: Registered Art Therapist, Board Certified

Attention Deficit Disorder (ADD): disorder characterized by a child exhibiting certain specific characteristics such as, among others, high distractibility, short attention span, poor organization skills, difficulty following directions, and low tolerance for frustration

Attention Deficit Hyperactivity Disorder (ADHD): Attention Deficit Disorder that includes heightened motor activity

B.A.: Bachelor of Arts, four-year college degree

B.C.D.: Board Certified Diplomate

cerebral palsy: form of paralysis, accompanied by motor difficulties, caused by a prenatal brain defect or birth injury

child care: caring for children in a family day care setting or child care center to foster the child's social, emotional, physical, and intellectual needs

CHILDFIND: federally funded program for testing for developmental delays in young children

cognitive development: intellectual development

cooperative preschool: a preschool managed and/or staffed by parents, with a hired director and teachers; parent participation preschool

C.P.C.: Certified Professional Counselor

dance therapy: therapy using dance and movement for evaluation and treatment

developmental delays: delays in a child's emotional, social, cognitive, verbal, or physical development

Down's Syndrome: a congenital disorder consisting of moderate to severe learning difficulties accompanied by physical abnormalities

dyslexia: an impairment of the ability to read due to a brain defect

EC: Early Childhood

ECE: Early Childhood Education

EC Professional: Early Childhood education director, teacher, aide, daycare provider, home care provider, consultant, mentor, trainer, specialist

epilepsy: disorganized electrical activity in the brain leading to transient attacks of disturbed motor and sensory functions

family child care: child care provided in caregiver's home

Head Start: national federally-sponsored program started in 1965 to give children from lower-income families a head start in preparing for school

L.C.S.W.: Licensed Clinical Social Worker

L.C.S.W.-C.: Licensed Clinical Social Worker, Clinical specialty

LD: see learning disability in glossary

learning disability (LD): a difficulty in learning to read, write, compute, or do school work that cannot be attributed to impaired sight or hearing, or to mental retardation

L.P.C.: Licensed Professional Counselor

L.S.P.: Licensed Speech Pathologist

M.A.: Master of Arts graduate degree

M.A.E.E.: Master of Arts in Elementary Education

M.A.T.: Master of Arts in Teaching

MCPPNS: Maryland Council of Parent Participation Nursery Schools

M.Ed.: Master of Education graduate degree

M.D.: Medical Doctor

Mental Health Practitioner: psychiatrist, psychologist, social worker, or specialist

Montessori School: teacher-centered school emphasizing the importance of cognitive growth and the importance of the senses in a child's development; multi-aged groupings; based on the philosophy originally developed by Italian educator Maria Montessori in 1907

motor impairment: diminished or damaged motor capabilities

movement therapy: therapy using movement or dance for evaluation and treatment

music therapy: therapy using music for evaluation and treatment

M.S.: Master of Science graduate degree

M.S.W.: Master of Social Work graduate degree

NAEYC: National Association for the Education of Young Children

nephrology: the branch of medical science that deals with kidneys

neural organization: organization of the nervous system

neurologist: physician specializing in the nerves and the nervous system

occupational therapy: therapy evaluating and treating perceptual and neuromuscular factors which influence function

ophthalmologist: physician dealing with the anatomy, functions, and diseases of the eye

optometrist: person skilled in testing the eyes for defects of vision and in prescribing glasses

O.T.R.: Registered Occupational Therapist

parent participation preschool: a preschool managed and/or staffed by parents, with a hired director and teachers; cooperative preschool

PEATC: Parent Education and Advocacy Training Center for families with special needs

Ph.D.: Doctor of Philosophy

physical therapy: therapy evaluating and treating orthopedic structure and neuromuscular functions

play therapy: therapy utilizing play for evaluation and treatment

psychiatrist: physician who treats mental diseases

psychologist: specialist in the mind, or mental states and processes

Psy.D.: Doctor of Psychology

P.T.: Physical Therapist

Reggio Emilia Preschool: child-centered preschool in which the physical environment and creative expression is important and in which parents play an important role; based on preschools in Reggio Emilia, Italy

respite care: temporary relief from caring for a family member with a disability

sensory integration: the organization of sensory input for use; through sensory integration, the various parts of the nervous system work together so a person can effectively interact with the environment

social worker: person trained to counsel people

special needs: emotional, social, cognitive, or physical concerns that require special treatment

strabismus: "cross" eyes

Tourette's Syndrome: neurological/behavioral disorder characterized by multiple motor tics and one or more vocal tics

vision therapy: therapy for improving visual functioning

visual training: training for improving visual functioning

Waldorf School: school emphasizing art, music, and handicrafts as well as reading, writing, and arithmetic; based on the educational philosophy of Austrian philosophy Rudolf Steiner

304

"How Can I Help My Child?" Early Childhood Resource Directory

Index

— A —

Accreditation 264
   Montessori Accreditation 266
   NAEYC Accreditation 266
ADD/ADHD 139
   Feingold Association 201, 202
   Mental Health Practitioners 124
   Parent Information/Support 201
   Specialists 96, 139
Adoption 195
Advocacy Groups
   General 15
   Organizations for EC Professionals 292
African-American Families 198
   National Black Child Development Institute 15
Aide Job Clearinghouses 291
Allergy and Asthma
   Allergists 97
   Parent Info 199
American Red Cross CPR and First Aid Courses 75, 76
Americans with Disabilities Act 42
Arabic Resources 119
ARC (Association for Retarded Citizens) 242
Art Supplies 57
Art Therapists 135
Asian-American Families .200
Assessment 141
   Assessments for Children 259
   CHILDFIND 141, 142, 144
Asthma
   Allergists 97
   Parent Info/Support .199
At-Risk Children: Low Income Resources 230
Autism 203

— B —

Babysitting Referrals 147
Background Checks for Child Care Providers 151
Bedwetting 203
Bi-lingual
   Hispanic Parent Education Classes 192
   National Assn for Bilingual Education 237
   Parenting Education Center 250, 251

   Testing: Multicultural Clinical Center 119
   Videos 301
Black Families 198
   National Black Child Development Institute 15
Books
   Book Finders 17
   Book Stores 17
   Catalogs 21
   Computer Online Services 37
   For EC Professionals .296
   Library Resources 23
   Magazines for Adults and Children 24, 25
   Personalized Books 29
   Resource Guides 30
Business Services for Child Care/Schools 255

— C —

Cancer
   Parent Info 203
   Special Love School for Cancer Patients 168
Carpets for Educational Spaces 52
Catalogs
   Book Catalogs 21
   Computer Software Catalogs 38
   Educational Supplies 52
   Toy Catalogs 52
Catholic Charities Family Services 230, 231, 233
Cerebral Palsy 204
Certification Courses: Maryland EC Professionals 286
CHADD (Children and Adults with ADD) 201
Challenging Children 204
Child Abuse
   Prevention 205
   Reporting 44
Child Care
   Babysitting Referrals .147
   Background Checks and Surveillance for Providers . .151
   Child Transportation .177
   Drop-In Child Care Centers 151
   Educational Resources for Child Care/Schools 259
   Insurance for Child Care/Schools 255
   Licensing and Regulation 264
   Nannies 160
   Referrals 148

Respite Care 153
Scholarships 152
Shared Child Care 148
Sick Children 153
Sliding Fee Child Care 152
Special Resources 151
Start-up Resources 257
Child Care
Business Management Resources 255
Educational Resources 259
Child Care Providers, see Teachers
Child Safety 175
Child Care Provider Background Checks 151
Child Photo-ID Registry 175
Child Safety Education 175
Environmental Safety 176
Home Safety 176
National Center for Missing & Exploited Children 15
Surveillance 151
Toy Safety 63
Child Transportation 177
CHILDFIND
District of Columbia 141
Maryland 142
Virginia 144
Childproofing 176
Children's Defense Fund 15
Children's Hospital .87, 88, 89
Chronically Ill Children 209
Classroom Supplies 52, 60
Clinics 86
College Programs in Early Childhood
Graduate Programs 277
Undergraduate Programs .279
Computer Online Services
Book and Literature Services 37
Children Services 37
College Programs 277
For EC Professionals 267
General 35
National Assn for the Education of Young Children . . .15
Parent Services 178
Security 37
Computers
Computer On-site Services 260
Computer Resources 34
Computer Resources for EC Professionals 267
Courses for Children and Adults 34
Software Catalogs 38
Software for Child Care Business Management 255
Conferences and Speaker Series
For EC Professionals 270
General 40

Consultants
Computers 34
Counseling Centers 113
Educational 155
Family 179
For Child Care and Schools 272
For Cooperative Preschools 274
For EC Professionals 272
For Reggio Emilia Preschools 274
Mental Health Practitioners 124
Multi-cultural 119
Multi-cultural Educational Consultants 157, 237
Play Equipment/Playgrounds 49
Special Needs 157, 242
Special Needs Family Consultants 180
Consumer Product Safety Commission 42
Continued Training Approval for Individuals
and Groups 288
Cooperative Preschools 165
Cooperative Preschool EC Professional Organizations 294
Cooperative Preschool Parent Organizations 182
Counseling Centers 113
Afro-American Counseling .114
Multi-cultural 119
Counseling Referral Services .124
Courses
Computer Courses 34
CPR/First Aid Courses 75
EC Certification Courses for Maryland 286
EC Professional Courses 282
Parent Education 183
CPR/First Aid 75
Bi-lingual: American Red Cross 75, 76
Craft Supplies 57
Crisis Centers 47
Curriculum 260
Bilingual 261
Curriculum Resources 260
Curriculum Units 261

– D –

Dance Therapists 136
Daycare Centers, see also Schools
Referrals 148
DCAEYC (DC Assn for the Education of
Young Children) 16
Deafness 106, 223
Death and Bereavement 207
Dentists 78
Dental Referral Services 77
Special Needs 77
Department of Health and Human Services
District of Columbia 42, 83
Maryland 43, 84
National 82
Virginia 43, 85

Dermatologists 99
Developmental Delays
        CHILDFIND: District of Columbia 141
        CHILDFIND: Maryland 142
        CHILDFIND: Virginia .144
        Mental Health Practitioners 139
        Pediatricians 96
        Testing and Assessment 141
Diabetes 208
Diet 90
Difficult Children 204
Directors' Organizations 295
Disabled and/or Chronically Ill Children 209
        Disability Information .44
Divorce and Separation 212
Down's Syndrome 216, 242
Drop-In Child Care 151
Drug Stores, Open 24 Hours 80
Dyslexia 229

– E –

Ear, Nose, and Throat Specialists 99
Early Childhood Consultation Center 155, 179, 184, 283
Educational Consultants 155
        Multi-cultural Educational Consultants 157
        Special Needs Educational Consultants 157
Educational Supplies, see also Toys
        Catalogs 52
        Stores 60
Emotionally Disturbed Children 217
Epilepsy 217
ERIC-Educational Resources Information Center 35, 249
Eye Tests 92, 259

– F –

Faber/Mazlish Workshops 70, 184
Family Day Care Organizations 295
Family Services Agency 186
Fathers 218
Feingold Association 90, 91, 201
Feltboards 56
Food Allergy Network 200
Foster Parents 219
Funding Resources for Child Care and Schools 255

– G –

Gastroenterologists 99
Gay and Lesbian Parents 220
GLOSSARY 303
Government Information/Resources 42
Grandparents 221
Grant Resources 255

– H –

Head Start
        Computer Online Service 36
        District of Columbia .169
        Maryland 170
        National 169
        Virginia 171
Health and Human Services .42
        Computer Online Services: U.S. Government 37
Health Information/Resources 82
Health Insurance for Nannies 162
Hearing Specialists 106
Hearing Testing for Schools 259
Hearing-Impaired Children .223
HELPLINES
        For EC Professionals 290
        General 44
        Multi-lingual 46
Hispanic Families 227
Home Safety 176
Home Schooling 225
Home visits
        Early Childhood Consultation Center 185
        Family Works Home Visitor Program 186
Hospitals 87
        Hospitalization Resources 86
HOTLINES 47
        Multi-lingual 48

– I –

Insurance
        For Child Care and Schools 255
        For Nannies 162
Interracial Families 238
Ivymount School, The .102, 143

– J –

Jewish Social Service Agency 115, 117, 270
Job Clearinghouses for EC Professionals 291
Journals and Magazines for EC Professionals 297

– K –

Kindergartens
        Private Schools 163
        Public Schools 169, 170, 171
        Referrals 163
Kingsbury Center, The 114
Korean Resources 119, 200

– L –

Lab School of Washington, The 166
Language Specialists 106
Latino Families 227

"How Can I Help My Child?"   Early Childhood Resource Directory

307

Learning Disabilities
    Parent Info 228
    Schools 166
Lesbian Parents 220
Library Resources 23
    For EC Professionals 299
    Special Needs Library 23
Licensing and Regulation
    Child Care 264
    Montessori Accreditation .266
    NAEYC Accreditation 266
    Schools 264
Lourie Center for Infants and Young Children 115
Low Income Resources 230
    Sliding Fee Child Care 152

– M –

MAEYC (MD Assn for the Education of
    Young Children) 16
Magazines for Adults 24
Magazines for Children 25
Management Resources for Child Care and Schools 255
    Start-up Resources 257
Maryland Committee for Children 16, 187
MCAEYC (MD Community Assn for Education of
    Young Children) 16, 294
MCPPNS (MD Council of Parent Participation
    Nursery Schools) 294
Mental Health Centers/Associations 121
Mental Health Information and Resources 121
Mental Health Practitioners 126
    Referral Services 124
    Special Needs 139
Mentoring 288
Montessori Schools
    Accreditation 266
    Listings in DC, MD, VA 165
    Organizations 262
    Teacher Training 287
Montgomery Child Care Assn., Inc. 187, 288
Montgomery County Crisis Center 47
Mothers 234
Movement Therapists 136
Multi-cultural
    Center for Multicultural Human Services 119
    Counseling Centers 119
    Educational Consultants 157
    Multi-lingual Helplines 46
    Multi-lingual Hotlines 48
    Parent Education Classes .192
    Parent Handouts for EC Professionals: Fairfax 299
    Parent Information 195
    Services 115
Music Therapists 137

– N –

NAEYC
    DCAEYC 16, 293
    MAEYC 16, 293
    MCAEYC 16, 294
    VAEYC 16, 294
NAEYC Accreditation 266
    Listings of NAEYC Accredited Programs 163
Nannies 160
    Agencies 160
    Health Insurance 162
    Hiring 162
    Newsletters 162
    Support and Training 162
    Tax Guidance for Household Employers 162
Ntl Assn for the Education of Young Children (NAEYC) . . .16
National Center for Missing and Exploited Children 15
Nephrologists 99
Neurologists 100
Newsletters 27
    About Books 26
    For EC Professionals 300
Newspapers 27
Nutritionists/Nutritional Resources 90

– O –

Occupational Therapists 102
Operation Resources for Child Care and Schools 255
Opthalmologists 100
Optometrists and Visual Training 92
ORDER FORM 311
Organizations
    For Directors 295
    For EC Professionals 292
    For Family Day Care Providers 295
    For Parents 182
    For Schools 262
    For Schools: Cooperative Preschools 263
    For Schools: Montessori .263
    For Teachers 292

– P –

PACT (Potomac Assn of Cooperative Teachers) 294
Parent Cooperative Preschool International
    (PCPI) 165, 294
Parent Education 183
    Faber/Mazlish Workshop Kits 21
    Multi-cultural, Multi-lingual Parent Education 192
    Special Needs Parent Education 193, 243, 251
Parent Teacher Association (P.T.A.) 169, 170, 171, 182
Parents
    Information and Support .195
    Organizations for Parents .182
    Parent Resource Centers .249

Parenting the Challenging Child 204
Parents Anonymous 247
Parents of Multiple Births 239
Single Parents 240
Support Groups 246
Working Parents 248
Parents Anonymous 247
Parents Stressline 44, 47, 205
PCPI (Parent Cooperative Preschools International) 165
Pediatricians 94
ADD/ADHD Specialists .96
Allergists 97
Dermatologists 99
Ear, Nose, and Throat Specialists 99
Gastroentrologists 99
Nephrologists 99
Neurologists 99
Opthalmologists 100
Orthopedists 100
Referral Services 94
Special Needs 101
Pharmacies, Open 24 Hours 80
Physical Therapists 102
Playground/Play Equipment 50
Consultants 49
Playgroups 240
Potomac Assn of Cooperative Teachers (P.A.C.T.) 294
Preschools, see also Schools
Cooperative Preschools 165
Licensing and Accreditation 264
Montessori Schools 165
Private Preschools 163
Public Preschools 169
Referrals 163
Reggio Emilia Preschools 165
Special Needs Schools 166, 172
Waldorf Schools 168
Private Schools and Kindergartens 163
Professional Organizations
Directors' Organizations 295
Family Day Care Organizations 295
General Organizations 292
Parent Teacher Associations (P.T.A.s) 169, 182
Psychiatrists 126
Psychologists 127
PTA (Parent Teacher Association) 169, 182
Publications for EC Professionals 296
Puppets 55, 56

– R –

Reggio Emilia Preschools 165, 287
Computer On-line Services 35
Professional Training .287
Resource Guides 30
Rides for Children 177

– S –

Safety
Child Care Provider Background Checks 151
Child Photo-ID Registry 175
Child Safety 175
Child Safety Education 175
Child Surveillance 151
Environmental Safety .176
Home Safety 176
Toy Safety 42, 63
Scholarships
For Child Care Provider Services 152
For Cooperative Preschools 152
For EC Professionals .263
Parent Encouragement Program 189
Schools, see also Preschools
Business Resources 255
Cooperative Preschool Information 165
Educational Resources 159
General Information 163, 169
Insurance for Schools .255
Licensing and Accreditation 264
Listings 163
Montessori School Information 165
Private Schools and Kindergartens 163
Public Schools 169
Reggio Emilia Preschools 165
Scholarships 152
Special Needs Schools Information 166, 172
Start-up Resources 257
Siblings 240
Sick Children
Child Care 153
Disabled and/or Chronically Ill Children 209
Hospitalization Resources 86
Hospitals and Clinics 87
Respite Care 154
Single Parents 240
Social Services 121
Social Workers 132
Software
For Business Management and Operation for
    Child Care and Schools 255
For Parents and Children 38
Speaker Series 40, 270
Special Needs
Computer online services 179
Consultants 157
Dentists 77
Mental Health Practitioners 139
Parent Advocacy Training 193
Parent Information 242
Pediatricians 101
Referrals: Schools/Child Care 163

Respite Child Care 154
School Information .166, 172
Special Needs Library 23
Speech Specialists 106
Start-up Resources For Child Care and Schools 257
Stepfamilies 245
Stuttering 245
Supplies
Craft Supplies 52, 57
Educational Supplies 52, 60
Support Groups 246
Surveillance of Child Care Providers 151

– T –

Tax Services
For Child Care/Schools 258
Tax Guidance for Household Employers 162
Teachers
Computer Resources 267
Conferences and Speaker Series 270
Consultants for EC Professionals 272
Courses: College Programs 277
Courses: General Training 282
Courses: Maryland Certification 286
Courses: Montessori 287
Courses: Reggio Emilia Preschools 287
Courses: Scholarships .263
Helplines 290
Job Clearinghouses 291
Mentoring 288
Organizations 292
Publications 296
Support Groups for Teachers 294
Videos 301
Television 24, 185
Testing/Assessment 141
CHILDFIND: District of Columbia 141
CHILDFIND: Maryland .142
CHILDFIND: Virginia 144
Class Assessments for Children 259
Counseling Centers 113
Mental Health Practitioners 124
Nutritionists 90
Optometrists 92
Pediatricians 94
Physical and Occupational Therapists 102
Speech and Hearing Specialists 106
Therapists
Art Therapists 135
Counseling Centers 113
Movement Therapists .136
Music Therapists 137
Occupational Therapists 102
Physical Therapists 102
Psychiatrists 126
Psychologists 127
Social Workers 137
Tourette's Syndrome 247
Toys
Catalogs 52
Craft Supplies 57
Educational Supply Stores 60
Recommendations 61
Rental 61
Replacement Parts 62
Safety 42, 63
Toy Safety 63
Toy Stores 64
Used Toys 69
Training for EC Professionals 282
Training for Trainers 288
Transporation for Children 177
Triplets 239
Twins 239

– U –

UPDATE FORM 311

– V –

VAEYC (Virginia Assn for the Education of
Young Children) 16
Videos 70
Bi-lingual 301
Faber/Mazlish Workshop Videos 301
For EC Professionals .301
Library Resources for EC Professionals 302
Video Reviews 72
Videos for Adults 70
Videos for Children 71
Virginia Cooperative Preschool Council
(VCPC) 165, 194
Vision and Hearing Testing for Schools 259
Visual Testing and Training 92, 259
Visually-Impaired Children 248

– W –

Waldorf Schools 168
Working Parents 248

– Z –

ZERO TO THREE
National Center for Infants, Toddlers, and Families 40

Resource Directory Update Form

I/My organization would like to have my/our listing included or updated in the *Early Childhood Resource Directory*.

Your name _____

Your phone no. W (_____)_____; H (_____)_____

Please ❑ include; or ❑ update page(s)_____ with the following information:

Individual/Organization _____

_____

Address _____

City_____ State_____ Zip_____

Please list additional locations on back of page

Telephone: (local) (_____)_____ Telephone: 1-800-_____

FAX: (_____)_____ TDD/TTY: (_____)_____

e-mail _____ www site _____

brief description of services _____

_____

_____

_____

Thank you for your information.

Please note that the editor reserves the right to edit or exclude entries as necessary.

Mail to: **EARLY CHILDHOOD RESOURCE DIRECTORY/UPDATE**
The Early Childhood Consultation Center
11506 Michale Court
Silver Spring, MD 20904-2704

Questions? Call 301-593-5992.

FORMS

Resource Directory Order Form

Name _____

Address _____

City _____ State_____ Zip_____

Telephone   H (_____)_____ W(_____)_____

Where did you hear about the Resource Directory? _____

Please send me _____ book(s): $25.00 per book .... total: $_____._____

MD residents, include 5% sales tax: $1.25 per book** .... $_____._____

** if tax-exempt, write tax-exempt#_____

postage and handling: $3.75 per book .... $_____._____

TOTAL: $_____._____

Questions? Call 301-593-5992.

Make check payable to: ECCC

Mail to: **EARLY CHILDHOOD RESOURCE DIRECTORY/ORDER**
The Early Childhood Consultation Center
11506 Michale Court
Silver Spring, MD 20904-2704

Please allow 6-8 weeks for delivery

FORMS